ADMISSIBILITY OF EVIDENCE IN EU CROSS-BORDER CRIMINAL PROCEEDINGS

This book provides a systematic and analytical account of the problems facing transnational criminal justice.

It details actual problems arising in the transnational prosecution of crimes; assesses existing obstacles on admissibility of evidence; in particular with regard to electronic evidence, assesses the impact that the impediment of free circulation of evidence has on fundamental rights of the defendants facing criminal trial; and finally drafts a proposal for the future of regulation for this complex topic.

The book therefore contributes to the debate on the creation of an Area of Freedom, Security and Justice in the EU. It offers insights on how to outline the main general rules that could be adopted at EU level in a manner that adequately balances the need for efficiency in prosecution and the protection of human rights.

With contributions of renowned experts in the field, the book addresses the discussion of a potential legislative proposal with the help of insight into the experience and conceptual context of the rules of evidence at the national level.

Volume 20 in the series Hart Studies in European Criminal Law

Hart Studies in European Criminal Law

Since the Lisbon Treaty, European criminal law has become an increasingly important field of research and debate. Working with the European Criminal Law Academic Network (ECLAN), the series will publish works of the highest intellectual rigour and cutting edge scholarship which will be required reading for all European criminal lawyers.

The series is happy to consider both edited and single authored titles. The series defines 'European' and 'criminal law' in the broadest sense, so books on European criminal law, justice and policy will be considered. The series also welcomes books which offer different methodological approaches.

Volume 1: *EU Criminal Law after Lisbon: Rights, Trust and the Transformation of Justice in Europe*
Valsamis Mitsilegas

Volume 2: *Challenges in the Field of Economic and Financial Crime in Europe and the US*
Edited by Vanessa Franssen and Katalin Ligeti

Volume 3: *Chasing Criminal Money: Challenges and Perspectives On Asset Recovery in the EU*
Edited by Katalin Ligeti and Michele Simonato

Volume 4: *Limits to EU Powers: A Case Study of EU Regulatory Criminal Law*
Jacob Öberg

Volume 5: *The Needed Balances in EU Criminal Law: Past, Present and Future*
Edited by Chloé Brière and Anne Weyembergh

Volume 6: *Redefining Organised Crime: A Challenge for the European Union?*
Edited by Stefania Carnevale, Serena Forlati and Orsetta Giolo

Volume 7: *White Collar Crime: A Comparative Perspective*
Edited by Katalin Ligeti and Stanislaw Tosza

Volume 8: *Criminal Liability of Managers in Europe: Punishing Excessive Risk*
Stanisław Tosza

Volume 9: *The European Union and Deprivation of Liberty: A Legislative and Judicial Analysis from the Perspective of the Individual*
Leandro Mancano

Volume 10: *The Legitimacy of EU Criminal Law*
Irene Wieczorek

Volume 11: *The Fight Against Impunity in EU Law*
Edited by Luisa Marin and Stefano Montaldo

Volume 12: *Controlling Immigration Through Criminal Law: European and Comparative Perspectives on 'Crimmigration'*
Edited by Gian Luigi Gatta, Valsamis Mitsilegas, and Stefano Zirulia

Volume 13: *The Principle of Mutual Trust in EU Criminal Law*
Auke Willems

Volume 14: *Surveillance and Privacy in the Digital Age: European, Transatlantic and Global Perspectives*
Edited by Valsamis Mitsilegas and Niovi Vavoula

Volume 15: *The External Dimension of the EU's Policy against Trafficking in Human Beings*
Chloé Brière

Volume 16: *Criminal and Quasi-criminal Enforcement Mechanisms in Europe: Origins, Concepts, Future*
Edited by Vanessa Franssen and Christopher Harding

Volume 17: *Data protection, Migration and Border Control: The GDPR, the Law Enforcement Directive and Beyond*
Teresa Quintel

Volume 18: *Corporations and the Privilege against Self-Incrimination*
Stijn Lamberigts

Volume 19: *EU Enforcement Authorities: Punitive Law Enforcement in a Composite Legal Order*
Edited by Michiel Luchtman, Katalin Ligeti and John Vervaele

Volume 20: *Admissibility of Evidence in EU Cross-Border Criminal Proceedings: Electronic Evidence, Efficiency and Fair Trial Rights*
Edited by Lorena Bachmaier Winter and Farsam Salimi

Admissibility of Evidence in EU Cross-Border Criminal Proceedings

Electronic Evidence, Efficiency and Fair Trial Rights

Edited by
Lorena Bachmaier Winter
and
Farsam Salimi

•HART•
OXFORD • LONDON • NEW YORK • NEW DELHI • SYDNEY

HART PUBLISHING

Bloomsbury Publishing Plc

Kemp House, Chawley Park, Cumnor Hill, Oxford, OX2 9PH, UK

1385 Broadway, New York, NY 10018, USA

29 Earlsfort Terrace, Dublin 2, Ireland

HART PUBLISHING, the Hart/Stag logo, BLOOMSBURY and the Diana logo are trademarks of Bloomsbury Publishing Plc

First published in Great Britain 2024

A catalogue record for this book is available from the British Library.

A catalogue record for this book is available from the Library of Congress.

Library of Congress Control Number: 2024931681

ISBN: HB: 978-1-50997-199-2
ePDF: 978-1-50997-201-2
ePub: 978-1-50997-200-5

Typeset by Compuscript Ltd, Shannon

This anthology is based on the ELI Project 'Admissibility of E-Evidence in Criminal Proceedings in the EU'.

ELI
EUROPEAN
LAW
INSTITUTE

PREFACE

Most legal systems do not have a consistent and comprehensive regulation on transnational criminal proceedings, and rules on the applicable law or conflicts of law rules are largely lacking. With regard to evidence obtained abroad, the practice varies greatly. In some cases, such evidence is admitted without any further control, whilst on other occasions it is subject to exhaustive domestic filters to check its compliance with domestic legal principles and sometimes also with the statutory provisions of the executing state.[1] This patchwork of rules, principles and practice not only increases the complexity of transnational justice, but undoubtedly has a negative impact on the protection of fundamental rights and the efficiency of international judicial cooperation, hindering the free circulation of evidence and also its admissibility at trial.

Until sufficient procedural harmonisation at the European level is reached, the best solution to ensure the admissibility of evidence would be for the executing authority, to the greatest extent possible, to respect the rules and formalities indicated by the issuing authority. However, this accommodation to the *lex fori* tends to become particularly complicated in relation to the gathering of e-evidence, where the huge amount of data accessed, which have to be filtered, follows different rules in each Member State and does not always allow the *lex fori* to be applied.

Three years ago, when we had the honour of being appointed Project Reporters of the European Law Institute (ELI) project on 'Admissibility of Evidence and E-Evidence in Criminal Proceedings in the EU', we could not imagine how complex and challenging the development of this project would be. Nevertheless, we started working with enthusiasm, confident that the goals of the project would be successfully achieved, since we had an outstanding team of experts working on and supporting the project, and could rely on the magnificent work and continuous support of the ELI staff.[2]

[1] On the stages and acts that encompass the transnational evidentiary procedure, see also S Ruggeri, 'Horizontal cooperation, obtaining evidence overseas and the respect for fundamental rights in the EU. From the European Commission's proposal to the proposal for a Directive on a European Investigation Order: Towards a single tool of evidence gathering in the EU?' in S Ruggeri (ed), *Transnational Inquiries and the Protection of Fundamental Rights in Criminal Proceedings* (Springer, 2013) 279, 287 et seq.

[2] The entire workforce of the ELI is highly professional and dedicated, in addition to being wonderful people, and we want to thank them all for their tireless commitment and support. Moreover, we would like to express our special gratitude to those persons in the ELI who were more intensely involved in the day-to-day progress of the present report: Christiane Wendehorst, Katja Kolman and Vanessa Wilcox.

The main objective of this project was to carry out a thorough analysis of the admissibility of cross-border criminal evidence in the European Union (EU), with the aim of presenting a draft proposal for an EU Directive. Thus, the exercise was not intended to resemble other projects, which collect information and data, analyse them and present the existing problems in the transfer of criminal evidence from one country to another in the EU. This study was conceived to address the most debated aspects of judicial cooperation in criminal matters relating to the gathering of evidence – and in particular electronic evidence – abroad, presenting a possible solution in the form of a Proposal for a Directive.

To this end, we relied on the numerous studies that had already identified diverse rules on evidence in EU Member States and complemented those findings with completely updated country reports in a few select countries, namely Austria, Italy, Luxembourg, the Netherlands, Portugal and the United Kingdom (excluding Scotland). The project was not aimed at compiling detailed information on the structure and functioning of the national criminal proceedings of all EU countries, nor at analysing in depth the rules applicable to the admissibility of EU cross-border evidence in each of the Member States. Since the project was focused on drafting common standards on admissibility of cross-border criminal evidence, with that aim in mind, it was sufficient to confirm the variety of systems and the typology of problems encountered in practice, when evidence collected in one country is to be used in a trial in another country. In any event, it was considered useful to take a closer look at at least a few countries, to assess whether the already existing information was still valid or not. The selection of these countries was not accidental but sought to include civil and common law legal systems, to cover different geographical areas and legal traditions, as well as countries with a more adversarial approach to the gathering of evidence and others with a more traditional approach to official inquiries. Another important factor that influenced our choice was the availability of excellent and experienced scholars and practitioners with already proven expertise in the field.

The study sought primarily to determine whether the principle of *lex loci*, and where necessary adjusted to the *lex fori*, could be defined as the main principle for the inclusion of cross-border evidence, or whether such a principle – known already from the Mutual Legal Assistance Conventions – should be reconsidered in the EU setting. The project also explored whether the principle of *lex loci* would have to be adjusted to a digital setting. When assessing the problems connected to the gathering and transfer of electronic evidence, the team realised that a quite common understanding on the protocols to be followed to ensure its integrity and authenticity already exists between Member States. Therefore, the Proposal reflects this common understanding and includes a particular focus on e-evidence, with precise rules on its gathering and storage, as well as safeguards for the defendant – rules that could ideally work as a blueprint for legislation at EU level based on Article 82 of the Treaty on the Functioning of the European Union (TFEU), or at least serve as soft law guidance for the parties involved.

Although the main objective was to secure precise principles for the admission of evidence – thus developing inclusionary rules of evidence – we could not ignore the case law of the European Court of Human Rights (ECtHR) and the Court of Justice of the European Union (CJEU), providing some very limited cases where the use of evidence would render the entire proceedings unfair. Those cases, where evidence has been gathered through grave violation of non-derogable human rights – mainly torture, entrapment and coerced confessions – should lead to the exclusion of such evidence.

The methodology applied in this project is in accordance with the standards of social sciences research. Once the reports were prepared, we undertook an analysis of the relevant literature and case law previously selected and compiled. The next step was to analyse such information together with acting practitioners in public prosecution as well as from the bar. The members of the project working in public prosecution and as criminal defence lawyers shed much light on practical questions, as well as facilitating access to other practitioners for their opinion on how to tackle existing problems. Such a qualitative method was considered much more useful than a quantitative study based on randomly selected practitioners.

Once all the information was compiled, analysed and studied, the Project Reporters focused on drafting a proposal for a legislative framework, which was presented to the Project Team and the Advisory Committee. The lively discussions, online as well as in-person, proved not only that we had made the right choice when selecting the team, but also that, in order to be successful, the right balance between the competing interests in criminal proceedings should be adequately reflected in a possible future EU Directive. This task was anything but easy, as accepting opposed interests and ideas, alien to the different national legislation, turned out to require not only a high degree of understanding of the underlying common interests, but also a great degree of pragmatism: if the right balance was not struck, the ELI Proposal would not have any chance of being considered as a discussion document to inspire and potentially trigger the legislative process in the EU.

Finally, the Draft Proposal was subject to several open debates with relevant stakeholders and academics, to assess its viability, to identify further shortcomings and to revise the text with the aim of improving prior versions. The draft was discussed at ELI Annual Conferences during the project's life cycle, at meetings of the ELI bodies as well as at bilateral meetings with key stakeholders. Prior to its adoption, final evaluations and/or comments were provided by the Project Team, Advisory Committee, ELI bodies, staff and the Scientific Director, as well as by key stakeholders. The ELI Proposal was adopted first by its Council on 23 February 2023 and, subsequently, by the ELI Fellows on 4 May 2023. This broad involvement of diverse legal vocations and European traditions within the ELI (which has a Membership base of about 1,600 natural persons and 135 institutions), as well as consultations, facilitated the integration of a variety of views and developments.

Discussions continued after the adoption of the Proposal, too, in a bid to disseminate it as widely as possible.[3]

The present book contains nine chapters, six of the chapters mainly reflect the questions addressed in the national reports, but which were updated as the project advanced. Thus, for example, several of the chapters addressing the national rules on cross-border admissibility of evidence already cover the problems that have arisen in connection with the evidence obtained in the much-debated EncroChat case, and some of the decisions of the courts with regard to its admissibility. The authors, as well as the editors of this book, have sought to lead the current discussions in the field of cross-border evidence gathering in criminal proceedings in the EU, addressing the main problems and trying to present solutions, as a forerunner to the legislative action of the EU.

In addition to the six chapters focused on the national rules on admissibility of evidence, this book includes two chapters addressing the particularities of electronic evidence (by Giulia Lasagni and Farsam Salimi, respectively), and one introductory chapter explaining the reasons for this exercise and why the Member States should not be reluctant to advance in this direction (by Lorena Bachmaier Winter).

Again, we thank all the authors for their excellent contributions, which show not only a high level of knowledge but also their intellectual generosity. Working with you all has been extremely enriching and productive, a real pleasure.

The output of the ELI project reflected in this book should not only serve to improve knowledge of the problems connected to cross-border criminal evidence and electronic evidence gathering – improving knowledge is the main objective of any scientific work – but it should also facilitate the work of the parties to criminal proceedings, by creating certainty and ensuring effectiveness, while increasing the protection of human rights. The EU should not give up in its role as a leader in the field of human rights by protecting them and by fighting efficiently against crime. We can only hope that this book contributes to that aim.

Lorena Bachmaier Winter, on behalf of the editors
Madrid
August 2023

[3] The ELI Proposal for a Directive of the European Parliament and the Council on Mutual Admissibility of Evidence and Electronic Evidence in Criminal Proceedings, available at www.europeanlawinstitute.eu/fileadmin/user_upload/p_eli/Publications/ELI_Proposal_for_a_Directive_on_Mutual_Admissibility_of_Evidence_and_Electronic_Evidence_in_Criminal_Proceedings_in_the_EU.pdf.

CONTENTS

LIST OF CONTRIBUTORS

Lorena Bachmaier Winter is Full Professor of Justice Systems and Procedure at the Law School of the Complutense Madrid.

Vânia Costa Ramos, LL.M. in Criminal Law and PhD Student at the Lisbon Law Faculty, is a Criminal defence lawyer in Portugal and Vice-Chair of the European Criminal Bar Association.

Gabriella Di Paolo is Full Professor of Criminal Procedure at the Faculty of Law of the University of Trento (Italy).

Daniel Gilhofer-Lenglinger is a Teaching and Research Associate at the Vienna University of Economics and Business (WU Vienna). He is working on a PhD on Admissibility of Evidence in Fiscal Penal Law.

John Jackson is Emeritus Professor of Comparative Criminal Law and Procedure at the University of Nottingham and Visiting Professor at the University of Lille.

J.M.W. Lindeman is Associate Professor in criminal law and criminal proceedings at Utrecht University, where he is also one of the programme leaders of the Montaigne Centre for Rule of Law and Administration of Justice.

M.J.J.P. Luchtman is Professor of economic and European criminal law at Utrecht University, the Netherlands.

Robert Kert is Professor for criminal law and criminal procedure and Head of the Institute for Austrian and European Economic Criminal Law at the Vienna University of Economics and Business.

Giulia Lasagni PhD is Senior Assistant Professor in Criminal Procedure at the University of Bologna.

Katalin Ligeti is Professor of European and international criminal law and Dean of the Faculty of Law, Economics and Finance at the University of Luxembourg and Vice-President of the International Association of Penal Law.

Farsam Salimi is Associate Professor and of criminal Law and criminal procedure at the Department of Criminal Law and Criminology at the University of Vienna and President of the Austrian Society of Criminal Law and Criminology.

Stanisław Tosza is Associate Professor in Compliance and Law Enforcement at the University of Luxembourg and Secretary General of the International Association of Penal Law.

D.A.G. van Toor is Assistant Professor in criminal law and criminal proceedings at Utrecht University, where he is also a member of the Montaigne Centre for Rule of Law and Administration of Justice.

1

The Quest for Evidentiary Rules in EU Cross-Border Criminal Proceedings: Electronic Evidence, Efficiency and Fair Trial Rights

LORENA BACHMAIER WINTER

I. Introduction

The issue of cross-border admissibility of evidence in criminal proceedings in the European Union (EU) has been debated for decades,[1] and currently a growing number of voices are calling for legislative action at the European level.[2] This is due to the increasing relevance of cross-border criminal evidence in the prosecution of crimes within the EU. Indeed, what initially could be seen as something unusual – that evidence would have to be requested outside national borders – and thus conceiving of cross-border evidence as a quite 'exotic' element within criminal proceedings, has gradually become commonplace, not simply due to the elimination of the internal borders in the EU, but mainly due to the increasing digitalisation of the entire society, including crime and, in consequence, criminal evidence too.

The increasing importance of transnational evidence in a large part of criminal proceedings has already been acknowledged by practitioners, as well as by legal

[1] For a brief summary of the various EU legislative initiatives on cross-border evidence, see J Vervaele, 'Lawful and fair use of evidence from a European human rights perspective' in F Giuffrida and K Ligeti, (eds), *Admissibility of OLAF Final Reports as Evidence in Criminal Proceedings* (Luxembourg University, 2019) 56, 62–67.

[2] See, eg, E Sellier and A Weyembergh, 'Criminal procedural laws across the European Union – A comparative analysis of selected main differences and the impact they have over the development of EU legislation', Study for the EP LIBE Committee (August 2018) at www.europarl.europa.eu/RegData/etudes/STUD/2018/604977/IPOL_STU(2018)604977_EN.p, 63 and 64; K Ligeti et al, 'Admissibility of Evidence in Criminal Proceedings in the EU' (2020) 3 *eucrim* 201 at https://eucrim.eu/articles/admissibility-evidence-criminal-proceedings-eu/; C Claverie-Rousset, 'The admissibility of evidence in criminal proceedings between European Union Member States' (2013) 3(2) *European Criminal Law Review* 152, 169.

scholars, for some time,[3] but it is only now that dealing with the problem of the admissibility of cross-border criminal evidence seems to have become crucial. In addition to the complexity surrounding the rules on admissibility of evidence and the effects and scope of exclusionary rules,[4] several additional factors explain the intensified interest in providing certainty to the question of admissibility of transnational evidence in criminal proceedings in the EU.

The first factor impacting the increased demand for common rules on admissibility of cross-border evidence in criminal proceedings may be found in the course of the discussions on the establishment of a European Public Prosecutor's Office (EPPO). This demand has continued to grow since the EPPO Regulation[5] entered into force and the EPPO initiated numerous cross-border investigations – the work of the EPPO that so far can only be described as a successful step forward in the battle to counter the fraud against the financial interests of the EU (PIF fraud). The activity of the EPPO, which mainly deals with cross-border fraud cases, reinforces the need for certainty regarding the evidentiary rules that will ultimately be applied before the trial court if proceedings finally proceed to trial before a national court.[6] The delegated public prosecutors who work in the EPPO are demanding that the rules for the admissibility of criminal evidence be clarified, since, if they are not, they realise that they will often have to commence actions without knowing whether they will lead to an effective prosecution of the crimes under investigation.

The uncertainty regarding the admissibility of cross-border evidence can ultimately reduce the effectiveness of work of the EPPO, since the handling prosecutors are unsure of the challenges they will have to face before the national courts. It must be borne in mind that public prosecutors in most EU countries are also responsible for ensuring the lawfulness of the proceedings, and therefore they are also accorded the role of protecting the fundamental rights of the suspect or accused by safeguarding the rights of the defence. This is all the more important

[3] There is a plethora of legal literature on the topic of the admissibility of evidence, cross-border evidence and electronic evidence (e-evidence), which it would be impossible and to a certain extent pointless to cite here. Therefore, bibliographical references will be kept to a minimum in this chapter, with the knowledge that many interesting and relevant scientific works will not be referenced, despite having been used in the elaboration of the ELI project.

[4] As stated by Charles McCormick about the US system, 'The great body of the law of evidence consists of rules that operate to exclude relevant evidence': EW Clearly, *McCormick On Evidence*, 2nd edn (West Publishing Co, 1972) § 121.

[5] Council Regulation (EU) 2017/1939 of 12 October 2017 implementing enhanced cooperation on the establishment of the European Public Prosecutor's Office ('the EPPO') [2017] OJ L283/1.

[6] On the rules of cross-border evidence in the EPPO Regulation, see L Bachmaier Winter, 'Cross-border investigations under the EPPO proceedings and the quest for balance' in L Bachmaier Winter (ed), *The European Public Prosecutor's Office: The Challenges Ahead* (Springer, 2018) 117; see also S Allegrezza and A Mosna 'Cross-border criminal evidence and the future European Public Prosecutor. One step back on mutual recognition?' in L Bachmaier Winter (ed), *The European Public Prosecutor's Office: The Challenges Ahead* (Springer, 2018) 141. Also F Giuffrida, 'Cross-border crimes and the EPPO' (2017) 3 *eucrim* 149; HH Herrnfeldt, 'Article 31: Cross-border Investigations' in HH Herrnfeldt, D Brodowski and C Burchard (eds), *European Public Prosecutor's Office* (Nomos, 2021) 282; and C Burchard, 'Article 37: Evidence' in HH Herrnfeldt, D Brodowski and C Burchard (eds), *European Public Prosecutor's Office* (Nomos, 2021) 345.

as Article 37 of the EPPO Regulation only provides for an inclusionary rule of evidence, according to which evidence presented to the court by the EPPO or the defendant cannot be denied admission on the mere ground that the evidence was gathered in another Member State or in accordance with the law of another Member State. This inclusionary rule, although very positive, does not clarify the scope of the exclusionary rules of evidence in a cross-border setting.

The calls for a more harmonised approach to the rules on the admissibility of evidence in criminal matters have also been fuelled by discussions about the cross-border production of e-evidence, culminating in the adoption of the Regulation on European Production and Preservation Orders.[7] This Regulation will have to be supplemented by international agreements with third states and by domestic legislation ensuring the production of e-evidence at national level. In this area, the issues regarding the admissibility of particular e-evidence remain a growing concern. Limits on the admissibility of cross-border evidence may have their origin, inter alia, in: (i) privileges and immunities; (ii) illegality of obtaining the evidence; (iii) fundamental rights as such. A more harmonised approach to exclusionary rules would be essential to ensure that judicial cooperation works in practice, precisely as regards the exchange of e-evidence within the criminal justice system.

The third element that has brought the debate on the need for EU admissibility rules to the forefront is the recent *EncroChat* case, where the infiltration of the messaging service by French intelligence has led to thousands of arrests and multiple prosecutions across Europe.[8] This case has highlighted the problems of accessing and using criminal evidence in a cross-border scenario, transferred via a European Investigation Order (EIO). The case has already triggered the filing of a preliminary reference to the Court of Justice of the European Union (CJEU) by a German court,[9] asking, amongst other things, whether the transfer of evidence obtained without probable cause in a foreign country is in accordance with EU law. For those prosecuting similar types of cross-border criminal cases, the issue whether such

[7] Regulation (EU) 2023/1543 of the European Parliament and of the Council of 12 July 2023 on European Production Orders and European Preservation Orders for electronic evidence in criminal proceedings and for the execution of custodial sentences following criminal proceedings, [2023] OJ L191/118. This Regulation was adopted once the European Law Institute (ELI) project for elaborating a specific proposal for a Directive (hereinafter ELI PD) on admissibility of cross-border evidence and e-evidence in criminal matters was finalised. Nevertheless, since the development of this legislative action was closely followed by the ELI project team, the provisions finally adopted in Regulation 2023/1543 were analysed and taken on board in the ELI project. So far, it can be stated that the text of the ELI PD is not affected by this new Regulation, in the sense that the principles and rules set out in the ELI PD shall also apply when e-evidence is obtained directly from the service providers. Of course, the references in the Explanatory Memorandum to the Proposal need to be understood now in light of the Regulation but the output of the ELI project and thus the text of the Proposal for a Directive is not affected by the adoption of Regulation 2023/1543. See further the annex to this volume.

[8] See in this volume Chapter 7 on the Netherlands. On the impact of the *Encrochat* case in Germany, see T Wahl, 'Verwertung von im Ausland überwachter Chatnachrichten im Strafverfahren' (2021) 7–8 *ZIS* 453. See further JJ Oerlemann and DAG van Toor, 'Legal Aspects of the EncroChat Operation: A Human Rights Perspective' (2022) 30(3–4) *European Journal of Crime, Criminal Law and Criminal Justice* 309 at doi.org/10.1163/15718174-bja10037.

[9] See Decision of the Berlin Regional Court (*Landgericht*) of 19 October 2022 at www.hrr-strafrecht.de/hrr/lg/22/279-js-30-22.php.

evidence will be admitted is also causing major concerns, since the prosecution of hundreds of members of organised crime groups could be hindered. This case clearly shows why some evidentiary rules are necessary at the EU level.

In this context, I believe that the principle of subsidiarity and proportionality in the adoption of rules on the admissibility of evidence in cross-border criminal proceedings can no longer be questioned, and it seems that the time is ripe to take decisive legislative action. The ELI project on the admissibility of cross-border evidence and e-evidence in criminal proceedings has sought to contribute to the necessary EU legislative process with a specific proposal for a Directive. The work of the excellent team that participated in this project on the drafting of a Proposal for a Directive was driven by the sole purpose of advancing towards a more effective Area of Freedom, Security and Justice (AFSJ), which means adequately balancing the need to effectively fight against crime and the protection of the fairness of the proceedings in cross-border settings.

For many years, a majority of the EU Member States have opposed any EU initiative linked to the rules on admissibility of evidence in criminal proceedings, thwarting the development of the necessary legislative measures in this field.[10] This opposing stance contrasts with widespread agreement concerning the benefits of regulating certain principles on cross-border criminal evidence – for the prosecution and for the defence – and the demands raised for years that the EU make use of the competences established under Article 82(2) of the Treaty on the Functioning of the European Union (TFEU).[11] The goal of this chapter is to explain why this traditional opposition of the national authorities to any type of European legislative initiative in this matter, rejecting outright and often with weak arguments European rules on the admissibility of cross-border criminal evidence, is not based on consistent and rational arguments.

To this end, I will first examine the reasons that led the ELI to present a Proposal for a Directive on the admissibility of criminal evidence, and the main principles upon which it is based.[12] Next, I will argue that the very few exclusionary rules that have been included in this Proposal for a Directive are not new, highlighting the fact that they are in line with the jurisprudence of the European Court of Human Rights (ECtHR) and the CJEU in matters relating to the admissibility of evidence.[13]

Finally, I will set forth the benefits of this Proposal for a Directive for both the prosecution of crime and the rights of defence. The efforts of the team, which are evident in the text finally adopted, aimed to strike the right balance between the interests of all parties involved in criminal proceedings. In the context of criminal

[10] See Ligeti et al (n 2) 202 ff.

[11] See, eg Vervaele (n 1) 91.

[12] The ELI Proposal for a Directive of the European Parliament and the Council on Mutual Admissibility of Evidence and Electronic Evidence in Criminal Proceedings, available at www.europeanlawinstitute.eu/fileadmin/user_upload/p_eli/Publications/ELI_Proposal_for_a_Directive_on_Mutual_Admissibility_of_Evidence_and_Electronic_Evidence_in_Criminal_Proceedings_in_the_EU.pdf.

[13] The justification and scope of the exclusionary rules of evidence have been and still are widely debated: see, eg, DE Wilkes, 'A Critique of Two Arguments Against the Exclusionary Rule: The Historical Error and the Comparative Myth' (1975) 32 *Washington & Lee Law Review*, 881. Also questioning the

law and cross-border evidence, it is equally important, from the point of view of the protection of human rights, that evidence is not excluded due to legal formalities imposed by courts in Member States and that evidence that violates human dignity is excluded. Both goals, ensuring human dignity and public safety, must go hand in hand if the EU aspires to be a fair and consistent AFSJ.

First, however, it is important to clarify some conceptual issues. With regard to the concept of 'evidence', the ELI PD opted for a very broad concept, as established in Article 3(a) ELI PD, meaning any information or object that might be relevant for the factual determination of a criminal offence. Therefore, the term 'evidence' is used for both the source of evidence and the means of evidence, as well as any materials that aim to prove facts in criminal proceedings. When defining the scope of application of the ELI PD, Article 2(1) includes evidence to be used in criminal proceedings 'or other proceedings defined in Article 4 of Directive 2014/41 EU regarding the European Investigation Order'.[14] This provision mentions a very precise type of sanctioning proceedings, namely those 'where the decision may give rise to proceedings before a court having jurisdiction, in particular, in criminal matters', covering, for example, the German *Strafbefehle*, where the sanction is primarily imposed by the Public Prosecutor but can be challenged before the criminal courts. The ELI PD does not cover evidence obtained for use in administrative punitive proceedings, since Article 82(2) TFEU applies only to criminal law *stricto sensu*.[15]

The second clarification regards the concept of 'admissibility' in the ELI PD, which is also used in a broad sense: it can mean that the evidence rendered inadmissible should not reach the trial stage (Article 11(a) ELI PD), or that, being affected by a 'non-absolute inadmissibility' rule, it cannot be used as a basis of a sentence against the defendant, thus either excluding or limiting its probative value. Only evidence that falls under the concept of 'absolute inadmissibility' (Article 5 ELI PD) shall not be used in any way, lacking any probative value.

II. Status Quo and Main Principles on Admissibility of Cross-Border Evidence in Criminal Proceedings: *Lex Loci Regit Actum* under Control

To date, the admissibility of evidence in criminal proceedings has been considered by the ECtHR and by the CJEU as an issue for national legal systems to determine.[16]

deterrent effect of the exclusionary rules of evidence and arguing for possible alternatives, see S Gless and L Macula, 'Exclusionary Rules – Is it Time for Change?' in S Gless and T Richter (eds), *Do Exclusionary Rules Ensure a Fair Trial? A Comparative Perspective on Evidentiary Rules* (Springer, 2019) 349, 362.

[14] Directive 2014/41/EU of the European Parliament and of the Council of 3 April 2014 regarding the European Investigation Order in criminal matters [2014] OJ L130/1 (hereinafter Directive on the EIO or DEIO).

[15] On this issue, see the excellent report by M Luchtman, A Karagianni and K Bovend'Erdt, 'EU administrative investigations and the use of their results as evidence in national punitive proceedings' in Giuffrida and Ligeti (eds) (n 1) 7, 21 ff.

[16] See Vervaele (n 1) 71 ff.

The ECtHR case law has repeatedly declared that any issues relating to the admissibility of criminal evidence is a matter of national law with which the Court will not interfere unless certain non-derogable rights are at stake. The ECtHR, as a supranational court, has refrained from setting standards on admissibility of evidence that could alter the systems of internal checks and balances of the national criminal justice systems and proceedings.

Thus, in general, no rules on the admissibility of criminal evidence are prescribed in the European Convention on Human Rights (ECHR) and the ECtHR, with the latter focusing on compliance with the fairness of the proceedings as a whole. This does not mean that the ECtHR is indifferent to compliance with the rules on the admissibility of evidence. The Court does expect any use of unlawful methods to obtain incriminating evidence to be condemned as a preliminary matter.[17]

This is also the position taken by several European legal systems for which illegal evidence does not automatically determine an exclusionary rule (admissible under a balancing test); while in other legal systems, any illegality will render the evidence void, and evidence obtained in violation of fundamental rights will be prohibited as incriminating evidence.[18] There are many studies that have highlighted this diversity of approach regarding the rules for the admissibility of criminal evidence.[19] There is also very useful research on the admissibility of European Anti-Fraud Office (OLAF) reports as evidence,[20] but I will not address this topic here.

[17] See, eg, *Hulki Güneş v Turkey* App no 28490/95 (ECtHR, 19 June 2003): 'Although it is not its task to examine in the abstract the issue of the admissibility of evidence in criminal law, the Court finds it regrettable that … the National Security Court did not determine that issue before going on to examine the merits of the case. Such a preliminary investigation would clearly have given the national courts an opportunity to condemn any unlawful methods used to obtain evidence for the prosecution' (para. 91).

[18] For an excellent overview in comparative view of the exclusionary rules of evidence, see SC Thaman, 'Balancing Truth Against Human Rights: A Theory of Modern Exclusionary Rules' in SC Thaman (ed), *Exclusionary Rules in Comparative Law* (Springer 2013) 403. This author stresses that only a few jurisdictions, 'notably those which have recently emerged from totalitarian or authoritarian regimes', have foreclosed all balancing in relation to the use of illegally obtained evidence (ibid 441). See also Gless and Richter (eds) (n 12).

[19] See, eg, EU Network of Independent Experts on Fundamental Rights (cfr-cdf), 'Opinion on the status of illegally obtained evidence in criminal procedures in the Member States of the European Union', 30 November 2003 at https://sites.uclouvain.be/cridho/documents/Avis.CFR-CDF/Avis2003/CFR-CDF.opinion3-2003.pdf; the report of The Law Society, 'Study of the laws of evidence in criminal proceedings throughout the European Union', Summary report October 2004 at https://es.scribd.com/document/144338382/The-Law-Society-Study-of-the-laws-of-evidence-in-criminal-proceedings-throughout-the-European-Union-Summary-ReportOctober-2004; G Vermeulen, W De Bondt and Y Van Damme, *EU Cross Border Gathering and Use of Evidence in Criminal Matters. Towards Mutual Recognition of Investigative Measures and Free Movement of Evidence?* (Maklu, 2010); G Vermeulen, *Free gathering and movement of evidence in criminal matters in the EU. Thinking beyond borders, striving for balance in search of coherence* (Maklu, 2011); SC Thaman (ed), *Exclusionary Rules in Comparative Law* (Springer, 2013); K Ligeti (ed), *Toward a Prosecutor for the European Union*, vol 1: *A Comparative Analysis* (Hart-Beck, 2013); S Ruggeri (ed), *Transnational Evidence and Multicultural Inquiries in Europe* (Springer, 2014) 231; A Ryan, *Towards a System of European Criminal Justice. The Problem of Admissibility of Evidence* (Routledge, 2014); M Kusak, *Mutual Admissibility of Evidence in Criminal Matters in the EU. A Study of Telephone Tapping and House Search* (Maklu, 2016) 243.

[20] See M Luchtman and J Vervaele (eds), *Investigatory Powers and Procedural Safeguards: Improving OLAF's Legislative Framework through a Comparison with Other EU Law Enforcement Authorities (ECN/ESMA/ECB)* (Utrecht University, 2017); Giuffrida and Ligeti (eds) (n 1).

It is also known that the rules of the admissibility of evidence are closely linked to the very structure of national criminal proceedings – more adversarial or more inquisitorial – and the importance of the principle of immediacy and the extension of the confrontation clause.[21] In general, there are two types of barriers to the admission of evidence in criminal proceedings: those that are believed to impede the fact-finding process (unreliable evidence), and barriers based on other reasons alien to the fact-finding process (illegally obtained evidence). The divide between common law systems and civil law systems is also visible in the rules on admissibility. Some exclusionary rules, such as the prohibition of character evidence or the rejection of probative information on the ground that it might be misused, are distinctive characteristics of common law evidence.[22] As put by Damaška, the adversarial party-driven gathering of evidence, characteristic of common law proceedings, has more exclusionary rules, while an officialised evidence-gathering system might experience a lower need to reject evidence that does not promote the fact-finding.[23] In general, it might be said that one of the main differences between common law and civil law systems is that the latter are more reluctant to adopt strict exclusionary rules, and more often opt for mitigating their impact on the fact-finding process,[24] while common law systems are concerned that propensity information could be accorded more weight than it deserves.[25]

Knowing the characteristics of the different criminal proceedings in the EU Member States, it is not necessary to define here their particularities. Suffice it to note that when presenting this proposal for a Directive on the admissibility of evidence, these diverse features and different structures, which have already been reflected in numerous studies, have been taken into account.

To summarise, there is currently a great variety of rules on the admissibility of evidence, as is the case with the specific regulation of the different investigative measures, which are subject to different requirements in terms of motivation, duration or scope of application. It is true that there is some harmonisation as a result of the impact of the jurisprudence of the ECtHR but, as already stated, such harmonisation is limited, for the Court has decided that, as a rule, this is matter for national law. A view with which I can only agree.

The diversity regarding the rules on the admissibility of evidence among the national legal systems is also apparent at the level of the admissibility of cross-border evidence: while some systems will apply strict admissibility checks to

[21] M Damaška, 'Evidentiary Barriers to Conviction and Two Models of Criminal Procedure: A Comparative Study' (1973) 121 *University of Pennsylvania Law Review* 506; E Billis, *Die Rolle des Richters im adversatorischen und im inquistorischen Beweisverfahren* (Duncker&Humblot, 2015); L Bachmaier Winter, 'Principio de inmediación y *confrontation*: paralelismos, diferencias y tendencias' in K Ambos and G Malarino (eds), *Fundamentos de Derecho Probatorio* (Tirant lo Blanch 2019) 279.

[22] M Damaška, *Evidence Law Adrift* (Yale University Press, 1997) 17.

[23] ibid 99.

[24] See L Bachmaier Winter, 'Rights and methods to challenge evidence and witnesses in civil law jurisdictions' in DK Brown, J Iontcheva Turner and B Weisser (eds), *The Oxford Handbook on Criminal Process* (Oxford University Press, 2019) 841.

[25] Damaska (n 21) 17.

evidence that has been collected abroad, other states will admit it without subjecting it to any legality or proportionality control.

After this broad overview of the current situation regarding the admissibility of criminal evidence at the EU level, it is necessary to clarify the scope of the principle of mutual recognition in matters of cross-border evidence.[26]

On the one hand, the principle of non-inquiry would reflect the perfect implementation of the mutual recognition principle: evidence will be admitted in the forum state, without questioning the reliability or the legality of such evidence, nor the methods used to obtain it. The principle of non-inquiry would therefore amount to an almost automatic application of the principle of mutual recognition.[27] In the past, the principle of non-inquiry was based on the impossibility of checking the application of the foreign law by the foreign authorities in a foreign country – together with the understanding of the principle of national sovereignty and international comity. However, within the EU AFSJ, such arguments can no longer be considered as valid for the following reasons:

(a) because, in the virtual world, it is possible to check what rules are applicable in another Member State;
(b) because technology nowadays allows almost instant communication with foreign authorities in order to share information on the applicable law and the ways to carry out the investigative measures that are needed in the forum state; and
(c) because, in a common European AFSJ, the principles deeply rooted in the traditional concept of sovereignty are somewhat out of place and require reinterpretation. While in the past it would not have been beneficial to question how the cooperating state had obtained evidence, as such a question could have been understood as reflecting distrust and lead to damage to the smooth relations among the states involved, and thus to their willingness to cooperate, within the EU AFSJ this is no longer the case, as there is an obligation to cooperate and every Member State has to accept that its legal system operates in a common area of justice.

Finally, while the principle of non-inquiry, as noted earlier, might generally be useful for the 'free circulation of evidence' and justified on the basis of mutual trust between judicial and prosecutorial authorities of the various Member States involved, such principle should not cause a kind of 'mutual recognition principle' restricting the rights of the defence. In fact, when faced with incriminating evidence obtained abroad, if it is admitted without any control as to its legality, the defence would be placed in a position of clear disadvantage, compared to the possibility of checking the legality of evidence obtained in the forum state according to the rules of the state in which the trial takes place.

[26] See further, Luchtman, Karagianni and Bovend'Erdt (n 14) 13 ff.
[27] In the same sense, see Sellier and Weyembergh (n 2) 65.

The principle of mutual recognition – and before it, the principle of non-inquiry – of cross-border criminal evidence cannot be imposed upon the defence, as this would mean demanding that they limit their rights to exercise an effective defence, which implies controlling the lawfulness and the reliability of the evidence, regardless of whether it was collected in the national territory or abroad. Mutual trust can exist and can be built up among prosecuting and judicial authorities from the different EU Member States, but trust in the work performed by the investigating authorities is not a principle upon which defence lawyers work or should work. On the contrary, their duty is to distrust, and thus look for any possible infringement of the law – national or foreign – that might benefit their client.

While it is true that Member States may be required to presume that fundamental rights have been observed by other Member States, as this is the meaning of mutual trust, which is the basis of the principle of mutual recognition,[28] this has to be reinterpreted or restricted when it comes to incriminating cross-border evidence.

In the AFSJ, it can no longer be accepted that the free circulation of evidence occurs at the cost of limiting the rights of the defence. This has been acknowledged repeatedly in studies on transnational evidence with almost absolute unanimity, and the experience of the European Arrest Warrant also shows that blind trust ultimately needs to be accompanied by measures of control to prevent violations of human rights.[29] In fact, the Directive on the EIO already departed from the automatic application of the mutual recognition principle, introducing checks of the mutual legal assistance mechanisms.[30] In analogy, the 'blind' admission of foreign evidence without checking its legality, to my mind, is no longer acceptable as a general practice.

Furthermore, it is relevant to recall the arguments set out in the judgment of the CJEU in *Dzivev*[31] – although relating to domestic evidence – where the Court stated that the effectiveness of EU law in fighting criminal PIF offences does not impose on national courts the obligation to admit evidence that has been obtained in breach of a legal rule, namely, that the judicial authorisation for an interception of communications had been issued by a judge without jurisdiction. While the Court determined that excluding such evidence is not contrary to EU law, it added an important rider: imposing on Member States an obligation to admit such evidence would be contrary to the rule of law. This reasoning is relevant since it underpins the position stated in Article 4 ELI PD, establishing the principle of *lex loci* for the admissibility of cross-border evidence. On the other hand,

[28] See CJEU judgment of 25 July 2018, Case C-216/18 *LM*, ECLI:EU:C:2018:586, para 192.

[29] See A Klip, 'The European Arrest Warrant, from mutual recognition to mutual supervision' (2022) 12(1) *European Criminal Law Review* 82.

[30] On the nature of the EIO, keeping some controls known from the Mutual Legal Assistance systems, see para 6 of the Explanatory Memorandum of the Directive on the EIO; see also L Bachmaier Winter, 'Transnational evidence: towards the transposition of the Directive 2014/41 regarding the European Investigation Order in criminal matters' (2015) 2 *eucrim* 47.

[31] CJEU judgment of 17 January 2019, Case C-310/16 *Dzivev and Others*, ECLI:EU:C:2019:30.

this argument would determine that cross-border rules on inclusion of evidence without checking the legality of the evidence obtained abroad could also be seen as a breach of the rule of law, as envisaged in Article 2 of the Treaty on European Union (TEU).

Once it is accepted that the principle of non-inquiry is not in accordance with the level of protection of fundamental rights guaranteed in the EU Charter[32] and in the ECHR, the next step is to determine the principles that must be respected with regard to the admissibility of criminal evidence obtained abroad. It appears to be logical to claim that the basic principle is that evidence should be admissible if the rules applicable in the executing territory have been complied with. This is the well-known principle of *locus regit actum*. As formulated in the ELI PD, this principle does not operate as an exclusionary rule of evidence, in the sense of rendering inadmissible any evidence that does not comply strictly with the principle of *lex loci*, but rather as an inclusionary rule of evidence: if the foreign evidence has been obtained in accordance with the *lex loci*, as a rule, its admissibility in the forum state should not be denied for not complying with the exact formalities required in the law of the forum state.

This is set out in Article 4(1) ELI PD, which provides that 'evidence obtained in compliance with *lex loci* shall be admissible in criminal proceedings of the forum State'.[33] However, this principle has been softened in the ELI PD in order to leave a certain margin for national courts to challenge evidence collected abroad in spite of respecting the *lex loci*, when its use would violate a fundamental constitutional principle of the forum state. This sort of 'emergency brake', which should only exceptionally be invoked in practice, has been introduced to overcome the traditional opposition of the Member States towards any rules on admissibility of criminal evidence: there would still be a possibility to refuse evidence if it violated constitutional principles of the forum state. I am aware that this 'emergency clause' could lead to abuses, and ultimately result in maintaining the current uncertainty with regard to the admissibility of cross-border evidence. Despite this risk, and even if I do not consider the proposed solution to be ideal, it was still considered advisable to retain it in the ELI PD as a compromise, to prevent potential objections to the adoption of a directive on the admissibility of cross-border evidence in criminal proceedings.

Adopting the principle of the *lex loci* as the general admissibility rule for evidence obtained abroad does not prevent the requesting state from requiring the executing state to follow certain rules of the forum state when executing the order to gather evidence. This means that the principle of *lex loci* does not exclude the possibility of combining it, when possible, with the principle of *lex fori*.[34]

[32] Charter of Fundamental Rights of the European Union [2000] OJ C364/01.

[33] In favour of a mandatory inclusion rule, like that provided in the OLAF Regulation 883/2013, which could be flanked by rules of exclusion derived from the European human rights law, also Ligeti et al (n 2) 206.

[34] As already provided in Art 4 of the EU Convention on mutual assistance in criminal matters between the Member States of the European Union of 29 May 2000 (Council Act of 29 May 2000

If it is considered that the most rational approach to regulate the common standards on the admissibility of cross-border criminal evidence is to comply with the principle of the *lex loci regit actum* – with the necessary adjustments to the forum state legislation – the next step would be to determine who should examine the compliance of the evidence with the *lex loci* and how should this be done.

Obviously, it is the authority in charge of the criminal investigation that should ensure that all procedural acts – including the gathering of evidence – are carried out in accordance with the law. Ultimately, the principle of mutual recognition in cross-border evidence is based precisely on the assumption that all actors in the criminal justice system comply with the law, respect fundamental rights, and apply the necessary checks to ensure that national and international law is respected.

The requesting authority receiving the evidence collected in another EU country shall act according to this premise, but not in a 'blind' way.[35] It should be reasonable that the court in the forum state can ask the executing authority to describe in detail all facts and incidents that would also be accessible to the judge confronted with an investigative act carried out in its own jurisdiction: the measures taken to obtain the evidence, the actions carried out during its execution; the legislation applied; the parties involved in obtaining the evidence; or how the chain of custody was guaranteed. It does not seem unreasonable that the judicial authority of the forum state itself, upon such information, will carry out a minimal verification of the lawfulness of the evidence submitted by the executing state.

This is what is provided under Article 4(3) ELI PD: the judge of the forum state, upon receipt of information from the executing authorities, can check whether the evidence prima facie complies with sufficient guarantees for safeguarding the fairness of the proceedings. It should be noted that this control would not entail an exhaustive check on compliance with each of the requirements and formalities provided by the *lex loci* for the execution of an investigative measure. The forum judge would only be required to assess, even if only prima facie, that the right to a fair trial has been respected.

A similar standard is already envisaged in the Directive on the EIO,[36] which is aimed not only at facilitating the execution of the requested measures but also at ensuring that they are admissible later in the criminal proceedings for which they have been requested. Therefore, the admissibility of evidence obtained will certainly be facilitated if, in the execution of the EIO, the *lex fori* is also respected – at least those formalities explicitly indicated by the issuing authority that do not contradict fundamental principles of the state of execution. Article 14.7 of the

establishing in accordance with Article 34 of the Treaty on European Union the Convention on Mutual Assistance in Criminal Matters between the Member States of the European Union [2000] OJ C197/1), and in Art 9(2) of the Directive on the EIO.

[35] Luchtman, Karagianni and Bovend'Erdt (n 14), at 21, states that under the EU Charter of Fundamental Rights regarding the protection of the right to respect for private and family life, it should be considered that 'the courts of the forum state may have a bigger responsibility for dealing with unlawfully obtained evidence from other jurisdictions than follows from the Strasbourg caselaw'.

[36] Directive 2014/41/EU (n 13).

Directive on the EIO does not include rules on admission or exclusion of evidence but states that the trial court shall take into consideration the way evidence was obtained in a foreign country in order to assess its evidentiary value. Thus, the control provided under Article 4(3) ELI PD is consistent with the rules adopted in the Directive on the EIO.

In addition to the judicial authority, the defence must be granted the opportunity to verify whether the evidence gathered abroad respects the *lex loci*, and eventually also whether it complies with the requirements of the requesting authority regarding the *lex forum*. How can a defence lawyer assess whether the evidence gathered in another Member State has been lawfully collected? How can this assessment be performed? The answer, of course, depends on the type of investigative measure carried out. In the case of a witness or expert witness who is to be questioned abroad – and who will not appear at trial in the forum state – the defence lawyer should be notified in advance to allow them to participate – either remotely or in person – during the questioning and to be able to cross-examine the witness.

If the defence are faced with a measure that needs to be adopted and executed without prior notification – such as an entry and search or an interception of communications – this control can obviously only be carried out *a posteriori*. In this case and in all other situations where the participation of the defence during the obtaining of evidence abroad is not possible, it is unclear how a defence lawyer will be able to assess the lawfulness of the procedure used in order to obtain evidence. To that end, it would be important for the defence to have access to the relevant applicable law and to be provided with a description of the procedures followed in the gathering of such evidence. This might be cumbersome, but this would be exactly the way in which a defence lawyer would act when confronted with evidence gathered in their own country. Why should the same approach not be promoted in the case of evidence gathered abroad? Arguing that this procedure to ensure the appropriate safeguards in the gathering of cross-border evidence is too cumbersome, complicated, not feasible or too costly appears completely unsubstantiated and, furthermore, unacceptable when what is at stake is the protection of fundamental rights.

Indeed, the obstacle usually invoked is the lack of knowledge of the applicable law in the foreign country. However, this does not represent an insurmountable problem. It would suffice if the requesting state were provided with the legal provisions and the protocol followed in the execution of the investigative measure, and this could also be made accessible to the defence lawyer. Language problems should not, in the current state of development of artificial intelligence (AI) translating software, be a significant problem. With such information, the defence could at least have some indication as to whether or not the legal rules have been complied with and whether the admissibility of the evidence might cause a constitutional problem in the forum state. If there are doubts, a defence lawyer could decide to hire an expert to confirm the lawfulness of the evidence obtained abroad.

Is such an approach so complicated? In a globalised and interconnected world, this way of proceeding might involve, at least at the beginning, some additional efforts on the part of all actors involved. But once conduct protocols have been consolidated, I cannot see that the requirement of providing more detailed information of the *lex loci* and the execution abroad of the investigative measure could be invoked to oppose the adoption of the principles set out in Article 5 ELI PD. In any event, it goes without saying that within the EU, the application of the principle of non-inquiry in the admissibility of evidence obtained abroad is completely outdated, resembling an old-fashioned and unjustified remnant of the nineteenth-century criminal codes of procedure.

III. Admissibility/Exclusion of Evidence from the Perspective of the Case Law of the ECtHR and the CJEU

The ECtHR has constantly reiterated that in ensuring the observance of the ECHR by the Contracting States, it is not its function to deal with factual or legal errors allegedly committed by the national courts, unless they have infringed the rights and freedoms protected by the ECHR. While Article 6 ECHR guarantees the right to a fair hearing, it does not lay down any rules on the admissibility of evidence as such, which is primarily a matter for regulation under national law.[37]

Certainly, the mere fact that evidence has been obtained illegally will not lead to the proceedings being considered as unfair. As a result, the ECtHR will not regard proceedings to be unfair where the evidence on which a conviction was based was obtained in breach of the rights guaranteed by Article 8 on account of the means used not having been 'in accordance with the law' as required by paragraph 2 of that provision. Rather, the concern in such instances will be whether the rights of the defence have been respected and the weight of the evidence, especially where there are doubts as to its authenticity.

Nevertheless, the ECtHR has identified a number of cases where the type of infringement in the gathering of evidence will lead to rendering the proceedings unfair as a whole, and thus the Court prohibits the use of such evidence.[38] Therefore, there are exclusionary rules stemming from the Strasbourg case law, which have to be applied by all members of the Council of Europe. These cases are, namely, when the evidence has been obtained (i) under torture and severe

[37] See *Akbay and Others v Germany* App nos 40495/15, 40913/15, 37273/15 (ECtHR, 15 October 2020); *Schenk v Switzerland* App no 10862/84 (ECtHR, 12 July 1988) paras 45–46; *Teixeira de Castro v Portugal* App no 25829/94 (ECtHR, 9 June 1998) para 34; *Moreira Ferreira v Portugal (no 2)* App no 19867/12 (ECtHR (GC), 11 July 2017) para 83.

[38] See F Pinar Ölcer, 'The European Court of Human Rights: The fair trial analysis under Article 6 of the European Convention of Human Rights' in SC Thaman (ed), *Exclusionary Rules in Comparative Law* (Springer, 2013) 371.

cases of ill- or degrading treatment; (ii) by way of police entrapment or incitement; and (iii) through the violation of the right against self-incrimination, in certain circumstances.

A. Evidence Obtained Through Torture

The ECtHR case law has recognised for a long time that particular considerations apply in respect of the use in criminal proceedings of evidence obtained in breach of Article 3 ECHR. The use of such evidence, secured as a result of a violation of one of the core and absolute rights guaranteed by the Convention, always raises serious issues as to the fairness of the proceedings, even if the admission of such evidence was not decisive for securing a conviction.[39] The reason is because the prohibition of torture is a core value in democratic societies,[40] closely and inextricably linked with the respect for human dignity, which is part of the very essence of the ECHR.[41] This prohibition is absolute and it does not admit any derogation from it, even in the event of a public emergency threatening the life of the nation or in the most difficult circumstances, such as the battle against terrorism and organised crime, irrespective of the conduct of the person concerned.[42]

The obligation under Article 1 ECHR in conjunction with Article 3 ECHR requires states to take effective measures to ensure that individuals within their jurisdiction are not subjected to torture or inhuman or degrading treatment. All these arguments lead to the exclusion of any evidence obtained under torture, because, being an absolute right, there can be no weighing of other interests against it, such as the seriousness of the offence under investigation or the public interest in effective criminal prosecution. As stated in *Gäfgen v Germany*,[43] neither the protection of human life nor the securing of a criminal conviction may be obtained at the cost of compromising the protection of the absolute right not to be subjected to ill-treatment prescribed by Article 3, as this would sacrifice those values and discredit the administration of justice. The Court further declared that the admission of such evidence obtained as a result of an act characterised as inhuman treatment in breach of Article 3, but falling short of torture, will only breach Article 6. However, if it has been shown that the breach of Article 3 "had a bearing on the outcome of the proceedings against the defendant, that is, had an impact on his or her conviction or sentence", then such a remote breach will render the proceedings unfair as a whole.[44]

[39] See *İçöz v Turkey* App no 54919/00 (ECtHR, 9 January 2003); *Jalloh v Germany* App no 54810/00 (ECtHR, 11 July 2006) paras 99 and 104; *Harutyunyan v Armenia* App no 36549/03 (ECtHR, 28 June 2007) para 63; *Gäfgen v Germany* App no 22978/05 (ECtHR, 1 June 2010) para 165.

[40] *El-Masri v the former Yugoslav Republic of Macedonia* App no 39630/09 (ECtHR (GC), 13 December 2012) para.195.

[41] See *Bouyid v Belgium* App no 23380/09 (ECtHR (GC), 28 September 2015) paras 81 and 89–90.

[42] See *Khlaifia and Others v Italy* App no 16483/12 (ECtHR (GC), 15 December 2016) para 158.

[43] *Gäfgen v Germany* (n 38) para 176.

[44] ibid para 178.

In identifying whether treatment may be defined as torture, the ECtHR claims that it has to reach a minimum level of severity,[45] usually involving bodily injury or intense physical or mental suffering: 'however, even in the absence of those characteristics, where treatment humiliates or debases an individual, showing a lack of respect for or diminishing his or her human dignity, or arouses feelings of fear, anguish or inferiority capable of breaking an individual's moral and physical resistance, it may be characterized as degrading and also fall within the prohibition set forth in Article 3'.[46]

The prohibition of torture will render the proceedings unfair as a whole even when the torture has not been inflicted by state authorities but when the evidence has been obtained under torture by a private person. This was the case in *Ćwik v Poland*,[47] where statements recorded by members of an organised group during the torturing of one of its members – without any involvement of the state – had been used as evidence in proceedings against another defendant. The ECtHR, resorting to an analogy, considers that the same principles that impose the prohibition on using evidence obtained by the state by torture or ill-treatment also apply to the admission of evidence obtained from a third party as a result of ill-treatment proscribed by Article 3 ECHR, when such ill-treatment was inflicted by private individuals, irrespective of the classification of that treatment.[48]

In sum, there is already binding case law of the ECtHR that determines that evidence obtained by way of torture or ill-treatment is to be excluded as evidence. Including this exclusionary rule in an EU Directive would therefore not require the introduction of a new evidentiary rule but would reinforce the message that such an exclusionary rule is to be respected.

It could be argued that a rule excluding evidence obtained by torture is not necessary in the EU, since compliance with the respect for human rights is already ensured, and within the EU no citizen is subject to torture by the state. Apart from not being completely true (the judgments of the ECtHR against several Member States show that there are cases where violations of Article 3 ECHR were established), providing for a specific exclusionary rule at the EU level ensures its compliance in a more efficient way, and thus is more effective in preventing such evidence from being admitted in any domestic criminal procedure.

[45] See eg *Muršić v Croatia* App no 7334/13 (ECtHR (GC), 20 October 2016) para 97; *Paposhvili v Belgium* App no 41738/10 (ECtHR (GC), 13 December 2016) para 174.

[46] See *Bouyid v Belgium* App no 23380/09 (ECtHR (GC), 28 September 2020) para 87.

[47] *Ćwik v Poland* App no 31454/10 (ECtHR, 5 November 2020).

[48] See *Ćwik v Poland* (n 46) para 89, although the reasoning of the Court in applying the analogy between evidence obtained through torture by the state and by private individuals appears to be quite weak, since it lacks any further explanation. As explained in the Dissenting Opinion to this judgment, if the analogy is used as an argument to apply the same consequences to the state and private evidence obtained in violation of Art 3 ECHR, the elements for such analogical interpretation should be explained and elaborated. See Joint Dissenting Opinion of judges Wojtyczek and Pejchal (paras 11 and 16).

B. Evidence Obtained Through Police Entrapment or Incitement

According to Article 5(1)(c) ELI PD, evidence obtained as a consequence of police incitement or entrapment is also to be excluded. This is the aim of this provision, although its precise text is drafted in a broader way, as it refers to evidence obtained by 'deception and excessive interference with a person's freedom of will'.[49] The Strasbourg Court, in its well-established case law dealing with evidence obtained by way of police entrapment, has repeatedly stated that the public interest in the battle against crime cannot justify the use of evidence obtained as a result of police incitement. To do so would expose the accused to the risk of being definitively deprived of a fair trial from the outset; and thus for a trial to be fair within the meaning of Article 6(1) ECHR, all evidence obtained as a result of police incitement must be excluded, or a procedure with similar consequences as excluding the evidence must apply.[50] The Court clearly states that a person cannot be punished for a criminal activity that was the result of incitement on the part of state authorities.

The case law is very clear in differentiating between evidence gathered in legitimate undercover operations and evidence obtained by police entrapment, where officers do not confine themselves to investigating criminal activity in an essentially passive manner "but exert such an influence on the subject as to incite the commission of an offence that would otherwise not have been committed, in order to make it possible to establish the offence", and to provide evidence.[51]

While these differences might not have been the subject of discussion, until recently the consequences for evidence obtained by way of entrapment did not lead to the exclusion of such evidence. The German Federal Court of Justice applied a different 'dogmatic approach' to evidence obtained by way of police incitement. After recognising that police entrapment involved a breach of Article 6(1) ECHR, the Court decided that evidence obtained in violation of the Convention should not necessarily lead to its exclusion but could be treated as a ground to apply a significant reduction of the sentence. By applying the 'fixing of penalty' approach, the Federal Court of Justice considered that it was possible to afford the necessary redress for the breach of Article 6 of the Convention. This approach was not shared by the Strasbourg Court, as shown in the judgments in *Furcht v Germany* of 2014[52]

[49] As, for example, by exercising coercion or infringing a prohibition on interrogation or the right to refuse to testify.

[50] See, eg, *Teixeira de Castro* (n 35) paras 35–36; *Edwards and Lewis* App nos 39647/98 and 40461/98 (ECtHR, 27 October 2004) paras 46 and 48; *Vanyan v Russia* App no 53203/99 (ECtHR, 15 December 2005) para 46; *Ramanauskas v Lithuania* [GC] App no 74420/01 (ECtHR, 5 February 2008) para 54; *Bannikova v Russia* App no 18757 (ECtHR, 4 November 2010) para 34; and *Furcht v Germany* App no 54648/09 (ECtHR, 23 October 2014) paras 47 and 64; *Lagutin and Others v Russia* App nos 6228/09, 19123/09, 19678/07, 52340/08 and 7451/09 (ECtHR, 24 April 2014) para 117; *Grba v Croatia* App no 47074/12 (ECtHR, 23 November 2017) para 103.

[51] *Ramanauskas v Lithuania* (n 49), [GC] 5 February 2008, para 55.

[52] *Furcht* (n 49).

and *Akbay and Others v Germany* of 2020,[53] holding that 'where an applicant's conviction for an offence was based on evidence obtained by police incitement, even a considerable mitigation of the applicant's sentence cannot be regarded as a procedure with similar consequences to the exclusion of the impugned evidence'.[54]

In the judgment of 10 June 2015, the German Federal Court of Justice (Second Division), reversing its previous case law, held that an incitement to an offence in breach of the rule of law by members of the investigative authorities or third persons directed by them, as a rule, should lead not only to the exclusion of evidence so obtained but went even further: resorting to police entrapment should entail the barring of the criminal proceedings, which therefore had to be discontinued.[55] The Federal Court of Justice argued that a reversal of its case law was necessary in order to implement the *Furcht* judgment, according to which the 'fixing of penalty' approach was not sufficient to redress a breach of Article 6(1) of the Convention resulting from incitement. The Court went even further:

> The Federal Court of Justice noted that, according to *Furcht*, it was necessary either to exclude all the evidence obtained as a result of police incitement or to apply a procedure with similar consequences. This case law could best be integrated into the German law of criminal procedure by a finding that an unlawful incitement led to a bar to the criminal proceedings instead of an exclusion of evidence. It noted that the impugned measure, incitement, did not concern only the acquisition of evidence, but resulted in the offence as a whole. Recognising a bar to the criminal proceedings followed as a direct consequence from the fact that an offence was incited and thus from the unlawful conduct of the investigation authorities. It led to the discontinuation of the proceedings in respect of that offence (see, in particular, Article 260 of the Code of Criminal Procedure, at paragraph 45 above).
>
> In contrast, solely excluding the statements made by the agents provocateurs would often not lead to eliminating the results of incitement as required by the Court's case law because the sale of drugs was usually also observed by other police officers whose testimony would be sufficient to prove drug trafficking at the trial.[56]

These cases show that although the ECtHR had repeatedly stated that the use of police entrapment and the evidence obtained thereof were contrary to the Convention, national courts still continue to address this breach of the Convention by reducing the applicable penalty. It was not until 2015 that the German courts changed this approach and regarded the evidence obtained by police incitement not only as inadmissible, but also as a ground to discontinue the proceedings for being contrary to the principles of the rule of law.[57]

[53] *Akbay* (n 36).
[54] ibid para 50.
[55] File no 2 StR 97/14.
[56] *Akbay* (n 36) paras 53 and 54.
[57] See C Schmitt-Leonardy, 'Entrapment & Evidence. The Impact of the ECtHR's Judgment in the Case of *Furcht v Germany* on the Jurisprudence of the German Federal Court of Justice' (2017) 7(3) *European Criminal Law Review* 304.

The ELI PD should prevent other national courts from also considering that evidence obtained by police entrapment could still be used to convict a defendant, as long as the defendant was 'compensated' by some benefit in their sentence.

As with evidence obtained under torture or degrading treatment, although the case law of the ECtHR has clearly stated that the use of evidence obtained by police incitement renders the proceedings as a whole unfair, this has not resulted always in the exclusion of such evidence.

C. Evidence Obtained in Breach of the Right against Self-Incrimination

Breach of the *nemo tenetur* principle, as defined by the case law of the ECtHR in accordance with Article 6 ECHR, renders the evidence thus obtained inadmissible, without the possibility of applying a weighing test. As held by the Strasbourg Court, the privilege against self-incrimination lies at the very heart of the notion of a fair procedure under Article 6 ECHR.[58] This right, however, does not protect against the making of an incriminating statement *per se* but against the obtaining of evidence by coercion or oppression. It is the existence of compulsion that gives rise to concerns as to whether this right has been respected, and therefore the ECtHR had first to examine the nature and degree of compulsion used to obtain the incriminating statements.[59] According to the Court, the privilege against self-incrimination does not extend to the use in criminal proceedings of material that may be obtained from the accused through recourse to compulsory powers but which exists independent of the will of the suspect, such as documents acquired pursuant to a warrant, breath, blood and urine samples, and bodily tissue for the purpose of DNA testing.[60]

Article 5(1)(b) ELI PD seeks to reflect this case law by establishing the 'prohibition of unacceptable coercion on a person to incriminate oneself'. Aware that some types of coercion, such as, for example, imposing minor fines for not providing information or requested documents, are exerted upon individuals to provide certain information – for example, information on revenues and taxes – and are nevertheless considered admissible as evidence, the ELI PD qualifies the coercion that leads to an absolute exclusion of evidence as 'unacceptable', meaning coercion that is not legally foreseen and which has the primary aim of obtaining incriminating evidence. Since the concept of coercion is not easy to define, and some incentives to cooperate in the criminal investigation might be seen as coercive practices to waive the right against self-incrimination, it has been considered appropriate to clarify that the absolute rule applies only to those measures that constitute 'unacceptable' coercion. Being aware that this leaves a margin for interpretation,

[58] See Pinar Ölcer (n 37) 371, 381 ff.

[59] See Guide on Article 6 of the ECHR: Right to a fair trial (criminal limb) 38 at www.echr.coe.int/documents/d/echr/guide_art_6_criminal_eng.

[60] *Saunders v the United Kingdom* App no 19187/91, (ECtHR (GC)17 December 1996) para 69; *O'Halloran and Francis v the United Kingdom* App nos 15809/02 and 25624/02 (ECtHR (GC) 29 June 2007) para 47.

after many discussions on the drafting of this provision, it was decided that it was more beneficial to retain it, rather than deleting the whole paragraph due to the inability to provide an exact definition of 'unacceptable' coercion.

D. The Case Law of the CJEU

As to the case law of the CJEU, the Court has also recognised that issues regarding the taking of evidence and the use of that evidence in criminal proceedings fall within the competence of the Member States.[61] In the *Dzivev* case, the Bulgarian court asked whether applying a national exclusionary rule, where an interception of communications had been carried out with prior judicial authorisation as required by national law, but where that authorisation had been issued by a judge who did not have jurisdiction to do so, and thus was not in accordance with the law, was contrary to the principle of effectiveness of EU law. The CJEU has constantly held that Member States must ensure that domestic rules of criminal procedure permit the effective investigation and prosecution of offences linked to fraud and other illegal activities affecting the financial interests of the EU,[62] but, as recognised in *Dzivev*, 'the obligation to ensure the effective collection of the European Union's resources does not dispense national courts from the necessary observance of the principle of legality and the rule of law is one of the primary values on which the European Union is founded, as indicated in Article 2 TEU'.[63]

In brief, at a time when the EU law does not make provision for rules on the admissibility of domestic evidence, the CJEU holds, correctly, that Member States are free to exclude relevant evidence, even if such an exclusionary rule is based not on the violation of a fundamental right but on the breach of a legal rule on jurisdiction. The Court in Luxembourg underlines that respecting legality is a core element of the rule of law. Finding the truth or effective prosecution do not require the admission of evidence that has been obtained in breach of the law.

There are a few cases in which the CJEU has had the opportunity to address the issue of the admissibility of evidence in criminal proceedings in relation to the data retention rules.[64] In the Grand Chamber judgment of 2 March 2021,[65] the referring court asked about the compliance of national law on access to retained data with the proportionality principle. In particular, the national court asked whether Article 15(1) of Directive 2002/58,[66] read in the light of Articles 7, 8 and 11 and

[61] CJEU judgment *Dzivev and Others* (n 30); and judgment of 17 December 2015, Case C-419/14 *WebMindLicenses*, ECLI:EU:C:2015:832, both regarding the interception of communications and the admissibility of evidence in PIF and VAT fraud cases.

[62] CJEU judgment of 5 June 2018, Case C-612/15 *Kolev and Others*, ECLI:EU:C:2018:392.

[63] *Dzivev* (n 30) para 34.

[64] See, for example, CJEU judgment of 6 October 2020 in Joined Cases C-511/18, C-512/18 and C-520/18 *La Quadrature du Net and Others*, ECLI:EU:C:2020:791; and Grand Chamber judgment of 2 March 2021 in Case C-746/18 *Criminal proceedings against HK*, ECLI:EU:C:2021:152.

[65] *Criminal proceedings against HK* (n 63).

[66] Directive 2002/58/EC of the European Parliament and of the Council of 12 July 2002 concerning the processing of personal data and the protection of privacy in the electronic communications sector (Directive on privacy and electronic communications) [2002] OJ L201/37.

Article 52(1) of the EU Charter, must be interpreted as precluding national legislation authorising access to telecommunication data retained by service providers regardless of the severity of the crime – access not being confined to procedures to combat serious crime – and regardless of the quantity and nature of the data available.

In relation to this question, the judgment of the CJEU, citing its previous ruling in the case of *La Quadrature du Net and Others*, makes some statements on the issue of the admissibility of evidence in criminal proceedings:

> [A]s EU law currently stands, it is, in principle, for national law alone to determine the rules relating to the admissibility and assessment, in criminal proceedings against persons suspected of having committed criminal offences, of information and evidence obtained by general and indiscriminate retention of such data contrary to EU law[67] or by access of the national authorities thereto contrary to EU law.
>
> The Court has consistently held that, in the absence of EU rules on the matter, it is for the national legal order of each Member State, in accordance with the principle of procedural autonomy, to establish procedural rules for actions intended to safeguard the rights that individuals derive from EU law, provided, however, that those rules are no less favourable than the rules governing similar situations subject to domestic law (the principle of equivalence) and do not render impossible in practice or excessively difficult the exercise of rights conferred by EU law (the principle of effectiveness) (judgment of 6 October 2020, *La Quadrature du Net and Others*, C-511/18, C-512/18 and C-520/18, EU:C:2020:791, paragraph 223 and the case-law cited).
>
> As regards the principle of effectiveness in particular, it should be noted that the objective of national rules on the admissibility and use of information and evidence is, in accordance with the choices made by national law, to prevent information and evidence obtained unlawfully from unduly prejudicing a person who is suspected of having committed criminal offences. That objective may be achieved under national law not only by prohibiting the use of such information and evidence, but also by means of national rules and practices governing the assessment and weighting of such material, or by factoring in whether that material is unlawful when determining the sentence.[68]

And later in the same judgment, the Court mentions the elements to be taken into account when deciding on the admissibility or exclusion of information or evidence obtained in breach of EU law, namely the possibility to comment effectively on the lawfulness of the evidence gathered. The CJEU states that regard must be had to the risks that the admissibility of evidence might pose to the right to a fair trial; and finally, regarding the use of evidence obtained in breach of EU law on data retention, the Court decided as follows:

> If a court takes the view that a party is not in a position to comment effectively on evidence pertaining to a field of which the judges have no knowledge and that is likely to have a preponderant influence on the findings of fact, it must find an infringement of the right to a fair trial and exclude that evidence in order to avoid such an infringement.

[67] Quoting here the judgment in *La Quadrature du Net and Others* (n 63) para 222.

[68] *Criminal proceedings against HK* (n 63), paras 41 and 43.

> Therefore, the principle of effectiveness requires national criminal courts to disregard information and evidence obtained by means of the general and indiscriminate retention of traffic and location data in breach of EU law or by means of access of the competent authority thereto in breach of EU law, in the context of criminal proceedings against persons suspected of having committed criminal offences, where those persons are not in a position to comment effectively on that information and that evidence and they pertain to a field of which the judges have no knowledge and are likely to have a preponderant influence on the findings of fact.[69]

Therefore, the CJEU has already defined an exclusionary rule of evidence pertaining to the retention of digital evidence: when the defendant is not in a position to comment effectively on such evidence, and when such data are likely to have a significant influence on the assessment of the facts at stake in the criminal proceedings. However, the risk for the right to a fair trial would, according to the CJEU case law, only arise when, in addition to these two factors, a third one is present: that the evidence upon which the defence cannot comment pertains 'to a field of which the judges have no knowledge'.

This approach is quite interesting, since it appears that the CJEU will require evidence obtained in breach of EU law to be excluded when the evidence has an impact on the outcome of the case and the defence have not been able to challenge it, and where the adjudicating court is not able to counterbalance the absence of effective confrontation between the parties due to a lack of knowledge. The argument is strange, as it seems to link the exclusion of evidence to the role of judges – not being clear whether reference is being made to pre-trial investigating judges or adjudicating judges – in counterbalancing the absence of the possibility for the parties to comment on the evidence.

So far, I have attempted to reflect on the fact that the ELI PD does not add new exclusionary rules of evidence, and thus it does not interfere with the system of assessing illegally obtained evidence provided in the domestic rules of the criminal procedure of each of the EU Member States. In other words, it does not introduce new absolute exclusionary rules, but rather seeks to provide for effective implementation of those already recognised by the ECtHR and the CJEU.

IV. Further Rules on Inadmissibility of Evidence

As stated in the Explanatory Memorandum, Article 6 ELI PD provides for very limited situations in which evidence should be rendered inadmissible, albeit that this provision allows for exceptions in certain cases. These rules attempt to reflect an existing standard on human rights' protection and are widely accepted in the national legislation of the EU Member States. The ELI PD does not require Member States to adopt a new system on the admissibility of evidence. It is important to

[69] ibid. para 44.

stress that Article 6 ELI PD, in certain cases, could be read in conjunction with the provisions set out in Article 11(b) ELI PD (regarding the effectiveness of the remedies). As mentioned earlier in section III.C, under the rules of 'non-absolute' inadmissibility of evidence, the ELI PD still leaves a certain margin for the national courts on how to act in the face of evidence that should be rendered inadmissible but which is not subject to an absolute exclusionary rule. The ELI PD ensures that, at least when such evidence is not excluded from the file, it cannot be used to prove the crime and ensure a conviction.

Of course, in strengthening the rights of the defence, the drafters of the ELI PD would have preferred to introduce a higher threshold to completely exclude unlawful evidence, but this approach might have been seen as too ambitious to be accepted by the EU Member States. On occasion, a pragmatic approach to practice might lead to an increase in human rights' standards, even if the ideal level is not reached.

Under Article 6(1) ELI PD, incriminating statements made by a suspect during a police interrogation in the absence of a defence lawyer should not be admissible as evidence.

By including this rule, the drafters of the ELI PD seek to implement the so-called *Salduz* doctrine of the ECtHR,[70] according to which such confessions, made without ensuring access to a defence lawyer, are 'irretrievably prejudiced' and should not be used as evidence. Since the case law based on the *Salduz* doctrine is well known, it is not necessary to recall it here in all its aspects, which mainly seek to prevent the commission of any type of abuses by law enforcement agencies in obtaining forced confessions. The ELI PD aims to ensure that such pre-trial confessions made by the suspect to the police – detained or not – will not have any evidentiary value if a defence lawyer is absent. One important added value has to be highlighted here: the principle is that a lawyer has to be present for statements to be valid as incriminating evidence. Granting access to a lawyer will not be enough to sustain the validity of such confessions as incriminating evidence. This should be seen as a step forward in protecting the rights of suspects.

As to the protection of the right to lawyer–client privilege, this being a crucial aspect of the right to legal assistance and the exercise of an effective defence, as recognised in well-established case law of the Strasbourg Court, this protection should be reinforced by declaring inadmissible evidence obtained in breach of the privilege. Lawyer–client privilege is already included in the national Criminal Procedure Codes, but it is necessary to stress that Member States should ensure that evidence obtained in breach of the lawyer–client privilege is not used in criminal proceedings. The protection of the clergy–communicant privilege has also been added here, as there is absolute consensus that such communication is granted absolute protection in all Member States. Even if breaches of this right to

[70] *Salduz v Turkey* App no 36391/02 (ECtHR, 27 November 2008).

confidentiality are not relevant in practice – in contrast to the lawyer–client privilege – for systematic reasons the right has been included under Article 6 ELI PD, since it derives from the fundamental right to religious freedom.

Accordingly, other types of evidence, even if not lawfully obtained, could still be admitted and be assessed by resort to a balancing test if this is provided for under national law. This approach, which could be defined as '*de minimis*', should prevent unreasonable opposition from being raised by certain Member States, which might fear that their entire criminal justice system is going to suffer severe alterations due to new or unacceptable rules on the admissibility of evidence.

V. Common Rules on E-Evidence and the Regulation on E-Evidence Production Orders

According to the Explanatory Memorandum, the ELI PD includes a second part – namely Articles 7, 8 and 9 ELI PD – setting out concrete rules on the gathering of e-evidence. While with regard to other investigative measures the drafters refrained from moving towards a greater harmonisation of procedural rules, in the case of e-evidence, the approach is different.[71] What are the reasons behind these precise provisions on the collecting of e-evidence? Why should major harmonisation be reached of the national laws on the collection of digital data for evidentiary purposes?

Various reasons have been given why the drafters opted for this approach. The first is also a very pragmatic factor: regarding the impact of digital data and e-evidence in criminal investigations, very few systems have comprehensive rules regulating how to carry out access to digital data and to computer searches. Second, those that do provide for such rules have rarely adopted clear norms to prevent the disclosure of confidential communication between a lawyer and their client, or they lack an adequate procedure to sift and filter the privileged files. And finally, there is a wide agreement among IT experts as regards the protocols or guidelines to be followed in order to ensure the authenticity, integrity and completeness of digital data.

Attempting to ensure the free movement of criminal evidence within the AFSJ, it should not be overlooked that digitalisation is one of the major factors that has caused the 'transnationalisation' of criminal proceedings. If digital evidence is going to be transferred from one country to another, and there is no uniform or comprehensive regulation in the various Member States, it might be seen as

[71] The ELI PD has refrained from listing all the types or forms of e-evidence that may be adduced in a criminal procedure, and it does not enter into the nuances of proving computer errors and software evidence. In general, the applicable standards for cross-border e-evidence should apply *mutatis mutandis*. On all the particularities on e-evidence, with a focus on the UK case law, see the comprehensive analysis of S Mason and D Seng (eds), *Electronic evidence and electronic signatures* (School of Advanced Study, University of London, 2021) at https://humanities-digital-library.org/index.php/hdl/catalog/view/electronic-evidence-and-electronic-signatures/214/408.

appropriate to act beforehand, providing for certain rules that should prevent future obstacles to the question of admissibility because of the diverging legal rules applicable in each national legal system.

Nowadays, when cross-border e-evidence plays an increasingly important role, it is no longer sufficient to provide for the protection of procedural safeguards at the national level, because data and the communications electronically stored may be used in a different jurisdiction from where those communications took place.

As stated earlier, most legal systems do not have consistent and comprehensive regulation of transnational criminal proceedings, and rules on the applicable law or conflicts-of-law rules are, for the most part, lacking.[72] At the same time, IT forensic experts agree on common standards.[73] Given those generally accepted standards, what should prevent the EU from adopting them as legal rules?

The ELI PD attempts to reflect those standards, precisely those on accessing electronic storage devices, and the principles set out in ISO standards to ensure the integrity and authenticity of e-evidence.[74]

E-evidence is normally personal data the collection, storage or disclosure of which is subject to strict data protection rules, such as those implementing Directive (EU) 2016/680.[75] Also, general data protection law, mainly enshrined in the General Data Protection Regulation (GDPR) and in the e-Privacy Directive and the future e-Privacy Regulation,[76] may mean that the processing of personal data, for example by a provider of voice-control features for smart home devices, is illegal. Illegality may also follow on other grounds, including the obtaining of access to data in violation of criminal law, such as that enshrined in the Budapest Convention,[77] for example by hacking another person's account. Where such data are nevertheless

[72] See L Bachmaier Winter, 'Transnational criminal proceedings, witness evidence and confrontation: lessons from the ECtHR's case law', Utrecht Law Rev, Special issue, September 2013, vol 9–4, pp 126–148 at <http://www.utrechtlawreview.org | urn:nbn:nl:ul:10-1-112937>.

[73] A Stoykova, 'Standards for Digital Evidence: an inquiry into the opportunities for fair trial safeguards through digital forensics standards in criminal investigations', *Computer Law & Security Review* 2021, 42, 1–20.

[74] In drafting the ELI PD, many of the rules on e-evidence were inspired by the outcome of the DEVICES project, published in M Caianiello and A Camon (eds), *Digital forensic evidence. Towards common European standards in antifraud administrative and criminal investigations*, (Wolters Kluwer-Cedam 2021), free open access online.

[75] Directive (EU) 2016/680 of the European Parliament and of the Council of 27 April 2016 on the protection of natural persons with regard to the processing of personal data by competent authorities for the purposes of the prevention, investigation, detection or prosecution of criminal offences or the execution of criminal penalties, and on the free movement of such data, and repealing Council Framework Decision 2008/977/JHA [2016] OJ L119/89.

[76] Directive 2002/58/EC of the European Parliament and of the Council of 12 July 2002 concerning the processing of personal data and the protection of privacy in the electronic communications sector (Directive on privacy and electronic communications) OJ L 201, 31.7.2002; and Proposal for a Regulation of the European Parliament and of the Council concerning the respect for private life and the protection of personal data in electronic communications and repealing Directive 2002/58/EC (Regulation on Privacy and Electronic Communications), of 10 January 2017, COM/2017/010 final – 2017/03 (COD).

[77] Council of Europe Convention on Cybercrime (adopted 23 November 2001) ETS No 185.

procured as evidence in criminal proceedings, the question arises whether the fact that obtaining the data was illegal means that the data are excluded as evidence. Exclusionary rules are among the most highly contested issues in procedural law, both in criminal and in civil proceedings. Some jurisdictions would largely deny admissibility or follow something like an 'inevitable discovery' doctrine, while others take a more flexible approach and would admit the evidence, for example if it were the only available evidence and subject to a balancing of interests, taking into account, in particular, the nature of the illegality, the gravity of the offence at issue, the stage of the proceedings and possibly other factors.

On the other hand, the ELI PD has included measures to strengthen the defence rights, Article 8(2) requiring Member States to ensure that 'an IT expert is also involved in the production stage' of the e-evidence – of course, when this is possible – and, under Article 8(3), by putting the burden of proof of the authenticity and integrity of the e-evidence on the prosecution, showing that the protocols established under Article 7 ELI PD have been followed.

Finally, in Article 10 ELI PD, the drafters of the Proposal have striven to ensure that the right to access to a lawyer is facilitated in the state where the gathering of the evidence has taken place.

The recently adopted Regulation (EU) 2023/1543 of the European Parliament and of the Council of 12 July 2023[78] does not deal with exclusionary rules but includes two provisions that might have an impact on the admissibility of evidence. These provisions relate to the use of electronic communications in cross-border judicial proceedings and the documents transmitted through them:

> **Article 20: Legal effects of electronic documents**
>
> Documents transmitted as part of electronic communication shall not be denied legal effect or be considered inadmissible in the context of cross-border judicial procedures under this Regulation solely on the ground that they are in electronic form.
>
> **Article 21: Electronic signatures and seals**
>
> 1. The general legal framework for the use of trust services set out in Regulation (EU) No 910/2014 shall apply to electronic communication under this Regulation.
> 2. Where a document transmitted as part of the electronic communication under Article 19(1) or (4) of this Regulation requires a seal or a signature in accordance with this Regulation, the document shall feature a qualified electronic seal or qualified electronic signature as defined in Regulation (EU) No 910/2014.

Article 34(2) provides that Regulation 2023/1543 shall apply from 18 August 2026.

VI. Concluding Remarks

In the course of the discussions in the drafting of the ELI PD, it was clear that for some of the scholars and practitioners, such a legislative text should be more

[78] Regulation on European Production and Preservation Orders (n 7).

ambitious, expanding the exclusionary rules and even including additional rights for the defence. However, courts all over the world are reluctant to exclude evidence,[79] and even more so when such exclusion would allow a guilty person to go unpunished. This stance against exclusionary rules of admissibility is understandable, because, ultimately, legal systems prefer to allow the adjudicating court to apply a balancing test. This is the reason why the proposed Directive has tried to narrow the scope of exclusionary rules to those already prescribed by the ECtHR and the CJEU for the protection of human rights. Ultimately, the rules on the absolute inadmissibility of evidence set out in Article 5 ELI PD merely reflect the standards already defined by the ECtHR case law. Therefore, a question could arise as to the added value of regulating the already existing exclusionary rules in an EU Directive.

The issue of questionable added value was also raised during the discussions on the EU Directives on procedural rights in criminal proceedings for the accused and suspects; here, even if the ELI PD would not add essential elements to those already recognised by the case law of the ECtHR on absolute exclusionary rules on the admissibility of evidence, regulating them in a Directive offers clear advantages for its effective enforcement and thus for the protection of human rights. Among other things, this would allow for the common interpretation of the few exclusionary rules by the CJEU and the possibility to resort to EU instruments and institutions to enforce compliance. Even if the ELI PD could be more ambitious, its added value cannot be denied.

Furthermore, the ELI PD adds clarity to the principles to be applied to transnational cross-border evidence in criminal proceedings, and ensures that there will be a judicial remedy available in every Member State in the case of violation of the rules on admissibility of cross-border evidence.

In addition to these significant advances, not only will the rules on the gathering of e-evidence ensure an increased level of protection for defendants, as provided under Article 8 ELI PD, but the harmonisation in the gathering of e-evidence will also result in ensuring the inclusion rule. As to the question whether higher standards for the admissibility of evidence could have been reached, the response would be affirmative, but such would likely interfere with the constitutional traditions of the Member States and would not always be justified to ensure the effectiveness of EU law and the implementation of the principle of mutual recognition, as set out under Article 82(2) TFEU.

Finally, another important question that should be addressed in the future is whether the proposed rules on the admissibility of evidence should cover only cross-border evidence or should also apply to purely domestic cases, thus avoiding unequal treatment in the level of protection of the rights of defendants when facing a cross-border case or a domestic one.[80] In any event, even if the proposal for a Directive is only intended to apply to cross-border cases, as has been the case

[79] See Gless and Macula (n 12) 354.
[80] Vervaele (n 1) 56.

with the Directives on procedural rights, ultimately, a certain harmonisation of national rules will be reached.

Even if there are areas where the legislative action of the EU is more urgent and even more important, and being aware that the current European scenario needs to give priority to other more stringent issues – as, for example, the protection of victims of war crimes or the freezing of dubious Russian assets, or control of the immense amount of European funds allocated to the Member States to counter the consequences of the Covid-19 pandemic – the EU Commission should strive to further a legislative proposal on the admissibility of criminal evidence. I am convinced that once the advantages are understood by the Member States, a reasonable text that adequately strikes a balance between all interests at stake should not provoke adverse reactions. Rather the contrary: the quest to guarantee human rights and security should always be seen as a priority. Thus, the moment has arrived, and it can only be hoped that the common efforts of practitioners and scholars with policy makers can open the doors for the necessary legislative action at the European level.

2

Admissibility of Evidence in Criminal Proceedings: Lessons (and Problems) from the 'Data Retention Saga'

GIULIA LASAGNI*

I. Introduction

Admissibility rules lie at the crossroads of a number of essential questions that haunt whoever approaches the matter of evidentiary law, or, more broadly, inquires about the meaning of 'effective protection' of fundamental rights in all proceedings that see public authorities pitted against private individuals.[1] This is clearly even more so in cases of complex, multi-level legal systems, like the European Union (EU), where traditional aspects concerning the limits of public powers merge with diverging legal notions and qualifications, and with a pronounced cooperation dimension.

As the theme could be addressed from multiple perspectives, most of them requiring an analysis that goes well beyond the remit of this chapter, it is important to clarify from the outset the focus of the present contribution.

First, this analysis will focus on the EU dimension of admissibility rules for at least three reasons. To begin with, as pointed out since the establishment of the freedom of movement within the Union, a supranational approach is necessary in a context where economic, social and increasingly also political life, and the risks attached, are increasingly interconnected.[2] Moreover, looking for common supranational standards, or at their potential development, is justified by the practical need to keep pace with a reality where evidence is increasingly found in the form

* My heartfelt thanks to Dr Isadora Neroni Rezende for her intelligent and helpful comments on the drafts of this chapter. The Chapter is updated to May 2023.

[1] For a historical reconstruction of the principle and its role, J Skorupka, 'The rule of admissibility of evidence in the criminal process of continental Europe' (2012) 7(1) *Revista Brasileira de Direito Processual Penal* 93. The topic is significant in this sense not only at the national and regional level, but also in the dimension of international justice. For an analysis of this last dimension, not examined in this contribution, see M Caianiello, *Ammissione della prova e contradditorio nelle giurisdizioni penali internazionali* (Giappichelli, 2008).

[2] See, from the institutional perspective, European Commission, 'Green Paper on criminal-law protection of the financial interests of the Community and the establishment of a European Prosecutor' COM (2001) 715 final, 11 December 2001.

of data, often digital data, which itself is not limited by geographical boundaries. Lastly, the choice is also driven by a practical motivation, since the examination of admissibility rules present at the Member State level would undeniably require a much broader and in-depth study, due to their extreme variety.[3]

Second, due to the persistent lack of EU legislation on admissibility, this chapter will principally examine the rules drafted by the European courts, and in particular by the Court of Justice of the European Union (CJEU). As the CJEU has mostly tackled the issue of admissibility within a series of decisions – it might be called a 'saga' – concerning data retention and privacy rights (see section II), this further limits the scope of the analysis. On the one hand, this chapter will pay specific attention to admissibility rules drafted for a particular form of data, that is metadata of communications (traffic data, IP addresses and subscriber information). This inevitably leaves out a whole range of other data, such as banking or financial data, or digital data in general, which might be equally transnational and relevant in criminal proceedings, and for which, however, no specific standards have been developed yet. On the other hand, thanks to the chosen viewpoint, the discussion will highlight an aspect that is often not fully considered when looking at admissibility from a purely criminal law perspective, that is the (unclear) relationship between privacy and fair-trial violations, and the extent to which these aspects could, or should, overlap (section III).

At the same time, the European case law on admissibility exacerbates a classic theme, that is the difficulty, perhaps the impossibility, of drawing a clear line between preventive and *post-factum* investigations. The complexity of the problem will be exemplified in this chapter by looking at the field of financial supervision, a matter where, as it will be argued, the approach of the CJEU shows all its limitations (section IV).

Finally, some conclusive considerations will contextualise the lacunas of the applicable case law against a recent proposal for a Directive on admissibility of evidence, trying to delineate a possible way forward in a jungle of decisions and enforcement systems that make admissibility rules as essential as they are difficult to define (section V).

II. Admissibility Rules in EU Law: The CJEU Saga on Data Retention and its Repercussions on Criminal Proceedings

The absence of harmonised rules on admissibility of evidence, the 'great taboo' of European criminal justice as it has been called,[4] has been repeatedly stressed as

[3] See, for instance, S Gless and T Richter (eds), *Do Exclusionary Rules Ensure a Fair Trial? A Comparative Perspective on Evidentiary Rules* (Springer, 2019); SC Thaman (ed), *Exclusionary Rules in Comparative Law* (Springer, 2013).

[4] JAE Vervaele, 'Lawful and Fair Use of Evidence from a European Human Rights Perspective' in F Giuffrida and K Ligeti (eds), *Admissibility of OLAF Final Reports as Evidence in Criminal Proceedings* (University of Luxemburg, 2019) 56, 62.

critical, both from the perspective of defence rights and for impairing the effectiveness of judicial cooperation in criminal matters.[5] This consideration holds valid across the whole European dimension, encompassing the European Convention on Human Rights (ECHR), as well as the EU legal order.

On the side of the Council of Europe, the Court in Strasbourg has adopted a very self-restricting approach that leaves the matter almost entirely to the discretion of the national legislator. Even in cases of potential violation of Article 3 ECHR, the impact of torture or inhuman and degrading treatments on the admissibility of evidence has been assessed only to a limited extent by the Court, as famously showed in *Gäfgen*.[6]

Apart from this more extreme hypothesis, moreover, the Court has consistently stated that fair-trial violations do not automatically lead to the inadmissibility of the information gathered, and that Article 6 ECHR 'does not lay down any rules on the admissibility of evidence or the way it should be assessed'.[7] Similarly, the Court has not singled out significative admissibility elements from its case law

[5] See *Measures to improve cross-border access to electronic evidence for criminal investigations following the Conclusions of the Council of the European Union on Improving Criminal Justice in Cyberspace*, no 9543/17, 6 at https://home-affairs.ec.europa.eu/system/files/2020-09/20170522_technical_document_electronic_evidence_en.pdf; or the European Parliament, in Resolution of 3 October 2017 on the fight against cybercrime (2017/2068(INI)), P8TA(2017)0366 at www.europarl.europa.eu/doceo/document/TA-8-2017-0366_EN.html, §§ 59, 66, 67. The issue is not new, however, having been officially raised since the drafting of the Stockholm programme in the 'Green Paper on obtaining evidence in criminal matters from one Member State to another and securing its admissibility' COM/2009/0624 final, para 5.2, and extensively pointed out by legal scholars. See, amongst many, Vervaele (n 4) 56 ff; G Vermeulen, W De Bondt and Y van Damme, *EU cross-border gathering and use of evidence in criminal matters. Towards mutual recognition of investigative measures and free movement of evidence?* (Maklu, 2010) 145 ff; K Ligeti (ed), *Toward a Prosecutor for the European Union*, vol 1: *A Comparative Analysis* (Hart Publishing, 2013); M Kusak, 'Mutual admissibility of evidence and the European investigation order: aspirations lost in reality' (2019) 19 *ERA Forum* 391; S Gless, 'Mutual recognition, judicial inquiries, due process and fundamental rights' in JAE Vervaele (ed), *European evidence warrant – transnational judicial inquiries in the EU* (Intersentia. 2005) 121, 124; S Gless, 'Transnational Cooperation in Criminal Matters and the Guarantee of a Fair Trial: Approaches to a General Principle' (2013) 9(4) *Utrecht Law Rev* 95; Z Durdevic, 'Admissibility of evidence, judicial review of the actions of the European Public Prosecutor's Office and the protection of fundamental rights' in V Bazzocchi (ed), *Protecting Fundamental and Procedural Rights. From the Investigation of OLAF to the Future EPPO* (Fondazione L Basso, 2014) 123, 126; M Kusak, 'Common EU Minimum Standards for Enhancing Mutual Admissibility of Evidence Gathered in Criminal Matters' (2017) 23 *European Journal of Criminal Policy Research* 337; G Lasagni, 'Admissibility of Digital Evidence' in V Franssen and S Tosza (eds), *Cambridge Handbook of Digital Evidence in Criminal Matters* (Cambridge University Press, 2023).

[6] *Gäfgen v Germany* App no 22978/05 (ECtHR, 1 June 2010) paras 98–99, where the Court declared the extorted confession inadmissible but did not take a clear position on the evidence deriving from the latter; see, for all, SC Thaman, 'Fruits of the Poisonous Tree in Comparative Law' (2010) 16 *Southwestern Journal of International Law* 333.

[7] See, amongst many, *Garcia Ruiz v Spain* App no 30544/96 (ECtHR, 21 January 1999) para 28; *Schenk v Switzerland* App no 10862/84 (ECtHR, 12 July 1988) paras 45–46; *Miailhe v France (No 2)* App no 18978/91 (ECtHR, 26 September 1996) para 43; *Heglas v the Czech Republic* App no 5935/02 (ECtHR, 1 March 2007) para 84; *Hümmer v Germany* App no 29881/07 (ECtHR, 19 July 2012); *Moreira Ferreira v Portugal (no 2)* App no 19867/12 (ECtHR, 11 July 2017) para 83. Highlighting how, in this field, solutions of the ECtHR do 'not always offer the best protection to human rights', see S Allegrezza, 'Critical Remarks on the Green Paper on Obtaining Evidence in Criminal Matters from one Member State to another and Securing its Admissibility' (2010) 9 *ZIS* 575.

on digital evidence, which today represents one of the most fruitful grounds for raising admissibility issues at the supranational level. Most of the ECtHR decisions grounded on Article 8 show a rather self-restrictive approach as well, one that heavily relies on the 'overall' assessment of the harm concretely caused to the applicant and emphasises the roles of diverging rules established at the national level.[8]

At the EU level, no statutory regulation on the admissibility of evidence may be found yet,[9] except in very general or indirect terms, and thus with rather unpredictable harmonisation potential.[10] For instance, the Directive on the European Investigation Order,[11] Regulation 2018/1805 on freezing and confiscation orders[12] and the EPPO

[8] See, eg, *Sallinen and others v Finland* App no 50882/99 (ECtHR, 27 September 2005) paras 77 et seq; *Wieser and Bicos Beteiligungen GmbH v Austria* App no 74336/01 (ECtHR, 16 October 2007) para 53 et seq; *Robathin v Austria* App no 30457/06(ECtHR, 3 July 2012) paras 47 and 52; *Van Wesenbeeck v Belgium* App nos 67496/10 and 52936/12 (ECtHR, 23 May 2017) §§ 67–68; *Natunen v Finland* App no 21022/04 (ECtHR, 31 March 2009) paras 42–43; *Sigurđur Einarsson and o. v Iceland* App no 39757/15 (ECtHR, 4 June 2019) paras 85 et seq, on which see, also for a comparative analysis with CJEU case law, Lasagni (n 5); for an analysis of the relation between digital forensics best practices and national rules, and the interaction between administrative and criminal investigations with regard to digital evidence, see M Caianiello and A Camon (eds), *Digital Forensic Evidence: Towards Common European Standards in Antifraud Administrative and Criminal Investigations* (Wolters Kluwer/CEDAM, 2021).

[9] With the exception of the recent proposal for a Directive, which will be discussed further in section V.

[10] Although to facilitate the execution of measures issued within the Area of Security, Freedom and Justice, Member States may be informally incentivised to agree upon minimum common procedural standards. This way of proceeding towards harmonisation, however, is neither structural nor truly foreseeable in its development, and at the very least, it requires a certain amount of time before it produces consolidated results. Examples in this regard include, for the more consolidated practice of the European Arrest Warrant, aspects like safeguards in trials *in absentia*, on which see H Brodersen, V Glerum and A Klip, 'Improving Mutual Recognition of European Arrest Warrants for the Purpose of Executing Judgments Rendered Following a Trial at which the Person Concerned Did Not Appear in Person' at www.inabsentieaw.eu/wp-content/uploads/2020/02/InAbsentiEAW-Research-Report-1.pdf; and G Giudicelli-Delage and S Manacorda (eds), *L'intégration pénale indirecte. Interactions entre droit pénal et coopération judiciaire au sein de l'Union européenne* (Société de Législation Comparée, 2005). With regard to the Directive 2014/41/EU of 3 April 2014 regarding the European Investigation Order in criminal matters [2014] OJ L130/1 (EIO Directive) for instance, see the case of real-time monitoring of banking records; on which M Caianiello, 'L'attuazione della direttiva sull'ordine europeo di indagine penale e le sue ricadute nel campo del diritto probatorio' (2018) 6 *Cassazione penale* 2197. The phenomenon has recently started to be measured by Eurojust, again with regard to the EIO Directive; see Report on Eurojust's casework in the field of the European Investigation Order, November 2020, 28 at www.eurojust.europa.eu/publication/report-eurojust-casework-european-investigation-order.

[11] Among the extensive literature on the EIO Directive, see, amongst many, S Tosza, 'All evidence is equal, but electronic evidence is more equal than any other: The relationship between the European Investigation Order and the European Production Order' (2020) 11(2) *New Journal of European Criminal Law* 161; I Armada, 'The European investigation order and the lack of European standards for gathering evidence is a fundamental rights-based refusal the solution?' (2015) 6(1) *New Journal of European Criminal Law* 8; S Allegrezza, 'Collecting criminal evidence across the European Union: the European investigation order between flexibility and proportionality' in S Ruggeri (ed), *Transnational evidence in multicultural inquiries in Europe developments in EU legislation and new challenges for human rights-oriented criminal investigations in cross-border cases* (Springer, 2014) 51; C Heard, 'The European Investigation Order: Changing the Face of Evidence-Gathering in EU Cross-Border Cases' (2011) 2(4) *New Journal of European Criminal Law* 353; L Bachmaier Winter, 'European investigation order for obtaining evidence in the criminal proceedings study of the proposal for a European Directive' (2010) 9 *ZIS* 580.

[12] Regulation (EU) 2018/1805 of 14 November 2018 on the mutual recognition of freezing orders and confiscation orders [2018] OJ L303/1, on which see, for instance, A Bernardi (ed) and F Rossi (coord),

Regulation[13] all touch on the topic from the perspective of ensuring mutual recognition. However, they do not prescribe common requirements at the EU level that could integrate proper admissibility criteria. According to Article 31 of the EIO Directive, for example, findings involving the interception of telecommunications carried out without the technical assistance of the notified Member States 'may not be used, or may only be used under conditions which it shall specify, in cases where the interception would not be authorised in a similar domestic case'.[14] For its part, Article 37 of the EPPO Regulation excludes that evidence shall be 'denied admission on the mere ground that [it] was gathered in another Member State or in accordance with the law of another Member State'. In other words, those rules confer or deny relevance to the admissibility criteria established in national law, but they do not address the need to design common standards. Hence, the latter is a task that currently remains relegated to the national level, resulting in a highly divergent legal patchwork.[15]

Against this situation, the Court of Justice (CJEU) started to address the matter of admissibility, looking at it, as anticipated, mostly from a privacy-orientated perspective rather than a criminal procedure one. From a brief overview of such constantly developing jurisprudence, which stems from a cornerstone of the EU policies, a clear progression in its approach may be observed, with admissibility becoming an increasingly explicit issue as the saga has unfolded.

In its first decisions, *Digital Rights Ireland* (2014) and *Tele2/Watson* (2016), the CJEU started by merely stating the goal of ensuring 'effective protection of the data retained against the risk of abuse and against any unlawful access and use of that data'.[16] Thus, still in rather broad terms, the Court began to affirm the necessity to limit the use of collected data in light of the proportionality principle, even when such data are collected to meet important social needs, such as the fight against serious crime.[17]

Improving Confiscation Procedures in the European Union (Jovene, 2019); N Brandão, 'The right of defence under Regulation (EU) 2018/1805 on the mutual recognition of freezing orders and confiscation orders' (2022) 13(1) *New Journal of European Criminal Law* 28.

[13] Council Regulation (EU) 2017/1939 of 12 October 2017 implementing enhanced cooperation on the establishment of the European Public Prosecutor's Office ('the EPPO') [2017] OJ L283/1, on which see L Bachmaier Winter, *The European Public Prosecutor's Office: the Challenges Ahead* (Springer, 2018); H-H Herrnfeld, D Brodowski and C Burchard (eds), *European Public Prosecutor's Office: EPPO Regulation (EU) 2017/1939 implementing enhanced cooperation on the establishment of the European Public Prosecutor's Office. Article-by-Article Commentary* (Nomos, 2021).

[14] As highlighted by K Ligeti et al, 'Admissibility of Evidence in Criminal Proceedings in the EU' (2020) 3 *eucrim* 202.

[15] For a recent analysis of the variety of admissibility models across the EU, Vervaele (n 4) 59 ff.

[16] Joined Cases C-293/12 and C-594/12 *Digital Rights Ireland Ltd v Minister for Communications, Marine and Natural Resources and others*, ECLI: ECLI:EU:C:2014:238, para 66; Joined Cases C-203/15 and C-698/15 *Tele2 Sverige AB v Post- och telestyrelsen and Secretary of State for the Home Department v Tom Watson and others*, ECLI:EU:C:2016:970, para 122.

[17] 'Further, while the effectiveness of the fight against serious crime, in particular organised crime and terrorism, may depend to a great extent on the use of modern investigation techniques, such an objective of general interest, however fundamental it may be, cannot in itself justify that national legislation providing for the general and indiscriminate retention of all traffic and location data should be considered to be necessary for the purposes of that fight': *Tele2/Watson* (n 16) para 103; *Digital Rights Ireland* (n 16) para 51.

Proportionality then became the key argument in *WebMindLicenses* (2015), the only decision mentioned here in which the CJEU dealt with admissibility outside the domain of data retention (but still looking at it from a privacy perspective). In that case, the Court was facing admissibility problems deriving from information sharing between criminal and administrative proceedings concerning VAT frauds. Answering the referring judges, the CJEU established a double-proportionality test, according to which domestic courts shall verify whether 'the use [of the exchanged information] is proportionate to the aim pursued, examining whether all the necessary information could not have been obtained by means of investigation that interfere less' with the rights at stake; and if such requirement is not satisfied, 'the evidence obtained in the context of the criminal procedure and used in the administrative tax procedure must be disregarded and the contested decision which is founded on that evidence must be annulled if, as a result, the decision has no basis'.[18]

The Court then better detailed the limits of which information could be admitted to pursue which objective in subsequent cases, again on the matter of data retention. In particular, in *Ministerio Fiscal* (2015), the CJEU established some conditions for the use of metadata of communications, though without explicitly calling them admissibility criteria.[19] On the one hand, the Court slightly downplayed the relevance of the 'seriousness of the crime' criterion, to avoid a scenario in which abuses could be perpetrated in the name of a more efficient repression of whatever crime is considered more socially alarming at a given time or in a socio-political context. On the other hand, attention was shifted to the 'seriousness of the interference' caused by access to the data. According to the judges in Luxembourg, the latter shall be considered serious where it, 'taken as a whole, allow[s] precise conclusions to be drawn concerning the private lives of the persons whose data is concerned'.[20] The Court then combined the two conditions, basically establishing an admissibility scheme according to which the use of data gathered through serious interferences is allowed only in the case of the fight against serious crime, while non-serious crime could only justify access to data that did not entail the profiling of the affected subjects.[21]

The reference to admissibility finally became explicit in *La Quadrature du Net* (2020).[22] There, the CJEU stated that

> the objective of national rules on the admissibility and use of information and evidence is … to prevent information and evidence obtained unlawfully from unduly prejudicing

[18] Case C-419/14 *WebMindLicenses Kft v Nemzeti Adó- és Vámhivatal Kiemelt Adó- és Vám*, ECLI:EU:C:2015:832, paras 82–89, according to which the proportionality test is actually twofold: first, it shall be carried out by the criminal court where the evidence was collected, and then by the administrative court receiving that evidentiary material. On the possibility to apply this double test to the case where a piece of evidence is transferred from administrative to criminal proceedings, see S Tesoriero, 'Processo penale e prova multidisciplinare europea in materia di illeciti finanziari' (2016) 6 *Rivista di diritto processuale* 1526.

[19] Case C-207/16 *Proceedings brought by Ministerio Fiscal*, ECLI:EU:C:2018:788.

[20] ibid para 54; already in *Digital Rights Ireland* (n 16) para 27.

[21] *Ministerio Fiscal* (n 19) paras 48–63.

[22] Joined Cases C-511/18, C-512/18 and C-520/18 *La Quadrature du Net and Others v Premier ministre and others*, ECLI:EU:C:2020:791.

> a person who is suspected of having committed criminal offences. That objective may be achieved under national law not only by prohibiting the use of such information and evidence, but also by means of national rules and practices governing the assessment and weighting of such material, or by factoring in whether that material is unlawful when determining the sentence.[23]

Nonetheless, the Court continued, Member States' discretion encounters some limitations in this regard, in that national legislators are bound by the principle of effectiveness. Such principle – and this is the interesting connection made by the CJEU – is, in turn, linked with that of fairness, calling into question the 'adversarial principle and, therefore, the right to a fair trial'.[24]

The Court restated the idea in *Prokuratuur* (2021), where it became even more explicit, by saying that 'in deciding whether to exclude information and evidence obtained in contravention of the requirements of EU law, regard must be had, in particular, to the risk of breach of the adversarial principle and, therefore, of the right to a fair trial entailed by the admissibility of such information and evidence'.[25] If an infringement of the right to a fair trial is found, the Court must then 'exclude that evidence in order to avoid such an infringement. Therefore, the principle of effectiveness requires national criminal courts to disregard information and evidence obtained' by means of collection that are not in compliance with EU law.[26]

Now, in this regard it is necessary to clarify an important aspect. In the 'data retention saga', the CJEU established a series of requirements that allow national legislation to legitimately retain personal data, without infringing Articles 7 and 8 of the EU Charter.[27] These requirements take different shapes, stemming from the obligation to store the data within the EU, to the need of involving an independent and impartial authority, or to select the targets of the retention using a subjective or geographic perspective, just to mention a few. It is clear, from the Court's jurisprudence, that infringing such rules causes a violation of the rights to privacy and data protection. But does it also necessarily trigger the inadmissibility of the collected data? On a closer look at the decisions, the answer seems to be in the negative.

In *Commissioner of An Garda Síochána* (2022), in particular, the issue was explicitly brought to the attention of the Court in relation to criminal proceedings.[28] In that instance, the CJEU fell back on the 'national discretion' solution, considering that 'admissibility is, in accordance with the principle of procedural autonomy of the Member States, a matter for national law, subject to compliance, inter alia, with the principles of equivalence and effectiveness'.[29] Further applying

[23] ibid para 225.
[24] ibid para 226.
[25] Case C-746/18 *Prokuratuur (Criminal proceedings against HK)*, ECLI:EU:C:2021:152.
[26] ibid para 44.
[27] Charter of Fundamental Rights of the European Union [2000] OJ C364/01.
[28] Case C-140/20 *GD v Commissioner of An Garda Síochána and others*, ECLI: ECLI:EU:C:2022:258, paras 23–30.
[29] ibid paras 127–128.

the argument to the admissibility of evidence obtained by means of a retention scheme that did not comply with the necessary conditions, the Court declined to automatically declare a breach of fair-trial rights when the rights to privacy or data protection were also violated.[30]

The conclusion seems all the more necessary considering that some requirements listed by the CJEU to define a legitimate retention obligation are quite at odds with the exigencies of criminal investigations; or at least so it appears, reading an even more recent pronouncement on the saga. The reference is to *Spetsializirana prokuratura* (2022), where the Court considered that legislation violates Articles 7 and 8 of the EU Charter when it does not guarantee that persons whose data have been accessed are informed of such access and have a remedy if that access has been carried out unlawfully.[31] To support its assessment, the CJEU problematically added that the requirement imposing judicial authorisation to access the data is not sufficient without the data subjects' having been heard and, therefore, without the authorising court's having been able to examine the possible objections of those data subjects.[32] Hearing the data subjects before accessing the data, however, seems to be a requirement that would deprive the investigative measure of most of its meaning from a criminal investigation perspective. Thus, the only way to continue using communications metadata in criminal proceedings would likely be that of separating inadmissibility at trial from the assessment of the violation of the rights to privacy and data protection.[33]

Even setting aside this late decision, which in truth it presents some internal contradictions that make it rather difficult to interpret it on the point,[34] it seems at any rate established in the CJEU jurisprudence that only some breaches of the

[30] Talking about 'a victory for the law enforcement community, the surveillance powers of which have been significantly expanded', see V Mitsilegas et al, 'Data retention and the future of large-scale surveillance: The evolution and contestation of judicial benchmarks' [2022] *European Law Journal* 1, 10, who highlight that 'This flexibility is even extended to the admissibility of unlawfully collected evidence. After all, even if national data retention laws are violating EU law, national courts are given the discretion to accept such retained data as evidence in criminal proceedings, as the admissibility of evidence will largely depend on the national procedural rules'; as well as J Sajfert, 'Bulk Data Interception/Retention Judgments of the CJEU – a Victory and a Defeat for Privacy' (EU Law Blog, 26 October 2020) at https://europeanlawblog.eu/2020/10/26/bulk-data-interception-retention-judgments-of-the-cjeu-a-victory-and-a-defeat-for-privacy/.

[31] Case C-350/21 *Spetsializirana prokuratura*, ECLI:EU:C:2022:896, para 76, currently not available in English: 'les personnes dont les données ont fait l'objet d'un accès par [l]es autorités nationales en soient informées dans la mesure prévue par le droit de l'Union et sans qu'elles disposent d'une voie de recours à l'encontre d'un accès illégal à ces données'.

[32] ibid § 75: 'dans le cas où l'accès aux données conservées requiert une autorisation délivrée par une juridiction nationale, le principe d'effectivité ne semble pas être respecté. En effet … une telle autorisation ne suffit pas … sans que les personnes concernées aient été entendues et, partant, sans que la juridiction compétente pour délivrer une telle autorisation ait été en mesure de prendre en compte les possibles objections de ces personnes.'

[33] Though the situation would remain quite peculiar, as the absence of a right to be heard before issuing the authorisation would constitute a systemic violation in the legal order.

[34] Perhaps the decision could be interpreted with more flexibility, also allowing inclusion of the data subjects in the process after the measure has been carried out. For instance, at para 70 of its decision in *Spetsializirana prokuratura* the CJEU reasonably refers to the circumstance where notification is

conditions deriving from Articles 7 and 8 of the Charter may also cause inadmissibility at trial; hence, the question becomes that of their identification.

For its part, the Court does not provide a clear answer to the matter, and, from an institutional point of view, the choice is understandable. Deciding how to identify which breaches are so relevant as to affect the course of a criminal proceedings is a task with a clear policy content, which should better be assessed by a legislator rather than a court. Lacking any statutory norm in this respect at the EU level, the CJEU's reliance on national law also seems unavoidable. Nevertheless, this result evidently does not add to the requirement for ensuring legal certainty and uniformity of treatment within the Union: not only do Member States vary widely when it comes to procedural approaches and rules, especially in evidence law, but also the relationship between privacy violations and inadmissibility at trial is often an aspect significantly underrated in domestic systems. This state of affairs is therefore openly unstable, and clearly destined to evolve either by the introduction of harmonised rules at the EU level, or by the reluctant development of some further criteria by the CJEU. Incidentally, the two options are not necessarily alternatives; especially should the frequency of preliminary rulings continue to maintain the current pace in the data retention domain.

In this scenario, the leading role of the CJEU in shaping admissibility rules seems unchallenged, at least for the time being. And while the battle to bring the attempts to establish mass-surveillance mechanisms back within the boundaries of democracy is rightly recognised as one of highest peaks that contribute to defining the European identity and values,[35] the approach showed in the saga about certain fair-trial rights raises some worries.

What causes concern is the prominence given by the CJEU to the right for the parties to comment effectively on the evidence submitted. Both in *La Quadrature du Net* and *Prokuratuur*, the Court explicitly linked the issue of admissibility to the assessment of whether 'a party is not in a position to comment effectively on evidence pertaining to a field of which the judges have no knowledge and is likely

'susceptible de compromettre les enquêtes menées par ces autorités'; however, this possibility is not referred to again in the subsequent reasoning, nor does it form part of the decision of the Court. Also the wording of the decision (using *autorisation* instead of *contrôle*) does not literally support an interpretation of an *ex post* notification. In other related fields, however, the Court has explicitly (and reasonably) admitted the possibility of 'duly justified urgency' exceptions to the prior notification duty: see, eg, Case C-817/19 *Ligue des droits humains ASBL v Conseil des ministres*, ECLI:EU:C:2022:491, about passenger name record (PNR) data, at para 223, 'In particular, in order to ensure, in practice, that fundamental rights are fully observed in the system put in place by the PNR Directive and, in particular, the conditions set out in paragraphs 218 and 219 above, it is essential that disclosure of PNR data for the purposes of subsequent assessment be, as a general rule, except in the event of duly justified urgency, subject to a prior review carried out either by a court or by an independent administrative authority, and that the decision of that court or body be made following a reasoned request by the competent authorities submitted, inter alia, within the framework of procedures for the prevention, detection or prosecution of crime. In the event of duly justified urgency, the review must take place within a short time.'

[35] Perhaps one of the fields where the so-called 'Brussels Effect' is more pronounced. On the magnitude and impact of the phenomenon, see A Bradford, *The Brussels Effect: How the European Union Rules the World* (Oxford University Press, 2020).

to have a preponderant influence on the findings of fact'; in such cases, a court 'must find an infringement of the right to a fair trial and exclude that evidence to avoid such an infringement'.[36]

Conferring such a relevance to the right to be heard resembles the approach of the ECtHR, which includes it among the range of potential 'counterbalancing measures' capable of reducing the finding of violations of Article 6 ECHR.[37] Legal scholars have already pointed out the problematic aspects of this position: from the debasement of the individual aspects composing the right to a fair trial, a single violation of which could now be mutually compensated, to the loss of legal foreseeability about the minimum level of procedural rights protection, which could bring a court to declare their violation.[38] The idea that the CJEU could also start sharing a similar 'overall approach', and specifically that it could consider the right to be heard as a sort of 'admissibility trigger', cannot but shed a sinister light on the protection of fair-trial rights throughout the Union, and should be carefully avoided by judges in Luxembourg.

III. The Scope of Retention Obligations and Access to Data: A Significant but Uncertain Role for Admissibility Rules

Further critical aspects concerning admissibility in the CJEU case law emerge from the consideration that, in practice, the same piece of communications metadata may be exploited not only for *post factum* criminal investigations, but also for other purposes, mostly of a preventive nature. The classic problem of reconciling prevention and repression, or at least of trying to draw a foreseeable line between the two domains,[39] surfaces in the CJEU saga in relation to the scope of retention obligations.

In this regard, the dilemma stems from the difficulty in finding a balance between apparently incompatible statements. On the one hand, there is the

[36] *La Quadrature du Net* (n 22) para 226; *Prokuratuur* (n 25) para 44; and more recently, Joined Cases C-339/20 and C-397/20, *VD and SR*, ECLI:EU:C:2022:703, para 106 inspired by *Mantovanelli v France* App no 21497/93 (ECtHR, 18 March 1997) paras 34–36.

[37] See for all *Schatschaschwili v Germany* App no 9154/10 (ECtHR, 15 December 2015) paras 107, 114–116, 125–131; *Ibrahim and others v The United Kingdom* App nos 50541/08, 50571/08, 50573/08 and 40351/09 (ECtHR, 13 September 2016) para 274; *Murtazaliyeva v Russia* App no 36658/05 (ECtHR, 18 December 2018) paras 167–168. On the overall approach applied to surveillance matter, see *Big Brother Watch and others v The United Kingdom* App nos 58170/13, 62322/14 and 24960/15 (ECtHR (GC), 25 May 2021) paras 360 and 370; *Case of Centrum för Rättvisa v Sweden* App no 35252/08 (ECtHR, 25 May 2021) para 274. See further L Bachmaier Winter, 'Proportionality, surveillance and criminal investigation: Strasbourg Court facing Big Brother' in E Billis, N Knust and A Rui (eds), *The Principle of Proportionality in Crime Control and Criminal Justice* (Hart Publishing, 2021) 317.

[38] See, eg, T Mariniello (ed), 'Too Much Unfairness in the "Overall Fairness" Test (*Murtazaliyeva v Russia*)' in T Mariniello (ed), *Judge Pinto de Albuquerque and the Progressive Development of International Human Rights Law* (Brill-Nijhoff, 2021) 231; M Caianiello, 'You Can't Always Counterbalance What You Want' (2017) 25(4) *European Journal of Crime, Criminal Law and Criminal Justice* 283.

[39] See, for all, A Ashworth and L Zedner, *Preventive Justice* (Oxford University Press, 2014) 51 ff.

(laudable) intention of the Court to prevent the establishment of generalised and indiscriminate systems of mass surveillance, which would be at odds with democratic principles. On the other hand, there is the awareness that to meet legitimate preventive goals, and – at least in the current practice – to meaningfully apply several criminal investigation techniques, targeted retention of data represents a solution only in a limited number of cases. As explicated by the referring court in *Commissioner of An Garda Síochána*, the idea is that

> in essence, … only the general and indiscriminate retention of traffic and location data allows serious crime to be combated effectively, which the targeted and expedited retention (*quick freeze*) of data does not make possible.
>
> As regards targeted retention, [the question concerns] whether it is possible to target specific groups or geographic areas for the purposes of combating serious crimes, since some serious crimes rarely involve circumstances known to the competent national authorities enabling them to suspect the commission of an offence in advance. In addition, targeted retention could give rise to discrimination. As for expedited retention, … that that is only useful in situations where it is possible to identify a suspect in the very early stages of an investigation.[40]

Against such objection, repeatedly brought to the attention of the Court due to the lack of clarity of the current legal framework, the reply of the judges in Luxembourg has developed in two directions, starting from *La Quadrature du Net* and *Privacy International* (2020).[41] Those are indeed the decisions where, along the line already traced by the ECtHR,[42] and to a certain extent, the CJEU first admitted the circumscribed possibility of generalised data retention mechanisms. The political move of the Court was grounded on the need to address the position of several Member States, that EU law did not apply in the domain of national security,[43] and by the intent of submitting these systems to a centralised form of control and thus reducing potential abuses. Nonetheless, the opening introduced some intrinsic contradiction in the system or rules designed by the Court.[44]

[40] *Commissioner of An Garda Síochána* (n 28) para 26.

[41] *La Quadrature du Net* (n 22); Case C-623/17 *Privacy International v Secretary of State for Foreign and Commonwealth Affairs and others*, ECLI:EU:C:2020:790, on which see Mitsilegas et al (n 30) 2 ff: 'The CJEU, in a way, has initiated a perilous pas de deux, trying to ensure fundamental rights protection through the applicability of EU law while opening the back door to mass surveillance through "fifty shades" of public interests. The evolution of the Court's case-law highlights the intricate institutional architecture at play when it comes to defining the future of mass surveillance and democracy in the digital era, with a complex part played by the judiciary, the legislative and the executive in a multi-level polity such as the EU.'

[42] *Big Brother Watch and others v the United Kingdom* Appl no 58170/13, 62322/14 and 24960/15 (ECtHR, 13 September 2018); and *Big Brother Watch and others v The United Kingdom* App nos 58170/13, 62322/14 and 24960/15 (ECtHR (GC), 25 May 2021). See Bachmaier Winter (n 37) 318 ff.

[43] See, for instance, the intervention of the UK, Czech, Estonian, Irish, French, Cypriot, Hungarian, Polish and Swedish Governments in *Privacy International* (n 41) (para 32).

[44] Critical about the choice of the Court, Mitsilegas et al (n 30) 5 ff, and esp at 8: 'Perhaps, if the Court had taken on board previous criticism that bulk retention of telecommunications metadata amounts to a violation of the essence of the right to privacy and data protection and freedom of expression, then confusion regarding which interferences are particularly serious would not have occurred.'

The CJEU today identifies two concentric scopes for retention obligations, grounding the difference on the purpose pursued by the public authorities. In principle, general and indiscriminate retention is considered legitimate only where the aim is that of safeguarding national security;[45] all other goals, including crime prevention or repression, do not justify a similar limitation of fundamental rights. In this second domain, therefore, retention obligations are allowed only insofar as they are targeted.[46]

Within such a framework, two aspects emerge as problematic: first, the definition of 'national security', especially regarding objectives that are difficult to classify, such as the protection of financial markets (on which see section IV); second, the consideration that a single piece of data could be used for multiple, overlapping purposes, which are not known to the service provider who retains that piece of data. Hence, if service providers are not in the position of excluding that national security demands could ever be raised, a broader retention seems in practice the only practical solution. However, if retention obligations tend to remain generalised for practical reasons, the moment of selection inevitably shifts to that of access, and therefore of admissibility rules. This is not, however, the perspective of the Court, which insists on anticipating the *discrimen* at the level of setting the scope of the retention obligation.[47] The result is an interpretation that risks appearing more theoretical than practically applicable; and perhaps this is one of the reasons that fuel the massive number of preliminary references in the domain.

Naturally, the CJEU is aware of such problems. Starting from *Ministerio Fiscal*, and then more systematically from *La Quadrature du Net*, the Court tried to address them by proposing a classification, grounded on the profiling potential of the collected data.[48]

At the lowest level the CJEU put subscriber data, that is 'data relating to the civil identity of users of electronic communications systems', which information

[45] To prevent abuses, the Court also introduced conditions and procedural requirements that should apply in this case. In particular, retention obligation can be considered proportionate only where the threat to national security is proved 'to be genuine and present or foreseeable'; moreover, the decision to impose such a restriction shall be 'subject to effective review, either by a court or by an independent administrative body whose decision is binding, the aim of that review being to verify that one of those situations exists and that the conditions and safeguards which must be laid down are observed, [and] that instruction may be given only for a period that is limited in time to what is strictly necessary, but which may be extended if that threat persists'. See *La Quadrature du Net* (n 22) para 168; *Commissioner of An Garda Síochána* (n 28) § 58.

[46] Even though the European Commission would rather support a broader scope in this case, at least with regard to serious crime; see *Commissioner of An Garda Síochána* (n 28) para 60.

[47] In this sense, see also Mitsilegas et al (n 30) 11: 'The Court found that access for the purposes of the prevention, investigation, detection and prosecution of criminal offences to a set of traffic or location data that are liable to provide information regarding the communications made by a user of a means of electronic communications, or the location of the terminal equipment and thus to allow precise conclusions to be drawn concerning their private life is only permitted in relation to serious crimes. Consequently, any attempt to disassociate retention from access are destined to fail the legality test.'

[48] The classification was then confirmed in subsequent case law, see eg Joined Cases C-793/19 and C-794/19 *Bundesrepublik Deutschland v SpaceNet AG and others*, ECLI:EU:C:2022:702, paras 75 et seq.

is considered rather unproblematic and thus may be subject to generalised and indiscriminate retention to meet any of the legitimate objectives of general interests according to Articles 7 and 8 of the EU Charter.[49] On the opposite side of the scale one may find traffic and location data for which, due to their high profiling potential, retention may be allowed only 'on the basis of objective and non-discriminatory factors, according to the categories of persons concerned or using a geographical criterion, for a period that is limited in time to what is strictly necessary, but which may be extended'.[50]

The boundaries of the selection, however, continue to be somewhat ambiguous, despite the explanatory effort of the Court. For instance, to meet the perplexities raised by the referring court in *Commissioner of An Garda Síochána*, the CJEU clarified that targeted retention may also encompass the collection of data that is 'likely to reveal a link, at least an indirect one, with serious criminal offences, to contribute in one way or another to combating serious crime or to preventing a serious risk to public security or a risk to national security'.[51] Interestingly, the Court stressed that the measures could also address 'persons who have been identified beforehand, in the course of the applicable national procedures and on the basis of objective and non-discriminatory factors, as posing a threat to public or national security in the Member State concerned,' for instance 'persons who, on the basis of an identification, are the subject of an investigation or other measures of current surveillance or of a reference in the national criminal record relating to an earlier conviction for serious crimes with a high risk of reoffending'.[52] A similar interpretation clearly meets some of the investigative expectations about exploiting data potential, as mentioned above. At the same time, such criteria also open up significant risks of discrimination, as, for instance, the vagueness of the recalled notions (eg 'high risk of reoffending' or 'subject of an investigation') say nothing about how or after how long a person could be excluded from the reference group.[53]

The need to take the temporal dimension into account emerges more explicitly with regard to the geographical criterion. Indeed, the CJEU affirmed that the selection must be based on

> objective and non-discriminatory factors, that there exists, in one or more geographical areas, a situation characterised by a high risk of preparation for or commission of serious criminal offences. Those areas may include places with a high incidence of

[49] *Ministerio Fiscal* (n 19) para 60; *La Quadrature du Net* (n 22) para 168; *Commissioner of An Garda Síochána* (n 28) para 67.

[50] *La Quadrature du Net* (n 22) para 168; *Commissioner of An Garda Síochána* (n 28) para § 67; subject to 'effective judicial review' and for a 'specific period of time', national authorities can also issue an order addressed to service providers, requiring the 'expedited retention (*quick freeze*)' of such data.

[51] *Commissioner of An Garda Síochána* (n 28) para 76.

[52] *Commissioner of An Garda Síochána* (n 28) paras 77–78.

[53] Assessment that is currently left to a case-by-case evaluation by the Court; see, for instance, the reference to a 6-month period for PNR data in *Ligue des droits humains ASBL v Conseil des ministres* (n 34) paras 255–262.

> serious crime, places that are particularly vulnerable to serious crime, such as places or infrastructure which regularly receive a very high volume of visitors, or strategic locations, such as airports, stations, maritime ports or tollbooth areas … [eg by taking into account] the average crime rate in a geographical area, without that authority necessarily having specific indications as to the preparation or commission, in the areas concerned, of acts of serious crime.[54]

To avoid being considered discriminatory, the Court prescribed that such assessment 'be amended in accordance with changes in the circumstances that justified their selection'.[55]

In between these two classes of data, 'IP addresses assigned to the source of an internet connection' hold a sort of intermediate position.[56] Such data are indeed problematic, for two reasons. First, although they 'may allow precise conclusions to be drawn concerning the private life of the user',[57] IP addresses are not uniformly treated at the national level, being at times assimilated to subscriber data and at other times to traffic data.[58] Second, contrary to the general expectation of the Court towards metadata of communications,[59] access to IP addresses can in certain cases be the 'only means of investigation' enabling identification of the perpetrator,[60] for instance for offences committed online, like child pornography. Hence, to balance the need to protect privacy with that of not impairing investigation of serious crime, the CJEU designed a mixed model for IP addresses, allowing a generalised retention but then subjecting access to the stricter requirements established for traffic data.[61]

Looking comprehensively at the system, and trying to picture it in practice, all these rules seem once more to suggest a model where retention obligations tend to be generalised and untargeted, while only access to data may be tailored on the bases of the interests at stake. Still, after the annulment of Directive 2006/24

[54] *Commissioner of An Garda Síochána* (n 28) paras 79–81. See in particular ibid para 80, 'since a targeted retention using that criterion is likely to concern, depending on the serious criminal offences in question and the situation specific to the respective Member States, both the areas marked by a high incidence of serious crime and areas particularly vulnerable to the commission of those acts, it is, in principle, not likely moreover to give rise to discrimination, as the criterion drawn from the average rate of serious crime is entirely unconnected with any potentially discriminatory factors'.

[55] ibid paras 81–82, where the Court also states, perhaps a bit too drastically, that geographical targeting is not discriminatory as 'the criterion drawn from the average rate of serious crime is entirely unconnected with any potentially discriminatory factors'.

[56] *La Quadrature du Net* (n 22) para 168; *Commissioner of An Garda Síochána* (n 28) para 67.

[57] eg *Commissioner of An Garda Síochána* (n 28) para 73.

[58] As noticed by Mitsilegas et al (n 30) 10: 'Traffic data is interesting, as in Member States an IP address, port number for dynamic IP addresses and subscriber identification module (SIM) and device identification numbers (eg international mobile subscriber identity (IMSI) or international mobile equipment identity (IMEI)) are deemed either as subscriber data or traffic data.'

[59] *Commissioner of An Garda Síochána* (n 28) para 69, according to which, 'it must be observed, in the first place, that the effectiveness of criminal proceedings generally depends not on a single means of investigation but on all the means of investigation available to the competent national authorities for those purposes'.

[60] *La Quadrature du Net* (n 22) paras 153–154; *Commissioner of An Garda Síochána* (n 28) para 73.

[61] *La Quadrature du Net* (n 22) paras 155–156; *Commissioner of An Garda Síochána* (n 28) para 74. See however also AG Opinion in the same case, suggesting to extend the retention of IP addresses also beyond the case of serious crimes.

(the Data Retention Directive declared invalid by the CJEU), and given the lack of new European legislation on the matter, the Court never explicitly endorsed such a broad retention scheme. The result is a sort of disconnection between practice and principles; a system where access and admissibility rules must clearly play a crucial role, though exactly what this role should look like remains mired in uncertainty.

IV. Defining National Security: The Case of the Protection of Financial Markets

A last aspect to be examined concerns the definition of national security, which, in the interpretation of the Court, is decisive in shaping the scope of the retention obligation. According to the CJEU, the notion

> corresponds to the primary interest in protecting the essential functions of the State and the fundamental interests of society through the prevention and punishment of activities capable of seriously destabilising the fundamental constitutional, political, economic or social structures of a country and, in particular, of directly threatening society, the population or the State itself, such as terrorist activities.[62]

Moreover, 'unlike crime', a threat to national security 'must be genuine and present, or, at the very least, foreseeable, which presupposes that sufficiently concrete circumstances have arisen to be able to justify a generalised and indiscriminate measure of retention of traffic and location data for a limited period of time'.[63] Against these interpretative criteria, defining the precise scope of the notion is far from being straightforward. In particular, it is not clear what qualification should be given to cases where a goal is served by multiple lines of action, which cannot be *a priori* separated from one another. A significant example in this sense is offered by the financial sector, and in particular, by the supervision of financial markets.[64]

[62] *Commissioner of An Garda Síochána* (n 28) para 61.

[63] ibid para 62. See also ibid para 63, according to which 'criminal behaviour, even of a particularly serious nature, cannot be treated in the same way as a threat to national security. As the Advocate General observed in points 49 to 50 of his Opinion, to treat those situations in the same way would be likely to create an intermediate category between national security and public security for the purpose of applying to the latter the requirements inherent in the former.' On the same lines, see also *La Quadrature du Net* (n 22) para 63; *Spetsializirana prokuratura* (n 31) para 60, on which see I Neroni Rezende, 'Facial Recognition for Preventive Purposes: The Human Rights Implications of Detecting Emotions in Public Spaces' in L Bachmaier Winter and S Ruggeri (eds), *Investigating and Preventing Crime in the Digital Era. New Safeguards, New Rights* (Springer, 2022) 67, 86.

[64] The relevance of communications metadata in financial supervision can vary depending on the sector at stake. This chapter focuses on the supervision of financial markets, as this is the field where it is explicitly recognised. However, such metadata could also play a role in other financial sectors, for instance in banking supervision, especially in certain types of assessment where subjective features and interactions are more significant, such as in fit-and-proper or qualifying holdings procedures (Arts 4(1)(e) and 15, Council Regulation (EU) No 1024/2013 of 15 October 2013 (SSM R) and Arts 93 and 94, Regulation (EU) No 468/2014 of the European Central Bank of 16 April 2014 (SSM FR)). For example, Art 10 SSM R confers on the European Central Bank the power to require legal or natural persons to 'provide all information that is necessary' to carry out its institutional tasks. Among such

This is a domain where access to metadata of communications represents an important way of acquiring the information necessary to allow the competent authorities to carry out their institutional tasks. Actually, in some instances, like the fight against insider trading, communications metadata data represent a crucial, sometimes even the sole, element in proving the existence of types of conduct that counter the objectives pursued by the authorities.[65] The importance is mirrored in the relevant legal bases, which allow financial supervisors at the central and at the

subjects under the obligation to cooperate with the Single Supervisory Mechanism (SSM), there are also third parties to whom credit institutions of the participating Member States 'have outsourced functions or activities' (Art 10(1)(f) SSM R). The provision, although not directly related to metadata of communications, could be interpreted as also including the power to request service providers to give access to the data. A similar situation can be found also looking at the few harmonised powers of national banking supervisors. According to Art 65(3)(a) and (b) of Directive 2013/36/EU of the European Parliament and of the Council of 26 June 2013 (last consolidated text of 1 January 2022) ('CRD IV'), competent authorities shall have the power to request all relevant information from third parties to whom all potentially interested subjects (credit institutions, financial holding companies, mixed financial holding companies, mixed-activity holding companies) 'have outsourced operational functions or activities', and in any case, to 'conduct all necessary investigations … where necessary to carry out' their tasks. Also in this case, the scope of the provision is broad enough as to also allow inclusion in the list of 'third parties' service providers that store data related to the banking communications. Differently from the centralised level, though, national banking supervisors may also cumulate tasks that might make access to metadata of communications much more relevant. Consider, for instance, the power to sanction natural persons; the power to impose criminal law penalties, or to investigate money laundering or terrorist financing offences related to the banking activity. The precise scope of powers of each competent authority, hence, directly depends on the tasks attributed to it at the national level, and, as of today, varies widely from Member State to Member State. For a detailed study of several of such national systems, see S Allegrezza (ed), *The Enforcement Dimension of the Single Supervisory Mechanism* (Wolters Kluwer/CEDAM, 2020). Partially different considerations must be made with regard to anti-money laundering/countering the financing of terrorism (AML/CFT) systems. At the European level, the reference goes here mainly to the European Banking Authority (EBA), which has been granted a mandate in the field since 2019 (see for instance Art 8(1) of Regulation No 1093/2010, as amended by Regulation (EU) 2019/2175 of 18 December 2019), and to the soon-to-be-established Anti-Money-Laundering Authority (AMLA); see Proposal for a Regulation of the European Parliament and of the Council establishing the Authority for Anti-Money Laundering and Countering the Financing of Terrorism and amending Regulations (EU) No 1093/2010, (EU) 1094/2010, (EU) 1095/2010, COM/2021/421 final, Brussels, 20 July 2021. A distinction must be drawn in this regard. On the one side, although the EBA has been conferred with the power to sanction violations of AML/CFT regulation, its powers are rather general, and mostly concern coordination, monitoring and risk assessment (Art 9b (1) and Art 9a(1)(a), (c), (2) and (5), Regulation (EU) No 1093/2010). Hence, the EBA does not have specific investigatory powers, let alone about metadata communications. On the other side, according to the proposed Regulation, AMLA powers should encompass prerogatives quite similar to those already recognised to the SSM, and in particular to request information that is necessary to carry out its tasks from 'third parties to whom the selected obliged entities have outsourced operational functions or activities and natural or legal persons affiliated to them' (Art 16(1) of the Proposal). At the national level, competent authorities, and particularly Financial Intelligence Units, display high variety in their investigative powers; nonetheless, no harmonised power concerning access to communications metadata can be found in the relevant legal basis (Art 32(4), Directive (EU) 2015/849 of 20 May 2015 on the prevention of the use of the financial system for the purposes of money laundering or terrorist financing (last consolidated version of 30 June 2021)). On the powers and structure of the current AML/CFT systems, see B Vogel and J-B Maillart (eds), *National and International Anti-Money Laundering Law. Developing the Architecture of Criminal Justice, Regulation and Data Protection* (Intersentia, 2020).

[65] See Recital (65), Regulation No 596/2014 of 16 April 2014 on market abuse (market abuse regulation), as confirmed by the CJEU in *VD and SR* (n 36) paras 41, 66 and 77.

domestic level to access such data. On the one hand, according to Regulation (EU) No 600/2014, the European Securities and Market Authority (ESMA) can request service providers to release 'records of telephone and data traffic', subject, where so required by national law, to judicial authorisation.[66] On the other hand, national competent authorities must also be able to obtain the same information, at least when investigating market abuse conduct in accordance with Regulation (EU) No 596/2014. Specifically, national authorities shall have the power, as established by national legislation, to 'require existing data traffic records held by a telecommunications operator, where there is a reasonable suspicion of an infringement and where such records may be relevant to the investigation'.[67] But how should such powers relate to the principles established by the CJEU in the data retention saga? And what are the consequences in terms of admissibility?

The problems start from the very choice of the 'retention model' to apply. Indeed, one may consider that one of the financial authorities' tasks is to fight conduct, like insider trading or market manipulation, that is usually considered a criminal offence. To do so, supervisors are either directly entitled to impose sanctions of a criminal nature, or they can exercise administrative punitive powers or, in most cases, a combination of the two. Also, even where they are not directly granted criminal sanctioning powers, financial supervisors are usually bound by information-exchange duties, that allow or impose a sharing of data with criminal justice authorities.[68] Thus, information gathered by financial authorities may, in accordance with national law, be admitted as evidence in criminal proceedings too. Looking at the supervisory powers from this angle, one might conclude that retention and access to metadata of communications should follow the more restrictive rules established for crime prevention and repression.

Nevertheless, national security, as previously recalled, covers 'the primary interest in protecting the essential functions of the State and the fundamental interests of society through the prevention and punishment of activities capable of seriously destabilising the fundamental … economic … structures of a country'.[69] Thus, the protection of financial markets, which necessarily also passes through the contrast of conduct like insider trading or market manipulation, could well be included in the notion of national security. This is even more so considering, in the words of the Court, the potential for 'directly threatening society, the population or the State itself'.[70] One only needs to recall the impact of the 2006–08

[66] Art 38c(1)(e) and (5), Regulation (EU) No 600/2014 of 15 May 2014 on markets in financial instruments, as amended by Regulation (EU) 2019/2175 of 18 December 2019.

[67] See Art 23(2)(g), Regulation (EU) No 596/2014. According to para (h) of the same provision, competent authorities shall have also the power to access to certain communications content data, and in particular, 'to require existing recordings of telephone conversations, electronic communications or data traffic records held by investment firms, credit institutions or financial institutions'.

[68] Also recognised in *VD and SR* (n 36) paras 26 et seq. Analysing the phenomenon from the side of banking supervision, see S Allegrezza, 'Information Exchange Between Administrative and Criminal Enforcement: The Case of the ECB and National Investigative Agencies' (2020) 4 *eucrim* 302.

[69] *Commissioner of An Garda Síochána* (n 28) paras 61 et seq.

[70] ibid.

financial crisis and the role attributed to the lack of adequate financial supervision in spreading its dramatic effects.[71] According to this interpretation, therefore, data retention and access could follow a much more permissive regime.

In *VD and SR* (2022), a case concerning an insider trading investigation by the French financial market supervisor, the CJEU came close to taking a stand on the matter. The decision affirmed that 'legislative measures which, as a preventive measure, in order to combat market abuse offences including insider dealing, provide for the general and indiscriminate retention of traffic data' would be incompatible with Articles 7 and 8 of the EU Charter.[72] Be that as it may, in the decision, the referring court did not ask, and the Court of Justice did not really inquire, about the nature of financial supervisory tasks.

The CJEU did note that 'as regards the objectives pursued, the purpose of the legislation at issue is, *inter alia*, the investigation, detection and prosecution of criminal offences, including those relating to market abuse such as insider dealing'.[73] Nonetheless, it did not elaborate further on how the presence of multiple, overlapping goals could affect the retention regime, and, consequently, also the admissibility of the collected information.

Leaving this crucial aspect to the margin of appreciation of each Member State, however, reiterates the problems of a fragmented approach, which seems even less suitable in light of the harmonised enforcement of supervisory powers in the field.

V. Which Way Forward?

What emerges from this brief overview is a system that accords a great deal of relevance to admissibility rules, at the same time without explicitly taking the necessary steps to ensure the adequacy of those rules.

Certainly, the policy implications in establishing common admissibility standards require that the problem should not continue to be faced by the CJEU alone. In this regard it is well known that Article 82(2) TFEU[74] already provides for the legal bases that would allow the EU to adopt 'minimum rules' on the 'mutual admissibility of evidence'; but even so, no legislative initiative has been embraced by the European legislators. The recent Proposal for a Directive on Mutual Admissibility of Evidence and E-Evidence in Criminal Proceedings, formulated by the European Law Institute (ELI), thus represents at last a step forward.

The Proposal aims at eliminating, or at least sensibly reducing, the cases of declarations of inadmissibility arising from the different practices and legislation of

[71] On which see, for all, US Senate Permanent Subcommittee on Investigations, Wall Street and the Financial Crisis: Role of the Regulators, S.Hrg 111–672, April 16, 2010, at https://catalog.princeton.edu/catalog/6432020.

[72] *VD and SR* (n 36) §§ 43–44 and 69–95; moreover, the Court recalled that Regulation (EU) No 596/2014 could at most allow for the retention of data pertaining to financial operators, see para 75.

[73] ibid para 91.

[74] Consolidated version of the Treaty on the Functioning of the European Union [2012] OJ C326/47.

Member States.[75] Looking mostly at the horizontal level, the text does not directly tackle the question of how to coordinate admissibility rules already established at the national level with the principles and conditions deriving from EU law and the jurisprudence of the CJEU. Nor does it provide for specific rules concerning the partial overlapping of preventive and criminal investigations, which, as illustrated above, represents a crucial and problematic aspect emerging from the data retention saga. For the scope of the present analysis, there are, however, two elements of interest in the draft.

The first is the explicit reference to the proportionality principle in the admissibility assessment. According to Article 4(5) of the Proposal, Member States shall ensure that evidence collected by interfering with fundamental rights be used 'only to the extent' that such interference is proportionate. In this context, the seriousness of crime at stake, as well as other legitimate interests (of third parties, for instance), may be taken into account. The second element of interest is the extension of the general rules on admissibility of evidence to 'evidence produced in an administrative proceeding to be used in criminal proceedings'.[76] In particular, aiming at preventing the circumvention of procedural safeguards by obtaining evidence outside the criminal justice system (and then bringing it back via exchange of information duties) seems pivotal in the development of common standards on admissibility, given the multilayer structure of enforcement systems within the EU.[77]

By building on these two strands, it is compelling to finally address the vertical dimension of admissibility rules, looking at the relationship between fundamental rights and retention regimes, and keeping in mind the complexity of the matter at stake. That requires taking into account at least the following elements, recalled

[75] See the Explanatory Memorandum of the ELI Proposal for a Directive of the European Parliament and the Council on Mutual Admissibility of Evidence and Electronic Evidence in Criminal Proceedings, at 16 (https://www.europeanlawinstitute.eu/fileadmin/user_upload/p_eli/Publications/ELI_Proposal_for_a_Directive_on_Mutual_Admissibility_of_Evidence_and_Electronic_Evidence_in_Criminal_Proceedings_in_the_EU.pdf), in particular Art 4, which 'aims at ensuring two objectives: that the principle of *lex loci* in the gathering of evidence is complied with and that such compliance is checked by the adjudicating court (*enhancing respect for defendant's rights*); and also that evidence obtained under different rules as those provided in the *lex forum*, shall not lead to its inadmissibility, unless fundamental principles of the forum state are violated (*enhancing free circulation of evidence and thus effectiveness in the cross-border prosecution*). And these objectives are to be achieved in accordance with the human rights standards already defined by the European Courts. By defining those common standards at the EU level, the principle of mutual recognition shall be implemented.'

[76] Art 4(6) of the Proposal.

[77] Although the definition of 'administrative proceeding' shall be carefully tailored, in order to embrace the magnitude of the current interactions among different authorities. Actually the term currently includes 'administrative proceeding to be used in a criminal proceeding or other proceedings defined in Article 4 of the Directive 2014/41EU regarding the European Investigation Order in criminal matters' (Recital (1) of the Proposal); the reference to the EIO Directive, in that regard, however, could narrow the notion, as the interpretation of the term in that context is quite restrictive and does not cover several cases where administrative authorities gather information that could also become evidence in criminal proceedings at a later stage; see, for instance, Opinion of AG Campos Sánchez-Bordona delivered on 19 October 2016 in Case C-452/16 PPU *Openbaar Ministerie v Krzysztof Marek Poltorak*, ECLI:EU:C:2016:782, paras 47 et seq.

in the foregoing analysis: (i) the need to find a balanced approach between the assessment of privacy and fair-trial violations, which allows for autonomous evaluations without at the same time depriving the respective rights of their safeguarding function; (ii) the awareness that metadata of communications represent only a fraction of the data the admissibility of which could be investigated, and therefore that admissibility rules at the EU level, though developed so far mostly in this domain, should not look at such data exclusively; (iii) the consciousness that criminal justice principles aim at protecting specific needs that are essential to ensure individual freedoms, but which can be impaired by overall approaches that underestimate the importance of ensuring foreseeability for the consequences of their violation; (iv) the consideration that data are, by themselves, multifunctional, and could serve purposes of different relevance and natures, supported by a network of multi-level enforcement systems that are connected by cooperation mechanisms, duties to exchange information and, certainly, admissibility rules.

Certainly, creating a coherent and effective scheme that encompasses all these exigencies is far from being straightforward. *The devil is in the detail*, as the old saying goes, and it is precisely in such specificities that the difference lies between legitimate interference and violation of fundamental rights. The CJEU has embarked on a path leading in this direction. Reaching the destination, however, demands a collective effort, which cannot be delegated entirely to national legislators and which requires the EU to define, even more clearly than it has already done with data retention, the intangible boundary of fundamental freedoms and the consequences for their violation.

3

Legal Challenges in Dealing with Electronic Evidence in Criminal Proceedings

FARSAM SALIMI

I. Introduction

The term 'electronic evidence' is omnipresent. It is not surprising that the digitalisation process is also reflected in criminal proceedings. Hardly any criminal proceedings can get by without the aid of digital tools and digitally stored information. This applies not only to classic cases of cybercrime, where digital traces and thus electronic evidence have usually been the only investigative approach; today, electronic evidence is essential in almost all areas of combating crime, be it in white-collar criminal cases or in the fight against everyday crime.[1] However, if one analyses the discussions and current legislative plans in more detail, it soon becomes apparent that there are different ideas about what can be considered as electronic evidence. This study will provide a conceptual classification of the term 'electronic evidence'.

The next step is to examine what makes electronic evidence so special, that is, why special rules are required for the production and handling of it. And, finally, the special requirements that must be observed in a cross-border context have to be explored. All these national, as well as international, regulations should serve only one goal: ensuring effective investigations in criminal proceedings and, at the same time, safeguarding the rights of the accused and the rights of other parties affected by encroachments upon fundamental rights. These two – equally important! – goals must not be left out of consideration in any new proposal for a regulation.[2]

[1] B Lovejoy, 'Smartphone and smartwatch data led husband to confess to murdering his wife' (2021) *9to5Mac* at https://9to5mac.com/2021/06/18/smartphone-and-smartwatch-data-murder/.

[2] The ELI-proposal for a directive follows these premises, see https://www.europeanlawinstitute.eu/fileadmin/user_upload/p_eli/Publications/ELI_Proposal_for_a_Directive_on_Mutual_Admissibility_of_Evidence_and_Electronic_Evidence_in_Criminal_Proceedings_in_the_EU.pdf.

II. The Concept of 'Electronic Evidence'

Digitalisation plays a role in almost all areas of criminal proceedings. However, the mere fact that evidence is presented digitally in trial proceedings does not necessarily make it 'electronic evidence'.[3] Therefore, a document displayed on a screen for better illustration at trial remains a classic piece of evidence. Electronic evidence may be defined as digitally stored information. On the other hand, one should also think of evidence that is digitally stored only after it has been accessed by the law enforcement authorities. This includes, for example, image and sound recordings made during observation or an undercover investigation. Such recordings are also electronic evidence, because they exist solely in digital form as from the first step taken by the law enforcement authorities to process these data. It does not matter whether such electronic evidence is printed out or committed to paper later: it remains electronic evidence.[4]

Whereas all digitally stored information may be defined as 'electronic evidence in the broader sense', this term does not say anything about the content of the evidence. The content can be very different and may thus refer to digitally stored documents, but also to image recordings, sound recordings or other content data. Communication data, that is messages or other information related to telecommunications, such as traffic data, can be stored on digital devices. For the concept of 'electronic evidence in the broader sense', it also does not matter whether the information was processed by a private person (eg information on the defendant's notebook), by a cloud provider or by a telecommunication operator. If one wants to limit the content to certain data, such as data in connection with telecommunications, or data that was processed by certain persons (eg service providers), it is better to speak of 'electronic evidence in the narrow sense'.

First of all, it must be clarified which definition is to be used as the basis for the discussion. Probably the most central legal project in this area is the European Commission's proposal for an electronic evidence Regulation ('the e-Evidence Regulation').[5] The definition of 'electronic evidence' (or of 'e-evidence') used here is

evidence stored in electronic form by or on behalf of a service provider at the time of receipt of a production or preservation order certificate, consisting in stored subscriber data, access data, transactional data and content data.[6]

The reference in this definition to the specific instruments of the production or preservation order is obvious, which is related to the objective of the proposed Regulation. Moreover, the time restriction should to be considered. The proposal refers to the time of the first receipt of the evidence by the law enforcement

[3] C Momsen, 'Digitale Beweismittel aus Sicht der Strafverteidigung' in S Beck, B Meier and C Momsen (eds), *Cybercrime und Cyberinvestigations – Neue Herausforderungen der Digitalisierung für Strafrecht, Strafprozessrecht und Kriminologie* (Nomos, 2015) 67.

[4] ibid 67.

[5] Proposal for a Regulation of the European Parliament and of the Council on European Production and Preservation Orders for electronic evidence in criminal matter COM (2018) 225 final.

[6] ibid Art 2(6).

authorities. However, information that is stored electronically for the first time in the investigation file naturally falls outside of this definition. This inevitably follows from the fact that the entire concept of the proposed Regulation is based on access to data that has already been processed digitally. Therefore, this definition by the proposed Regulation has too narrow an approach and follows a very specific target, so it cannot provide a comprehensive definition of electronic evidence in general.

The types of data mentioned in the proposal, however, are more or less comprehensive. In addition to telecommunication-related subscriber data, access data and transactional data, content data are also mentioned, which basically covers all forms of stored information. However, a decisive restriction results from the fact that all these data only fall within the scope of application if they are stored by or on behalf of service providers.[7] Thus, all information stored by a private person other than professional service providers is not covered by this definition. In sum, the e-Evidence Regulation cannot provide a comprehensive definition of digital or electronic evidence. Therefore, if a regulatory proposal is to be envisaged seeking to regulate the cross-border usability of electronic evidence in general, another definition of 'electronic evidence' must be found. This new definition must ensure that all electronic evidence is covered, irrespective of the fact, whether it is stored in digital form at the time it is first obtained by law enforcement or is processed by special service providers.

However, the terms 'electronic evidence' and 'digital evidence' are generally used synonymously in the legal context.[8] While the term 'digital evidence' refers to the characteristic of the evidence, that is, the way the information is processed, and distinguishes it from analogue (ie physically tangible) evidence, the term 'electronic evidence' refers to the place where it is stored, that is, in electronic form on a data carrier.[9] Basically, however, there is no difference – at least from a legal point of view. As soon as information is stored on electronic data carriers, it is digitally processed electronic evidence. Making such a conceptual distinction does not provide any added value from a legal point of view, as digital evidence will always be stored electronically.

III. Specific Problems in the Investigation of Electronic Evidence

Law enforcement authorities can obtain electronic evidence in various ways. First, it is conceivable that information not initially stored in digital form will be

[7] ibid Art 2 (6).

[8] AF Moussa, 'Electronic evidence and its authenticity in forensic evidence' (2021)11 *Egyptian Journal of Forensic Sciences*, 20.

[9] Council of Europe, Electronic Evidence in Civil and Administrative Proceedings: Guidelines and explanatory memorandum (2019) 6: 'Electronic evidence means any evidence derived from data contained in or produced by any device, the functioning of which depends on a software program or data stored on or transmitted over a computer system or network.'

processed in digital form, for example when documents are digitalised. In this case, there is no problem associated with obtaining the evidence. Special problems arise, however, if the evidence has already been processed in digital form before the law enforcement authorities have access to it and the law enforcement authorities seize the data carrier, cloud systems or interfere with telecommunication processes in order to gather evidence. Already at this stage, one is confronted with manifold technical challenges and interferences with fundamental rights, which will be discussed in the sections A and B. But also, analysis of information that is only stored in digital form due to the investigative act, for example by using image- and sound-recording devices, poses new problems caused by technological progress, for example in connection with the use of drones (section C).[10] And finally, regulation is needed of the extent to which law enforcement agencies have access to open digital information available on the Internet (section D). In the future, the use of artificial intelligence (AI) can be expected to lead to a variety of investigative approaches, but also to a variety of interferences with areas relevant to fundamental rights.[11]

A. Access to Electronic Evidence Through Seizure

The classic method of access to evidence through seizure is done by accessing physical objects. This also applies to access to digitally stored data. Thus, the data carrier can be seized and evaluated, just as physical documents are seized and analysed. In many legal systems, precisely this parallel is drawn, and rules that were once designed for physical access to objects are applied to access to digital data carriers.[12] This transposition no longer seems appropriate. Data carriers are no longer just a single CD-ROM or a single data stick with manageable data quantity. On the one hand, huge amounts of data are stored on company servers, for example. In this case, one could argue that it is only a quantitative difference that does not justify special treatment. Since the proportionality of every investigative measure must be guaranteed,[13] sufficient consideration can also be given to the amount of data seized. However, this appears to be different with regard to communication devices, including smartphones in particular. A smartphone regularly contains much more than documents and pictures; it may store a great

[10] See C Orlando, 'The Use of Drones and the New Procedural Safeguards in Crime Control and Criminal Investigation' in L Bachmaier Winter and S Ruggeri (eds), *Investigating and Preventing Crime in the Digital Era* (Springer, 2022) 101.

[11] See also L Bachmaier Winter, 'Remote computer Searches under Spanish Law: The proportionality principle and the protection of privacy' (2017) 129(1) *Zeitschrift für die gesamte Strafrechtswissenschaft* 205.

[12] See, for Germany, I Zerbes and M El-Ghazi, 'Zugriff auf Computer: Von der gegenständlichen zur virtuellen Sicherstellung' (2015) 8 *Neue Zeitschrift für Strafrecht* 425; for Austria, I Zerbes and S Ghazanfari, 'Stellungnahme im Auftrag des Instituts für Anwaltsrecht der Universität Wien zur Sicherstellung und Auswertung von Daten und Datenträgern' (2022) 12 *Anwaltsblatt* 640.

[13] See E Billis, N Knust and JP Rui (eds), *Proportionality in Crime Control and Criminal Justice* (Hart Publishing, 2021).

amount of data providing information about the user's communication, consumer and sexual behaviour, and many other aspects of his or her private life. In addition, it is possible to create a movement profile based on the location data. Basically, the evaluation of the information stored on a smartphone often allows the creation of a personality profile for years.[14] In this case, the interference with fundamental rights is to be assessed differently from access to physical data carriers – be they analogue or digital – not only in regard to quantity but also as respects quality.

In addition, in many legal systems, access through seizure is not limited to the medium of communication and the information stored locally on it; access to external storage locations, such as cloud systems, is also allowed.[15] This means that seizure, which is traditionally based on physical access, completely loses its connection to physicality. The data pool that can be accessed then appears limitless.

In this context, it also seems necessary to examine whether and how the law enforcement authorities can convince the person concerned to disclose the access data to the respective smartphone. Smartphones are usually protected by a PIN, fingerprint or other biometric access barriers. If the law enforcement authorities do not succeed in seizing the smartphone in an unlocked state, for example by exploiting the surprise effect, they usually depend on obtaining the access data. As a rule, cracking the access barrier takes an enormous amount of time and money.[16] It can be easier to force the person to put his or her finger on the mobile phone, or to position his or her head in such a way that the facial recognition is triggered and the smartphone is unlocked.[17] Here again, the question arises whether the fundamental rights-preserving parameters are sufficient. Does the use of coercion require judicial authorisation, and must the use of force be proportionate? Is a distinction to be made between the accused, for whom the *nemo tenetur* principle must be observed,[18] and third parties, to whom this does not apply and who usually have a duty to cooperate with law enforcement authorities in criminal investigations?

All these measures need their own rules. From a fundamental rights perspective, access to smartphones and external digital storage spaces would have to be specifically regulated. From the perspective of Article 8 of the European Convention on Human Rights (ECHR)[19] and the right to data protection, the threshold for access

[14] C Stachl et al, 'Predicting personality from patterns of behaviour collected with smartphones' (2020) 117(30) *Proceedings of the National Academy of Sciences* 17680 at www.pnas.org/doi/full/10.1073/pnas.1920484117.

[15] See, for Germany, Zerbes and El-Ghazi (n 10) 425.

[16] L Koepke et al, 'Mass Extraction: The Widespread Power of US Law Enforcement to Search Mobile Phones' (2020) *Upturn* at www.upturn.org/work/mass-extraction/.

[17] B Fung, 'Analysis: What happens if police officer forces you to unlock your iPhone X with your face?', *Washington Post* (13 September 2017); T Brewster, 'Feds Can't Force You To Unlock Your iPhone With Finger Or Face, Judge Rules' *Forbes* (14 January 2019).

[18] The European Court of Human Rights (ECtHR) derives the *nemo tenetur* principle from Art 6 ECHR, see *Funke v France* App no 10828/84 (ECtHR, 25 February 1993) Series A no 256; as does the European Commission of Human Rights (EComHR), see *P. R. and H. v Austria* App nos 15135/89, 15136/89, 15137/89 (EComHR, 5 September 1989) 62 DR 319 and others.

[19] Convention for the Protection of Human Rights and Fundamental Freedoms, ETS 5.

should be higher than those for regular seizures of analogue documents or other (mere) digital storage media. There is also a need for separate rules on the extent to which and the conditions under which the person concerned can be physically compelled to unlock the smartphone. All these questions are related to access to these new digital sources of evidence and must be specifically regulated in the national legal systems. From the perspective of European law, and to guarantee minimum standards of fundamental rights and cross-border usability of the evidence obtained in this way, it must at least be ensured that the individual legal systems specifically and explicitly address these issues and do not apply the traditional rules of seizure to these new types of evidence investigations without the necessary adjustment. Of course, it is also possible to apply the rules of telecommunications surveillance to the access of such information processed by means of telecommunications equipment, even if the access does not take place on the transmission path but only after the communication process has been completed.

B. Access to Telecommunications and Secret Access to Stored Information

If access takes place without seizing the communication device, that is secretly, by accessing the telecommunication contents via the transmission path, the rules of telecommunication surveillance are applicable. Legal systems usually provide regulations on the surveillance of telecommunications traffic through cooperation with telecommunications providers for decades.[20] Traditionally, these were providers of voice telephony; today, e-mail providers and other Internet providers are also subject to this regulatory regime. However, due to the technological progress, there is a glaring gap in law enforcement in many jurisdictions here as well. Messenger services and Voice over Internet Protocol (VoIP) providers, such as WhatsApp, Telegram or Signal, usually offer end-to-end encryption.[21] Access on the transmission path by the provider, as was otherwise possible with classic voice telephony, is ruled out here. This leads to criminals' avoiding the use of classic voice telephony and specifically using these messenger services, which are widespread anyway.[22] Traditional telephone surveillance – one of the traditional surveillance measures that are essential in any law enforcement regime – is thus visibly losing its significance.

This mainly concerns areas of professionally acting perpetrators and groups of perpetrators, that is, especially the area of organised crime and terrorism.

[20] See U Sieber, N von zu Mühlen and T Tropina (eds), *Access to Telecommunication Data in Criminal Justice*, vol 2 (Duncker & Humblot, 2021).

[21] PPG Neogi, 'A Dive into WhatsApp's End-to-End Encryption' (2022) at doi.org/10.48550/arXiv.2209.11198.

[22] For Germany, see 'Verschlüsselung im Netz: Polizeibehörden schalten von Kriminellen genutzten Messenger ab' *Zeit Online* (6 February 2023) at www.zeit.de/digital/2023-02/exclu-kryptomessenger dienst-abgeschaltet-polizei-drogenhandel.

The only option for law enforcement authorities is to access the target's means of communication directly by infiltrating spy software that logs the content intended for transmission before it is encrypted, that is before the transmission process, and transmits it to the law enforcement authorities.[23] While some states provide extensive competences for law enforcement authorities,[24] others do not provide secret access to telecommunication systems *de lege lata*.[25] The European Union (EU) is aware of this problem. Consideration has already been given to banning the encryption of communications altogether, or at least to providing backdoors for law enforcement authorities.[26] However, all these efforts have failed so far.[27]

The creation of proportionate and thus fundamental rights-compliant competence to access means of communication before end-to-end encryption is therefore inevitable if law enforcement is still to function effectively in the future. However, here again, special rules and careful consideration are needed as to what limits should apply to such an interference with fundamental rights. There are many parameters that can be used to design an investigative measure compliant with fundamental rights, for example: pondering the seriousness of the offence to be prosecuted; certain technical precautions to keep the encroachment as limited as possible; and procedural requirements, such as the judicial authorisation of such a measure.

Similar problems arise outside the telecommunication processes. Access to stored information can also be gained by infiltrating the target's computer system with spying software. This is often referred to as online searches or online surveillance.[28] The aim of such measures may be to determine the digital information stored on the computer system without the knowledge of the person concerned. However, it is also possible to monitor the future behaviour of the user of the computer system; the determination of the IP address of the person concerned is also enabled in this way, without the involvement of a service provider.[29]

[23] F Freiling, C Safferling and C Rückert, 'Quellen-TKÜ und Online-Durchsuchung als neue Maßnahmen für die Strafverfolgung: Rechtliche und technische Herausforderungen' (2018) 1 *Juristische Rundschau* 9.

[24] For Germany, see S Henrichs and K Weingast in C Barthe and J Gericke (eds), *Karlsruher Kommentar StPO*, 9th edn (CH Beck, 2023) § 100a, para 42.

[25] For Austria, see S Oswald, 'Die Verfassungswidrigkeit des Staatstrojaners: Anmerkungen zu VfGH 11. 12. 2019, G 72/2019' (2020) 2 *Österreichische Zeitschrift für Wirtschaftsrecht* 85.

[26] K Biermann, 'Überwachung: Der Kampf der EU gegen die Verschlüsselung' *Zeit Online* (26 November 2020); for new initiatives concerning child abuse, see D Moßbrucker, 'Chatkontrolle der EU: Ihr Messenger soll Ihre Fotos durchforsten' *Zeit Online* (31 May 2022); JJ Vasel, 'Datenschutz versus Kinderschutz? Kommissionsvorschlag zur digitalen Bekämpfung von Kindesmissbrauch' (2022) 6 *Zeitschrift für Rechtspolitik* 191.

[27] A Proschofsky, 'Chatkontrolle: EU-Pläne zur Unterwanderung von Chat-Verschlüsselung verschieben sich weiter' Der Standard (29 March 2022) at www.derstandard.at/story/2000134489912/eu-plaene-zur-unterwanderung-von-chat-verschluesselung-verschieben-sich-weiter.

[28] F Salimi, 'Terrorbekämpfung durch Straf- und Sicherheitspolizeirecht' (2013) 11 *Juristische Blätter* 698; Freiling, Safferling and Rückert (n 20).

[29] See A Ghappour, 'Searching Places Unknown: Law Enforcement Jurisdiction on the Dark Web' (2017) 69 *Stanford Law Review* 1075.

Recently, the term 'lawful hacking' has also become common.[30] The problem that arises is the same as that when monitoring messenger services: should public authorities be allowed to gain access to a computer system without the knowledge of the person concerned? Internationally, there are very different approaches to this. Even within the EU, no harmonisation is apparent in this regard. While Spain, for example, provides such access only under certain conditions,[31] Germany not only provides such a competence in the Federal Criminal Police Office Act (*Bundeskriminalamtgesetz*), related to combatting terrorism, but also largely allows it in the corresponding State laws for security police purposes. In Austria, however, the measure is not even admissible for the prosecution of or defence against the most serious forms of crime.

C. The Use of Image- and Sound-Recording Devices – The Drone and AI

The use of cameras to record human behaviour, for example in the context of observation, is part of the standard repertoire of criminal investigation methods. Due to technological progress, new types of image- and sound-recording devices, and the means of transportation of these devices, have become available. The use of aerial drones is already a possibility not only to make personnel-intensive observations more cost-effective and more efficient, but also to effectively expand the field of vision and the possibility of tracking target persons.[32] Again, the use of the new instrument implies a different intensity of encroachment than the use of classic cameras, which are operated either stationary or mobile. As the aerial drone expands the investigator's field of vision, the scope of the data digitally generated in this way has a different dimension than that which can be obtained through classic camera use,[33] and therefore reaches a different level of interference with fundamental rights. Nevertheless, many legal systems do not yet provide any regulations specifically covering the use of such aerial drone systems.

In addition, in the near future – against the backdrop of AI – it seems realistic that systems will be used that do not require any human control at all, and that can record or transmit images and sound. This can be done by flying intelligent robotic systems, but also by such systems deployed on the ground. Apart from the question

[30] See C Liguori, 'Exploring Lawful Hacking as a Possible Answer to the Going Dark Debate' (2020) 26 *Michigan Technology Law Review* 317; M Schallbruch, 'Der Staat als Hacker' in T Klenk, F Nullmeier and G Wewer (eds), *Handbuch Digitalisierung in Staat und Verwaltung* (Springer 2020) 527.

[31] Bachmaier Winter (n 9) 205.

[32] On the question – not explored in depth in this chapter – of the digital forensic examination of drones as evidence, see K Al-Room et al, 'Drone Forensics: A Case Study of Digital Forensic Investigations Conducted on Common Drone Models' (2021) 13 *International Journal of Digital Crime and Forensics* 1.

[33] R Berkowitz, 'Robotics: Drones Could Spot Crime Scenes from Afar' *Scientific American* (1 May 2022).

of expanding the field of vision, the question generally arises to what extent operations conducted by AI, detached from human control, should be permissible. Such systems are not yet in use in the vast majority of jurisdictions, but it can hardly be doubted that their use may be possible and useful from a technical and investigative point of view in the future.[34] The Member States must therefore also consider a regulatory system for these areas.

D. Access to Open Internet Resources

In most countries, access to open sources on the Internet, even if structured and systematic (so-called OSINT searches – Open Source Intelligence), is largely unregulated. In most cases, the idea prevails that the gathering of generally available information does not interfere with any specific fundamental rights. However, the ECtHR has already ruled in older decisions that access to open sources and the structured processing of such openly accessible information may also constitute an interference with the right to respect for private life under Article 8 ECHR.[35] Therefore, a legal basis is also required for such Internet searches. There is no doubt that this form of encroachment is a less intensive intrusion than access to private data or even secret telecommunication surveillance, and that the thresholds for admissibility may therefore be lower.

However, the foreseeable use of AI in the future must also be taken into account in this area. By intelligently searching for and interlinking all possible information available on the Internet about a person, it is possible to create a detailed behavioural profile of that person. It is also almost impossible to determine whether the content processed was lawfully available in the open area of the Internet or unlawfully found its way onto the Internet. The somewhat outdated term 'Big Data'[36] gains importance through this possible use of AI to extract targeted information from this Big Data pool. Here again, Member States will have to consider legal frameworks for dealing with such tools and such searches; retreating to the position that all information available on the Internet can be exploited without any particular barriers is no longer compatible with our fundamental rights standards. Instead, clear parameters are needed for defining to what extent law enforcement agencies should be able to conduct structured and targeted evaluations of information available on the Internet about a specific person.[37] In this context, however, it is important not to impose barriers that are far from being practical.

[34] For such a drone system, which was unveiled at Intersec Dubai 2023, see 'World's first AI drone for police cars unveiled, to make patrolling easier' *Hindustan Times* (26 January 2023).

[35] *Rotaru v Romania* App no 28341/95 (ECtHR, 4 May 2000).

[36] *Cambridge Dictionary*: 'very large sets of data that are produced by people using the internet, and that can only be stored, understood, and used with the help of special tools and methods'. See at https://dictionary.cambridge.org/dictionary/english/big-data.

[37] See L Bachmaier Winter, *Revue International de Droit Pénale*, vol 85, XIXth International Congress of Penal Law, Information Society and Penal Law (Edition Erès, 2014) Section II, General Report 89.

There is no doubt that a simple Internet search on a person at the beginning of any investigative activity, but also online police patrols,[38] can certainly be deemed permissible without special barriers, for example by a general clause-like authorisation. However, targeted and systematic searches of a person's behaviour over a certain period of time are to be assessed differently. In this case, the greater dimension of the interference with fundamental rights would also have to be reflected by stricter legal prerequisites.

IV. Particularities in Dealing with Already Identified Electronic Evidence

The special features of electronic evidence must be taken into account. This primarily concerns the handling of investigated electronic evidence. First of all, it should be borne in mind that electronic evidence can be manipulated or falsified more easily than traditional evidence that exists in analogue form, without leaving corresponding traces.[39] A digital tape recording, for example, can be manipulated more easily than a magnetic tape recording, and a digitally stored document can theoretically be forged more easily than a physical document, without leaving any visible traces.[40] The necessary programs and applications can often be obtained free of charge on the Internet. For more sophisticated programs rather obviously serving an illegal purpose, the darknet offers a corresponding marketplace. Thus, any electronic evidence is subject to greater uncertainty as to the reliability of the conclusions drawn from it.

The manipulation can take place at various levels. It is possible, for example, that an already existing data set, such as a video in an electronic file, may be subsequently digitally edited and distorted so that it suggests false evidence. It must be remembered, however, that digital data must first be processed before it can be perceived by humans at all and thus be usable at the trial hearing. Manipulations or falsifications of the content are also conceivable during this transformation process.[41] However, manipulations are also possible at an earlier stage, when the electronic evidence has not yet come within the prosecuting authorities' power of disposal. Thus the evidence may have been created in the first place with the intention of generating false conclusions.

This type of evidence falsification can also occur much more easily in the area of digital information than in relation to physical evidence. The danger of so-called 'deep fakes' falls within this problem.[42] Thus, it is clear that in order to investigate

[38] For Germany, see J Biemann, *Streifenfahrten im Internet: Die verdachtsunabhängigen Ermittlungen der Polizei im virtuellen Raum* (Boorberg, 2013).

[39] Moussa (n 6).

[40] Momsen (n 2) 73.

[41] ibid 74.

[42] R Chesney and D Citron, 'Deep Fakes: A Looming Challenge for Privacy, Democracy, and National Security' (2019) 107 *California Law Review* 1753 at doi.org/10.15779/Z38RV0D15J.

the material truth in criminal proceedings, it is essential to ensure that a piece of electronic evidence was neither created with the intention of enabling false conclusions, nor tampered with after this point, whether before or after it was obtained by law enforcement. This guarantee is often classified under the catchword 'authenticity'.[43] Of course, if there is even a suspicion that a piece of traditional evidence is the result of manipulation and forgery, it must be verified. In the case of electronic evidence, however, the risk of manipulation and forgery is so evident that it would be advisable to check the authenticity of the evidence by taking appropriate measures in every case, and not only when there are corresponding suspicions or objections from a party.

Furthermore, electronic evidence regularly poses special challenges for law enforcement agencies due to the volume of data. In many cases, digital data are available in a very large quantities, so that at a certain stage of the proceedings, law enforcement authorities have to decide which crucial content they want to process and use at the trial hearing. At this stage, there is the possibility of impairing the original evidentiary value of a piece of information by omitting individual data.[44] This problem also exists, in principle, in the same way with traditional evidence, but it is present to a particular degree when selecting individual data sets from a large amount of digital data. In addition, the evidential value of the data can be subsequently impaired by deleting individual data records even after the investigative act. Securing the original volume of the data is therefore another challenge that arises to a particular degree for electronic evidence.

To ensure the authenticity and completeness of electronic evidence, law enforcement authorities must take measures to ensure 'forensic readiness'. This means guaranteeing the usability of electronic evidence in a possible criminal trial.[45] This can be achieved by adhering to certain process sequences avoiding unauthorised access, logging any access that has taken place and storing the raw data even in the event of subsequent processing for the main proceedings. The guarantee of this 'forensic readiness', a special form of the so-called 'chain of custody',[46] can therefore only be ensured by defining certain formal process sequences. How these processes run in order to prevent misuse during the period of custody or during transmission between individual actors in law enforcement can only be regulated at the national level, because both the technical equipment of the national law enforcement authorities and the actors involved (police authorities, public prosecutors, experts, courts) may differ. However, the traceability of access to digitally stored evidence through the storage of log data is crucial in any case.

[43] Moussa (n 6).

[44] Momsen (n 2) 75.

[45] R Rowlingson, 'A ten step process for forensic readiness' (2004) 2(3) *International Journal of Digital Evidence* 1; Momsen (n 2) 78.

[46] L Bachmaier Winter, 'The Handling of Digital Evidence in Spain' in M Caianiello and A Camon (eds), *Digital Forensic Evidence* (Wolters Kluwer, 2021) 170.

V. The Cross-Border Handling of Electronic Evidence

Due to economic interdependencies, on the one hand, and the digitalisation of economic and social life, on the other, criminal proceedings are often no longer a purely national matter. Access to evidence located in another state – whether by direct access or by request via means of mutual legal and administrative assistance – and the utilisation of this evidence in domestic criminal proceedings are therefore playing an increasingly important role. While the European legislator intends to achieve far-reaching harmonisation for direct access to electronic evidence processed by a service provider by proposing an e-evidence Regulation,[47] the question of the usability of electronic evidence that is not processed by a service provider, and is therefore transmitted in the course of traditional mutual legal assistance or an investigation order, is hardly regulated. This is surprising, since Article 82(2) of the Treaty on the Functioning of the European Union (TFEU)[48] empowers the EU to issue rules on the admissibility of evidence. The goal of a functioning area of freedom, security and justice must therefore also be to ensure that evidence obtained in another country can also be used domestically. Electronic evidence is much more often used in a cross-border context. In this regard, it is particularly important to establish minimum requirements in all Member States of the Union. Uniform minimum standards should ensure that evidence is not considered inadmissible in another state simply because it does not meet the legal requirements or data security requirements of the forum state. The introduction of uniform standards, whether concerning the gathering or the analysis of evidence, is therefore of the utmost importance for the functioning of mutual recognition and the conduct of criminal proceedings in a cross-border context.

VI. Conclusion

Electronic evidence requires specific parameters not only as regards its acquisition, but also as regards its handling and cross-border exchange. The creation of largely uniform national frameworks for the handling of electronic evidence, based at least on minimum requirements, is of crucial importance for the functioning of cross-border criminal proceedings. The present project on 'Admissibility of Evidence and E-Evidence in Cross-border Criminal Proceedings in the EU' has created a first regulatory proposal for an EU directive. Discussion of the scope and degree of standardisation in this area, based on Article 82(2) TFEU, is just as necessary as efforts at the national level to create a more secure and compliant technological standard legal framework for the acquisition and analysis of electronic evidence.

[47] European Commission, Proposal for a Regulation of the European Parliament and of the Council on European Production and Preservation Orders for electronic evidence in criminal matters, COM(2018) 225 final.

[48] Consolidated version of the Treaty on the Functioning of the European Union [2012] OJ C326/47.

4

Admissibility of Evidence and E-Evidence in Cross-Border Criminal Proceedings in Austria

ROBERT KERT AND DANIEL GILHOFER-LENGLINGER

I. The Legal Framework on Admissibility of Criminal Evidence in Austria

A. General Rules on the Admissibility of Evidence in Criminal Proceedings

Austrian criminal procedure law does not contain an exhaustive list of evidence. Rather, everything that is suitable for discovering the truth may be used as evidence. This principle is limited by prohibitions on the use of evidence, which are in particular stipulated in the Austrian Code of Criminal Procedure (*österreichische Strafprozessordnung*, öStPO).[1]

For Austrian criminal proceedings, prohibitions on collecting evidence have to be distinguished from prohibitions on using evidence, because the violation of these prohibitions triggers different legal consequences. On the one hand, prohibitions on the collection of evidence prohibit the collection of certain evidence by the prosecution authorities or restrict the authorities in the choice or manner of carrying out the investigative measure.[2] If law enforcement authorities violate a prohibition on the collection of evidence, this may result in criminal and disciplinary consequences for the individual who has carried out the investigative measure.[3] Prohibitions on the use of evidence, on the other hand, do not apply when the evidence is collected but prohibit the later assessment of the evidence in

[1] OGH 08.09.1992, 11 Os 62/92 RIS-Justiz RS0097206 (T3).

[2] K Kirchbacher and A Sadoghi in H Fuchs and E Ratz (eds), *Wiener Kommentar zur StPO* (Manz Verlag, 2020) § 246 para 50.

[3] R Soyer, 'Beweisverwertungsverbote im künftigen strafprozessualen Vorverfahren' [1999] *ÖJZ* 829, 833.

criminal proceedings.[4] If the judge disregards a prohibition on the use of evidence, this may result in the nullification of the judgment.[5]

Although prohibitions on evidence collection and prohibitions on use of evidence will be considered separately, in certain cases they can also be interrelated in such a way that a violation of a prohibition on collecting evidence results in a prohibition on the use of that evidence. Such prohibitions on the use of evidence are referred to in legal doctrine as dependent prohibitions on the use of evidence, because they presuppose an infringement of the provisions of evidence collection.[6] In order not to restrict the principle of substantive truth too much, violations of prohibitions on evidence collection that are subject to nullity will in principle result in a prohibition on the use of the evidence.[7] This means that unlawfully conducted investigative measures will only have a very limited effect on the level of the use of evidence. The following violations of the Austrian Code of Criminal Procedure generally result in the nullity of the investigative measure:[8]

- Securing of written records or data storage devices in order to circumvent a statutory confidentiality right (Section 112 para 1 öStPO).
- Services rendered by an expert witness if a conflict of interest under Section 47 para 1 subparas 1 and 2 öStPO exists (Section 126 para 4 öStPO).
- The seizure of letters where directions and approvals were not made lawfully or in order to prove a criminal offence that was not committed intentionally (Section 140 para. 1 subpara. 2 and 4 öStPO).
- The disclosure of data concerning the transmission of messages where directions and approvals were not made lawfully or in order to prove a criminal offence that was not committed intentionally (Section 140 para 1 subparas 2 and 4 öStPO).
- The localisation of a technical device where directions and approvals were not made lawfully or in order to prove a criminal offence that was not committed intentionally (Section 140 paras 1 subparas 2 and 4 öStPO).
- The surveillance of communications where directions and approvals were not made lawfully or in order to prove a criminal offence that was not committed intentionally (Section 140 para 1 subparas 2 and 4 öStPO).
- Video and audio surveillance of persons where directions and approvals were not made lawfully or not in order to prove a felony (Section 140 para 1 subparas 2 and 3 öStPO).

[4] A Michel-Kwapinski in H Fuchs and E Ratz (eds), *Wiener Kommentar zur StPO* (Manz Verlag, 2022) § 166 para 1.

[5] K Schmoller in H Fuchs and E Ratz (eds), *Wiener Kommentar zur StPO* (Manz Verlag, 2016) § 3 paras 91 et seq.

[6] R Kier, 'Die Geltendmachung von Beweisverboten durch die Verteidigung im österreichischen Strafverfahren' in R Soyer and A Stuefer (eds), *Effektive Strafverteidigung* (nwv Verlag, 2011) 67, 71.

[7] K Schmoller, 'Beweise, die hypothetisch nicht existieren' [2002] *JRP* 251, 251.

[8] Exceptions and restrictions may apply to individual investigative measures but are not addressed in this overview for reasons of clarity.

- Video surveillance of persons where directions and approvals were not made lawfully (Section 140 para 1 subpara 2 öStPO).
- Any investigative measure used to bypass the official confidentiality of clergy (Section 144 para 1 öStPO).
- Gathering of evidence in order to circumvent the provisions concerning the questioning of the accused and of witnesses (Section 152 para 1 öStPO).
- The questioning of clerics about anything shared with them during confession or otherwise under the pledge of official confidentiality of clergy (Section 155 para 1 subpara 1 öStPO).
- The questioning of government officials about matters protected by official confidentiality, unless they have been discharged from that duty (Section 155 para 1 subpara 2 öStPO).
- The questioning of persons who have been granted access to classified information of the National Assembly or the Federal Council, as far as they are obliged to maintain confidentiality by law (Section 155 para 1 subpara 3 öStPO).
- The questioning of persons who are unable to state the truth because of mental illness, mental impairment or for another reason (Section 155 para 1 subpara 4 öStPO).
- Any investigative measure used to circumvent a person's right to refuse to answer questions granted on the basis of a recognised professional duty of confidentiality or electoral secrecy (Section 157 para 2 öStPO).
- Answers of a witness in proceedings against a relative where the person has not expressly relinquished the duty to answer questions (Section 159 para 3 öStPO).
- Answers given by a witness who has the right to refuse to give answers, granted on the basis of a recognised professional duty of confidentiality or electoral secrecy, but who has not been informed about that right in time (Section 159 para 3 öStPO).
- Answers given by the accused, as well as answers of witnesses, that came about or were obtained under torture or by illegally influencing a person's freedom of decision-making or the freedom to use his or her will, or by using inadmissible methods of questioning if these violate fundamental principles of procedure and if the exclusion of these answers is vital to repair this violation (Section 166 paras 1 and 2 öStPO).

The bridge between statutory nullity and the prohibition on using evidence can be drawn by the procedural objections available as remedy under Section 281 para 1 subparas 2 and 3 öStPO.[9] If void evidence is taken into account in the reasoning

[9] C Pilnacek, 'Überblick über die Grundsätze der Beweisermittlung und der Beweisverbote im österreichischen Strafverfahren' in F Höpfel and B Huber (eds), *Beweisverbote in den Ländern der EU und vergleichbaren Rechtsordnungen* (Edition iuscrim Verlag, 1999) 99, 107; W Platzgummer, 'Gesetzliche

of a judgment when reaching a verdict, this can subsequently lead to the judgment's also being void.[10] Consequently, it is prohibited for the judge to use such evidence in the judgment.[11] In the context of the unlawful collection of evidence, nullity comprises two aspects: on the one hand, the legislator expresses the inadmissibility of the use of the evidence; on the other hand, nullity also serves as an explicit indication that such procedural errors can lead to the contestability of the judgment.[12] If such rules of evidence collection are violated, in general, a challenge may be brought via the procedural objection pursuant to Section 281 para 1 subparas 2 and 3 öStPO. Which of the two clauses is applicable depends on whether the violation of the law occurred in the preliminary proceedings or in the main proceedings.[13] Material evidence from the preliminary proceedings must be introduced into the main hearing by reading it out. If the results of the evidence imported into the main hearing are void due to their unlawful collection in the preliminary proceedings, the procedural objection under Section 281 para 1 subpara 2 öStPO stipulates that the defence counsel must object to the reading in order to successfully assert the ground for nullity. If, on the other hand, the procedural error that is subject to nullity arose during the main hearing, this mistake can be asserted under Section 281 para 1 subpara 3 öStPO, and no objection by the defence counsel is necessary in this instance.

Other violations of provisions of evidence collection may exceptionally also lead to a prohibition on the use of the evidence. However, the Austrian Supreme Court only recognises non-explicit prohibitions on the use of evidence if they are approximately equivalent to those that are subject to nullity.[14] In legal doctrine, this is assumed for the results of a physical examination. Violations of the law in the case of physical examinations are not subject to nullity, but in the process of drafting the provision, the legislator took the provisions on visual and acoustic surveillance as a model, which foresees nullity in the case of non-compliance with certain provisions on collection.[15] Therefore, it can be assumed that the results of a physical examination cannot be used as evidence if they have been collected unlawfully.[16]

Such violations of the law cannot be asserted via Section 281 para 1 subparas 2 or 3 öStPO, because the unlawful taking of evidence is not subject to nullity.

Beweisverbote im österreichischen Strafverfahren' in H Haller et al (eds), *Staat und Recht – Festschrift für Günther Winkler* (Springer Verlag, 1997) 797, 799; K Schmoller, 'Beweisverwertungsverbote im Diskussionsentwurf zur Reform des strafprozessualen Vorverfahrens' [2000] *RZ* 154, 154 ff.

[10] K Schmoller, 'Heimliche Tonbandaufnahmen als Beweismittel im Strafprozeß?' [1994] *JBl* 153, 153.

[11] Schmoller (n 5) § 3 para 69.

[12] Kirchbacher and Sadoghi (n 2) § 246 para 156.

[13] H Hinterhofer and B Oshidari, *System des österreichischen Strafverfahrens* (Manz Verlag, 2017) paras 9.69ff.

[14] OGH 27.08.2008, 13 Os 83/08t RIS-Justiz RS0124168.

[15] JAB 406 BlgNR 22. GP 18.

[16] A Birklbauer in H Fuchs and E Ratz (eds), *Wiener Kommentar zur StPO* (Manz Verlag, 2013) § 123 para 56.

In this respect, the procedural objection by the appellant under Section 281 para 1 subpara 4 öStPO complements the other two possibilities for asserting procedural violations. Under this subparagraph, procedural violations in the preliminary proceedings, as well as in the main proceedings, can be taken up, as long as they are objected to in time and are similar in severity to the violation consisting of a taking of evidence subject to nullity.[17]

In addition to dependent prohibitions on the use of evidence, the Austrian Code of Criminal Procedure also contains prohibitions on the use of evidence that apply independently of the legality of the process of evidence collection. Such prohibitions on the use of evidence are known as independent prohibitions on the use of evidence and can be found, inter alia, in Section 258 para 1 öStPO.[18] According to this provision, in the rendering of the judgment, the court may only take into consideration those matters that featured in the main trial. Documents may only serve as evidence if they have been read out loud in the main trial, or if the presiding judge has presented them. Evidence that is only included in the court files, but which was not featured in the main trial, must therefore not be considered in the judgment even if it has been lawfully obtained.[19]

If these provisions are violated, this cannot be asserted with the procedural complaints under Section 281 para 1 subparas 2, 3 or 4 öStPO, because the violation of this prohibition on the use of evidence is not based on an unlawful process of evidence-gathering. However, in this case the objection of errors according to Section 281 para 1 subpara 5 öStPO and the objection of facts according to Section 281 para 1 subpara 5a öStPO are applicable. With the objection of errors under Section 281 para 1 subpara 5 öStPO, the parties to the proceedings can assert that the court relied on unusable evidence in its reasoning. If a finding in the judgment is based solely on evidence that cannot be used, this reasoning is insufficient and may be challenged.[20] Furthermore, the judgment may also be challenged under Section 281 para 1 subpara 5a öStPO, since the case file reveals considerable doubts about the correctness of decisive facts.[21]

The prohibitions on the use of evidence described so far have in common that they are designed as legal prohibitions, which are applied in connection either to an unlawful collection of evidence or to the use of evidence. However, there are also prohibitions on the use of evidence in the Code of Criminal Procedure that are not stipulated as such, but which are the result of another legal consequence. For example, in several provisions it is required that evidence obtained must be destroyed. Since destruction basically means to physically get rid of the evidence, it can no

[17] E Ratz in H Fuchs and E Ratz (eds), *Wiener Kommentar zur StPO* (Manz Verlag, 2020) § 281 para 337; E Steininger, *Nichtigkeitsgründe im Strafverfahren*, 7th edn (Verlag Österreich, 2019) 265.

[18] Schmoller (n 5) § 3 para 60.

[19] K Kirchbacher in H Fuchs and E Ratz (eds), *Wiener Kommentar zur StPO* (Manz Verlag, 2021) § 252 para 1.

[20] E Ratz, 'Die Handhabung von Beweisverboten durch den OGH' in C Grafl and U Medigovic (eds), *Festschrift Manfred Burgstaller* (Neuer Wissenschaftlicher Verlag, 2004) 307, 313.

[21] ibid 310.

longer be used to substantiate a decision.[22] According to the Code of Criminal Procedure, evidence collected is to be destroyed in the following situations:

- if a complaint concerning the inadmissibility of certain investigative measures (seizure of letters, disclosure of data concerning transmission of messages, localising a technical device, event-specific data storage, surveillance of communication, video and audio surveillance of persons, data matching supported by electronic data collection) is approved (Section 89 para 4 öStPO);
- if a physical examination is conducted in the event of imminent danger and based on a direction by the prosecution authority, but is later not approved by court (Section 123 para 3 öStPO);
- if molecular genetic testing has been conducted and the test material belonging to a specific person, or likely to belong to a specific person, and test results can no longer be attributed to the trace material or determine the person's identity or ancestry (Section 124 para 4 öStPO);
- if monitoring results cannot be of any relevance for any criminal proceedings, or if they must not be used as evidence (Section 139 para 4 öStPO);
- if data matching has been implemented and a complaint against the approval of a direction is granted, or if the direction of data matching through electronic data collection is revoked for other reasons (Section 142 para 5 öStPO);
- if a clandestine investigative measure has been carried out and the Commissioner for Legal Protection (*Rechtsschutzbeauftragter*) requests the destruction, due to irrelevance or unusability, of the evidence collected (Section 147 para 4 öStPO);
- if answers were given by a witness who has the right to refuse to give answers, granted on the basis of a recognised professional duty of confidentiality or electoral secrecy, but who has not been informed about that right in time (Section 159 para 3 öStPO).

Likewise, Section 75 para 1 öStPO contains the general requirement that unlawfully obtained personal data must be deleted. If this request were to be taken seriously, the reference to the person would have to be removed from all evidence falling within the scope of this provision, which would probably eliminate the evidentiary value of the evidence. However, both the legislator[23] and the currently prevailing opinion in Austria[24] assume that Section 75 para 1 öStPO does not apply to the contents of criminal files.

[22] E Ratz, 'Führung von Ermittlungsverfahren und Ermittlungsakt' [2020] *ÖJZ* 865, 869 ff; Schmoller (n 7) 253; Soyer (n 3) 835.

[23] ErläutRV 25 BlgNR 22. GP 108.

[24] Hinterhofer and Oshidari (n 13) para 1.207; V Lechner, *Die Stellung des Beschuldigten und seines Verteidigers im reformierten Vorverfahren* (Manz Verlag, 2010) 177; M Rohregger in A Birklbauer et al (eds), *Linzer Kommentar zur StPO* (Verlag Österreich, 2020) § 75 para 4.

In its case law, the Austrian Supreme Court has also elaborated a special form of prohibitions on the use of evidence. Normally, prohibitions on the use of evidence have an effect throughout the entire criminal proceedings.[25] This means that evidence that is subject to a prohibition on the use of evidence may not only not be used when passing the judgment in the main trial, but must also be disregarded when making decisions in the investigation proceedings. The Austrian Supreme Court now has started to recognise, in certain cases, prohibitions on the use of evidence with partial effect that the law does not stipulate.[26] The prohibition on the use of evidence only has partial effect because it applies only to decisions in the investigation proceedings; it does not prohibit the assessment of the evidence in the main trial. A prohibition on the use of evidence with partial effect has been affirmed where certain requirements for a house search were violated and the search was later declared unlawful. The Court ruled that the objects or data that had been found in the course of the search did not have to be given back to the owner. Although the evidence has been collected unlawfully, it does not have to be destroyed, since this is not explicitly foreseen by law. Furthermore, the Court pointed out that a violation of prohibitions on the collection of evidence does not necessarily mean that such evidence may not be used subsequently in the investigation proceedings or in the main trial. However, in the case of an illegal house search, the Austrian Supreme Court limited the use of such evidence insofar as it may not be used for the decision on the termination of the investigation proceedings or for the substantiation of a suspicion of an offence underlying the arrest or remand of the accused.

Prohibitions on the use of evidence can either have an effect on the entire criminal proceedings or refer only to the investigation proceedings. In any case, a prohibition on the use of evidence means that only the evidence affected by the prohibition may not be assessed. Accordingly, the prosecution authorities are allowed to use the evidence as the basis for further investigations, despite the existence of a prohibition on the use of evidence. Therefore, subsequently obtained evidence can be used in criminal proceedings without any difficulty.[27] The 'fruit of the poisonous tree' doctrine is generally not applicable in Austrian criminal proceedings.[28] Only in exceptional cases will the Austrian Code of Criminal Procedure prohibit the use of the evidence as well as to collect subsequent evidence. An example of this can be found in Section 112 para 2 öStPO, which requires the sighting of records seized from a person who is granted a statutory confidentiality right. After the sighting, records that are not added to the file must be returned to the person affected. Any insights of the prosecution authorities gained from sighting records that are returned to the person affected must not be used for further investigations or as evidence, otherwise any further use will be void.

[25] Schmoller (n 5) § 3 para 81.
[26] OGH 21.07.2009, 14 Os 46/09k RIS-Justiz RS0125171.
[27] OGH 13.05.2015, 11 Os 48/15s RIS-Justiz RS0130052.
[28] Kirchbacher and Sadoghi (n 2) § 246 para 58.

B. Rules for Cross-Border Evidence

Whether prohibitions on the use of evidence in criminal proceedings also apply to evidence collected in another country (cross-border evidence) depends on the type of prohibition on the use of evidence. Independent prohibitions on the use of evidence apply regardless of the way and where the evidence was collected, which is why they are also applied to cross-border evidence. If, for example, foreign evidence is to be used in Austria, it must also feature in the main hearing according to Section 258 para 1 öStPO. If it does not, it must not be used. Thus, for the applicability of an independent prohibition on the use of evidence, no distinction is made as to whether the evidence is collected domestically or abroad.

The situation is different for dependent prohibitions on the use of evidence. These only apply to a limited extent to evidence collected by foreign prosecution authorities, because only domestic prosecution authorities are the addressees of the Austrian Code of Criminal Procedure. Therefore, foreign evidence can be used in the main trial even if it was obtained through a (foreign) investigative measure that would have been void under domestic law.[29]

II. Rules on Admissibility of E-Evidence in Criminal Proceedings

The Austrian Code of Criminal Procedure is technology-neutral.[30] Therefore, no other rules apply to e-evidence as to other evidence. Likewise, there are no special rules on the admissibility of e-evidence in criminal proceedings. If the e-evidence obtained is subject to a general prohibition on the use of evidence, it may not be used. Similarly, e-evidence may be used if no prohibition on the use of evidence applies.

Difficulties arise with the question of which investigative measure should be taken to gather e-evidence. This difficulty exists because the application of some investigative measures was originally focused on physical objects, which have an inherent probative value. However, these investigative measures are now also used to obtain data that are not stored on the device itself but in the cloud of a service provider. There is disagreement in legal doctrine as to whether, for accessing data in a cloud, the rules on securing should be applied or whether the stricter requirements for surveillance of communication have to be met. Some scholars argue that the provisions on the surveillance of communication apply, since the data had to be transmitted to the provider and therefore can be seen as transmitted information or communications.[31] According to another opinion, the provisions on

[29] I Zerbes, 'Grenzüberschreitende Beweiserhebung der Europäischen Staatsanwaltschaft' [2022] *ÖJZ* 1193, 1200.

[30] ErlRV 25 BlgNR 22. GP 156.

[31] S Reindl-Krauskopf, F Salimi and M Stricker, *IT-Strafrecht* (Manz Verlag, 2018) para 5.11 and 5.102.

securing should apply under certain conditions. Especially from the point of view of the user of a mobile phone or computer, it is often not recognisable whether the data are stored on the device or in a cloud, because the user interface displays and organises the data in a uniform manner, regardless of the storage location. As long as the cloud is accessed via the secured device and not by any other means, the device has not been secretly secured and only the files available at the time of the securing are evaluated, data in the cloud can be accessed by securing the mobile phone or computer.[32]

Depending on which investigative measures are used for accessing data in the cloud, different requirements must be fulfilled to collect the evidence lawfully. Whilst securing is allowed without approval by a court, surveillance of communication requires such individualised approval. Prohibitions on the use of evidence also differ. In the case of securing, the non-fulfilment of formal requirements has no effect on the usability of the evidence. In the case of surveillance of communication, certain formal and substantive requirements must be met for the evidence to be admissible.[33]

III. Case Law Regarding Transnational Electronic Evidence and its Admissibility

Regarding the question whether transnational e-evidence is admissible, a distinction must be made between e-evidence collected in coordination with other law enforcement agencies and e-evidence that was not so collected. For those scenarios in which Austrian and foreign prosecution authorities cooperate, no specific case law can be found or problems identified. In general, transnational investigations do not seem to be strictly standardised, but it depends on the case and the country involved which instruments are used. Beside classical mutual assistance, most prosecutors seem to prefer direct contact with the person working on the case in the other state. This direct contact seems to accelerate and facilitate investigations, as it is the least complicated way to get the information needed.

Those scenarios in which evidence was collected without the cooperation of the prosecution authorities have already been the subject of case law. For example, the Austrian Supreme Court had to decide whether wiretap protocols based on a surveillance order issued by the Turin public prosecutor's office could be used in Austria.[34] In this case, the Turin public prosecutor's office was conducting criminal proceedings against the defendants for several offences. The investigative work had been started via the order of an Italian public prosecutor. The police authorities in Italy conducted acoustic surveillance of the two accused by installing microphones

[32] I Zerbes, 'Beweisquelle Handy' [2021] *ÖJZ* 176, 182 ff.
[33] For a list of all explicit prohibitions on the use of evidence, see chapter I. A.
[34] OGH 25.05.2004, 14 Os 47/04 RIS-Justiz RS0119110.

and GPS tracking devices in the car of one of them. The accused subsequently crossed the border into Austria in this car, resulting in recordings of conversations also taking place on Austrian territory. When the Italian police became aware of that, they informed the Austrian security authorities. The results of the acoustic surveillance were transmitted to the Austrian prosecution authorities and the Austrian judge used this evidence in the judgment. The defendants challenged the judgment, arguing, amongst other things, that the foreign prosecution authorities had not complied with the domestic provisions on acoustic surveillance and that this violation was subject to a prohibition on the use of evidence. The Austrian Supreme Court, on the other hand, stated that the Austrian Code of Criminal Procedure is in principle only directed at Austrian law enforcement agencies. An investigative measure of foreign law enforcement agencies that is to be judged as acoustic surveillance in Austria is not subject to nullity, as there is no explicit prohibition on the use of evidence in this respect. However, the use of foreign evidence in domestic criminal proceedings could possibly have been opposed by the accused, claiming a violation of the right to a fair trial under Article 6 of the European Convention on Human Rights (ECHR).

IV. Exclusionary Rules of Evidence in Criminal Proceedings at the EU Level?

As already pointed out, there is a tendency in Austria to be allowed to use the evidence in the criminal proceedings as a matter of principle. This is already shown by the fact that only a few errors in the collection of evidence have the explicit consequence that the evidence may not be used subsequently. Non-explicit prohibitions on the use of evidence have only recently been recognised by the Austrian Supreme Court. However, the case law is very restrictive in this respect. For example, the Austrian Code of Criminal Procedure sometimes orders that illegally collected evidence must be physically destroyed. If the prosecution authorities ignore this legal obligation to destroy the evidence and leave it in the court file, the evidence can nevertheless be used in further proceedings.[35]

Many of the prohibitions on the use of evidence that exist in Austria do not derive from fundamental rights but can be reasonably assigned to them.[36] Since there is a large overlap of fundamental rights in relation to other EU Member States, sanctioning of serious violations of fundamental rights with a prohibition on the use of evidence could be considered. Exclusionary rules of evidence could be agreed on, for example, if procedural rights were circumvented or the fairness of the criminal proceedings was severely violated. Also, the European Court of Human Rights (ECtHR) has already concluded that in some cases,

[35] OGH 27.08.2008, 13 Os 83/08t RIS-Justiz RS0124162.
[36] Kirchbacher and Sadoghi (n 2) § 246 para 62.

the use of unlawfully obtained evidence can constitute a violation of Article 6 ECHR. In cases where the law enforcement authorities tortured the suspect[37] or used an agent provocateur to induce a person to commit a crime,[38] the accused was deprived, right from the outset, of the right to a fair trial, which rendered the collected evidence inadmissible. It could be considered that other major violations, for example of Article 8 ECHR, might also lead to the inadmissibility of the evidence collected.

V. Admissibility of Evidence Obtained in an Administrative Procedure in Criminal Proceedings

There are usually no specific rules in the Austrian Code of Criminal Procedure on the usability of evidence that originates from administrative proceedings, which is why the general principles must be adhered to. If administrative evidence is to be used in criminal proceedings, dependent prohibitions on the use of evidence cannot be applied. The Austrian Code of Criminal Procedure requires such prohibitions on the use of evidence where the violation of the evidence collection provision is subject to nullity. However, such violations subject to nullity are usually found in the Austrian Code of Criminal Procedure and not in other procedural codes, such as those for administrative proceedings.[39] Applying dependent prohibitions on the use of evidence analogously on administrative evidence is also not possible as there is no unplanned gap in the law. The enumeration of void evidence is exhaustive and thus cannot be extended to include other violations of the law.[40] Therefore, administrative evidence, such as documents, must be introduced in the main trial, and it is for the court to evaluate this evidence independently.

As far as personal evidence is concerned, the inapplicability of dependent prohibitions on the use of evidence is mitigated by the fact that witnesses must re-make their statements in the main trial and that the transcript of the questioning of the witness from the administrative proceedings cannot simply be read out loud. The examination of a witness in the main proceedings constitutes a collection of evidence according to the provisions of the Austrian Code of Criminal Procedure, which can result in a prohibition on the use of evidence in the case of errors that are subject to nullity.[41] However, the situation is different in cases in which the administrative authority has questioned the accused. Here, the provisions on the examination of witnesses do not apply due to the different procedural positions, which is why records of statements made by the defendant earlier in

[37] *Jalloh v Germany* App no 54810/00 (ECtHR, 11 July 2006) para 99.
[38] *Furcht v Germany* App no 54648/09) (ECtHR, 23 October 2014) para 68.
[39] D Gilhofer, 'Use of Administrative Evidence in Criminal Proceedings in Austria' [2022] *eucrim* 266, 268 ff.
[40] OGH 06.08.1980, 9 Os 79/80 RIS-Justiz RS0099088 (T1).
[41] Gilhofer (n 39) 269 ff.

administrative proceedings must be read out loud and are thus usable in any case. This cannot be changed by the fact that in certain administrative proceedings, such as asylum proceedings, there are firm obligations to cooperate, because these obligations in themselves do not justify a prohibition on the use of evidence that could be derived from the principle of *nemo tenetur*.[42]

Independent prohibitions on the use of evidence can be applied to evidence from administrative proceedings, because for this type of prohibition it is irrelevant in which proceedings the evidence has been collected. In some cases, investigative measures contain provisions on how to deal with evidence from other proceedings. For evidence from administrative proceedings, the provisions on physical examinations are particularly important in practice. Results of physical examinations carried out for reasons other than criminal procedure may only be used as evidence in criminal proceedings if this is necessary to prove a criminal offence for which orders for a physical examination could have been given (Section 123 para 7 öStPO). The main application of this prohibition on the use of evidence is the taking of blood samples from alleged drunk drivers. If blood is taken from the driver according to the provisions of the Road Traffic Act (öStVO), the results can only be used in criminal proceedings if the blood sample would also have been admissible according to the provisions of the öStPO. Since there is a restriction in the Austrian Code of Criminal Procedure with regard to those offences that can be proved with a physical examination, the results obtained in the administrative proceedings may be used in the criminal proceedings if, for example, a person was injured in a car accident, whereas they may not be used if only property damage occurred.[43]

VI. Use of Results of Internal Investigations Carried Out in the Field of Compliance Programmes

In Austria, there is no law that conclusively regulates internal investigations. For criminal proceedings too, there are no provisions on the usability of results of internal investigations. However, it can be derived from the Austrian Code of Criminal Procedure that the private gathering of evidence is permissible in itself, since evidence that was collected privately can also be taken by making use of the right to request evidence.[44]

For the applicability of dependent prohibitions on the use of evidence, a distinction must be made between whether the internal investigations can be attributed

[42] OGH 13.11.2018, 14 Os 65/18t RIS-Justiz RS0132342.

[43] G Muzak, 'Die Blutabnahme nach Verkehrsunfällen zwischen der StPO und Verfassungsbestimmungen in der StVO' in E Bernat et al (eds), *Festschrift Christian Kopetzki* (Manz Verlag, 2019) 399, 407.

[44] P Madl, 'Unternehmensinterne Untersuchungen im Wirtschaftsstrafverfahren' in R Kert and G Kodek (eds), *Das große Handbuch Wirtschaftsstrafrecht*, 2nd edn (Manz Verlag, 2022) 891, 908 ff.

to the prosecuting authorities or not. If, for example, private investigators conduct interviews with employees on behalf of the prosecution authorities, this procedure may be considered to be circumventing the provisions on interrogation in the öStPO, which results in the evidence's being unusable.[45]

If the conduct of internal investigators cannot be attributed to the state, dependent prohibitions on the use of evidence under the Austrian Code of Criminal Procedure do not apply because the collection of evidence by private investigators does not fall within the scope of application of the öStPO. The addressees of the provisions on the collection of evidence are the prosecuting authorities or courts and not private investigators.[46] In this case, fundamental rights could restrict the admissibility of the results of internal investigations. For example, the ECtHR assumes a prohibition on the use of evidence if a private person obtained the evidence through torture.[47]

[45] K Dangl, *Unternehmensinterne Untersuchungen* (Linde Verlag, 2019) 222.
[46] Madl (n 44) 930.
[47] *Ćwik v Poland* App no 31454/10 (ECtHR, 5 November 2020) paras 80 ff.

5

Admissibility of E-Evidence, Transnational E-Evidence and Fair-Trial Rights in Italy

GABRIELLA DI PAOLO

I. General Legal Framework on Admissibility of Criminal Evidence

Inspired by the Anglo-American criminal procedure system, the reform enacted with the Italian Code of Criminal Procedure of 1988 (CCP) has had a great impact in the field of evidence too. Driven by a wish to leave behind the French model (from the investigating judge to the freedom of proof)[1] and implement the principles of the accusatorial system, the Code has established separation between the prosecutor's and the court's functions[2] as well as between pre-trial and trial phases.[3] It has also introduced clarity into the evidentiary rules, overcoming the

[1] E Grande, 'Italian criminal procedure: borrowing and resistance' (2000) 48 *American Journal of Comparative Law* 227, 244; L Luparia, 'Model code or broken dream? The Italian criminal procedure in a comparative perspective' in L Luparia et al (eds), *The Italian Code of Criminal Procedure. Critical Essays and English Translation*, 2nd edn (Wolters Kluwer & Cedam, 2017) 1, 2–3.

[2] Following the adversarial model of Anglo-American criminal procedure, the 1988 CCP has abolished the '*judge d'instruction*' (investigating judge) – the central figure at the preliminary stage of criminal proceedings in the Continental tradition – in order to avoid the centralisation of investigative, prosecution and adjudication roles in the hands of the judge. Consequently, under the 1988 CCP, it is duty of the prosecutor to make thorough investigations of criminal complaints and to prepare cases for trial. In the pre-trial stage, the judge for the preliminary investigations intervenes only in exceptional cases – usually at the request of the prosecutor, when the restraint of fundamental rights is involved and judicial authorisation (prior or subsequent to the coercive measure) is needed. This judge, however, does not have control of the investigation. Similarly, the presentation of evidence at trial is party driven, and the trial court has *ex officio* evidentiary powers only in exceptional cases. See E Amodio and E Selvaggi, 'An accusatorial system in a civil law country: the 1988 Italian code of criminal procedure' (1989) 62 *Temple Law Review* 1211,1213.

[3] As a consequence of the reform, the 1988 CCP distinguishes between the investigation phase (pre-trial) and the adjudication phase (trial). Most of the information collected in the pre-trial phase is not admitted or used as evidence at trial. Compared with the 1930 CCP, this is a great change. The new Code breaks the chain between preliminary investigation and the trial, putting an end to the 'communicating vessel system' of the 1930 CCP, under which the dossier of the pre-trial phase was known

unregulated discretionary powers that the previous system had given judges at different stages of the proceedings (the admission, gathering and assessment of evidence). From this perspective, a complex law of evidence has been developed, aimed primarily at safeguarding the principle of legality in the gathering of evidence.[4]

From a systemic point of view, the new procedural framework has produced a complete set of rules on evidence – an entire chapter of the Code, namely book III – establishing an independent *corpus* that encompasses fundamental principles of criminal evidence.[5] Book III is divided into three Titles, dealing respectively with the general principles (Articles 187–193); the single means of proof (testimony, examination of parties, confrontation, identification, judicial simulation,[6] expert evidence, documentary evidence) (Articles 194–243); and measures for obtaining evidence (inspection, searches, seizure, interceptions of communications) (Articles 244–271).[7] Title I includes a series of provisions outlining the fundamental principles of the evidentiary procedure regarding the admissibility (Articles 187–190), the gathering and production (Article 188) and the assessment of evidence (Article 192), as well as the consequences of the violation of evidentiary prohibitions (Article 191, regarding unlawfully gathered evidence).

Finally, books V and VII of the CPP are dedicated to the gathering of evidence: book V concerns investigative measures, rules on the preliminary investigation and preliminary hearing; book VII concerns the rules applicable at trial. Consistent with the adversarial principle, the production of evidence at trial is the task of the parties, conducting direct examination and cross-examination of witnesses and expert witnesses (Articles 498–499), and of the accused as well, if the accused agrees.[8]

To understand the rules on admissibility of evidence, it might be useful to start by explaining the impact of the newly introduced structure of the criminal proceedings, with the clear separation of the pre-trial and trial stages. Such separation has been

and used by the trial court in reaching its decision. See E Amodio, 'The accusatorial system lost and regained: reforming criminal procedure in Italy' in A Eser and C Rabenstein (eds), *Criminal Justice Between Crime Control and Due Process. Convergence and Divergence in Criminal Procedure Systems* (Duncker & Humblot 2004) 23, 24.

[4] In compliance with the Constitution (Art 111.1), according to which 'Jurisdiction is implemented through due process regulated by law.' See E Amodio, 'Libero convincimento e tassatività dei mezzi di prova' (1999) 1 *Rivista italiana di diritto e procedura penale*, 3; M Gialuz, 'The Italian code of criminal procedure: a reading guide' in Luparia et al (eds) (n 1) 17, 39.

[5] This microsystem has no precedent in the codifications of the European Continent. See Amodio (n 3) 24.

[6] The definition of 'judicial simulation' (*esperimento giudiziale*) is provided for under Art 218 CPP: '1. The judicial simulation shall be admitted when it is necessary to ascertain whether a fact has or could have occurred in a specific way. 2. The simulation [shall] consist in the reproduction, as exact as possible, of the situation in which the fact is said or believed to have occurred and in the reenactment of the way in which the fact has taken place.' For this translation (and for an unofficial translation of the CPP, updated to 5 July 2017), see Luparia et al (eds) (n 1) 116–565.

[7] F Ruggieri and S Marcolini, 'Italy' in K Ligeti (ed), *Toward a Prosecutor for the European Union*, vol 1 (Hart Publishing, 2013) 368, 370.

[8] See Gialuz (n 4) 36.

ensured by way of the 'double dossier system': the investigative dossier, available only to the parties; and the trial dossier, which is the one that will be forwarded to the adjudicating court. Such division of the files has been designed to prevent the trial judge from having access to the records of the pre-trial phase, thereby guaranteeing that only evidence produced during the trial stage can influence the court's decision.[9]

Building a 'firewall' between the pre-trial and the adjudication stages obviously has significant, far-reaching implications, as it lays the foundations for what has been called the 'accusatorial golden rule', now also enshrined in Art. 111.4 of the Constitution.[10] This means that, as a general rule, out-of-court statements may not be admitted and used as substantive evidence for ascertaining the truth of facts, but only to challenge the credibility/reliability of the witness.[11] However, this rule is not absolute and has some exceptions, mentioned in the Constitution too (Article 111.5), admitting the use of out-of-court statements as substantive evidence when the accused consents to it, or where it is objectively impossible to produce the evidence at trial (ie unavailable or protected witnesses, or the records of interceptions of communications) or when unlawful conduct by a third party against the witness has been proved (ie witness intimidation).

With regard to the phase of the admission of evidence, unlike the former criminal procedure model, where evidence was essentially collected by the investigating judge and produced in court before the trial judge, the CCP of 1988 has taken the opposite approach, envisaging a system of adjudication in which evidence gathering is to be done by the parties[12] and each of the parties is responsible for presenting it at trial.

Article 190 of the CCP of 1988 therefore provides that 'evidence shall be admitted [by the court] upon request of the party' and may be admitted on the judge's own initiative only in exceptional cases set by law.[13] In deciding whether to admit the evidence requested by the parties, the law provides for certain criteria and also sets out certain prohibitions, as, for example, when evidence is manifestly superfluous (ie redundant) or concerns facts that are not the object of the proceedings (irrelevant or not pertinent). In other words, there has to be a connection between evidence and *res iudicanda*,[14] as outlined in Article 187 CPP.[15]

[9] M Caianiello, *Chapter 9, Italy* at https://canestrinilex.com/assets/Uploads/en/Italy-country-report.pdf accessed 20 July 2022.

[10] Art 111.4, 'In criminal law proceedings, the formation of evidence is based on the principle of adversary hearings.'; and see para 3, establishing the confrontation clause. For the English translation of the Italian Constitution, see the website of Senato della Repubblica at www.senato.it/documenti/repository/istituzione/costituzione_inglese.pdf accessed 22 July 2022.

[11] The Italian law of evidence is therefore framed on the hearsay rule. See Amodio and Selvaggi (n 2) 1223.

[12] ibid 1220–21; Grande (n 1) 244.

[13] For example, see Art 507 CCP: '1. Upon completion of the evidence gathering, the court may order, also of its own motion, the admission of new evidence, if absolutely necessary.' For this translation, see Luparia et al (eds) (n 1) 437.

[14] G Ubertis, *Profiles of Judicial Epistemology* (Giappichelli & Nomos, 2018) 110.

[15] Under Art 187 CCP, '1. Facts concerning accusations, criminal liabilities and determination of either the sentence or the security measure are facts in issue. 2. Facts on which the application of

Regarding the prohibitions on evidence, in distancing itself from the French model, in which the principle of the freedom of evidence continues to be applied – '*les infractions peuvent être établies par tout mode de preuve*' (Article 427 French CCP) – the Italian Code of 1988 opted for an intermediate approach:[16] the Code includes a list of specific types of evidence and investigative measures that are admissible, but leaves some leeway for the judge to admit evidence not expressly included in the list (so-called 'atypical evidence') if it is deemed apt to determine the facts and does not compromise the moral freedom of the person (Article 189 CCP). This creates a flexible approach, allowing for new means of evidence to be admitted even if not specifically regulated, once their epistemological adequacy has been assessed, as well as the lack of any prejudice to the moral freedom of the person.

Last but not least, with the aim of guaranteeing the legality principle during the evidence gathering stage, Article 191 CCP states that illegally obtained evidence – evidence gathered in violation of prohibitions set by the law – shall not be used by the judge in deciding the case. While the former CCP, under the influence of the French model, was governed by the '*nullité*' regime (including the option of a '*purge de la nullité*'), the Code of 1988, inspired by the US concept of an exclusionary rule of evidence, has introduced the prohibition on using the illegally obtained evidence. Although the case law of the Supreme Court of Cassation[17] and of the Constitutional Court[18] has adopted a restrictive interpretation of the exclusionary rule – rejecting the 'fruit of the poisonous tree' doctrine for the objects seized during an illegally performed search – this rule is still considered one of the most important innovations experienced in evidence law.[19]

A. Evidence Obtained in Different Proceedings (Administrative Investigations and Internal Investigations in the Field of Compliance Programmes)

During an administrative investigation, when the prosecuting authorities have enough evidence to establish a reasonable suspicion that the alleged administrative

procedural rules depends are also facts in issue. 3. Facts concerning civil liability resulting from an offence are also facts in issue if a civil party joins the criminal proceedings.' For this translation, see Luparia et al (eds) (n 1) 217.

[16] Amodio (n 4) 6–7.

[17] C Cass 27 March 1996, Sala, in Cass pen, 1996, 3268.

[18] C Cost, judgment 3 October 2019, no 219. For a commentary see R Casiraghi, 'La Corte costituzionale non esclude l'invalidità derivata in materia probatoria' in *Sistema penale* (2019) at www.sistemapenale.it/it/scheda/invalidita-derivata-materia-probatoria accessed 20 July 2022; N Galantini, 'Note a margine di Corte cost., sent. 3 ottobre 2019, n 219, e a Corte cost, sent 26 novembre 2020 n 252' in *Sistema penale* (2021) at www.sistemapenale.it/it/sentenza/galantini-inutilizzabilita-derivata-corte-costituzionale-219-2019-e-252-2020?out=print accessed 20 July 2022; see also C Cost, ord 9 May 2022 no. 116. For a commentary on the ordinance that raised the question of constitutionality, see N Galantini, 'L'art. 191 c.p.p. a confronto con la 'inutilizzabilità derivata' in un nuovo giudizio costituzionale' *Sistema Penale* (2022) at www.sistemapenale.it/it/scheda/tribunale-lecce-qlc-191-inutilizzabilita-derivata accessed 15 July 2022.

[19] Amodio (n 4) 3; Gialuz (n 4) 39.

infringement could be a crime, the officers shall proceed according to the rules of criminal procedure (Article 220 Disp Att CCP). This means that evidence gathered after the suspicion of a crime has arisen may be introduced and used within criminal proceedings only if respecting the higher safeguards laid out in the CCP. Any other evidence obtained before that, under the administrative procedural rules, may be introduced in criminal proceedings as documentary evidence.[20]

This system aims to ensure, at least in theory, better protection for suspects, although this is questionable, because in practice it is very difficult to determine the point at which the line between administrative investigations and criminal investigations has been crossed. The duty to apply the CCP is only triggered when elements of crimes have appeared, but very often the nature of the offence is far from clear.

With regard to the information gathered during internal investigations in the field of compliance programmes (ie investigations carried out by supervisory bodies, often through lawyers), it is important to note that these procedures might have a preventive role or the aim of assessing reported infringements, and may establish facts that might entail the civil, administrative or criminal liability of the corporation or its employees. These investigations usually involve the examination of company documents, computer files, emails and interviews.

They can be carried out only for internal or 'restorative' purposes (to ascertain whether company policies were followed and identify any organisational deficiencies that can be rectified quickly through organisational changes; to assess the prerequisites for taking any disciplinary action; to handle correctly a report from a whistleblower); or for 'external' purposes (to collect and manage information to be examined by the court; to develop a defensive strategy; to research and gather items of evidence for the defence or for civil or criminal proceedings; to put in place 'restorative actions' in accordance with Articles 12 and 17 of Legislative Decree 231/2001).[21]

In the first case (investigations for purely internal purposes), evidence gathered through the above-mentioned measures – and in accordance with labour laws on employees' protection[22] and the provisions on data protection[23] – is definitely admissible in criminal proceedings as documentary evidence. In the

[20] L Bartoli and G Lasagni, 'The handling of digital evidence in Italy' in M Caianiello and A Camon (eds), *Digital forensic evidence. Toward common European standards in antifraud administrative and criminal investigations* (Wolters Kluwer & Cedam, 2021) 87, 120–21.

[21] See E Mancuso, 'Le investigazioni interne nel sistema processuale italiano: tra vuoto normativo e prassi applicative incerte' in F Centonze and M Mantovani (eds), *La responsabilità 'penale' degli enti: dieci proposte di riforma* (Il Mulino, 2016) 217; D Stendardi, 'Disposizioni del D. Lgs. 231/2001 a matrice riparativa e possibili intrecci con gli strumenti tipici della Restorative Justice' in *Giurisprudenza penale* web (2020) at www.giurisprudenzapenale.com/2020/04/16/disposizioni-del-d-lgs-231-2001-a-matrice-riparativa-e-possibili-intrecci-con-gli-strumenti-tipici-della-restorative-justice/ accessed 25 May 2023.

[22] Law no 300/1970, the so-called Workers' Statute.

[23] Privacy Code, ie Legislative Decree of 30 June 2003 no 163; and Regulation (EU) 2016/679 of the European Parliament and of the Council of 27 April 2016 on the protection of natural persons with regard to the processing of personal data and on the free movement of such data, and repealing Directive 95/46/EC (General Data Protection Regulation) (Text with EEA relevance) [2016] OJ L119/1.

second case (investigation for external purposes), the outcome could be admitted in court and used as documentary evidence under Article 234, if applicable (for example, in the case of the production of documents belonging to public administration). If internal investigations (for example interviews or taking statements) were conducted by a lawyer following procedural rules on defence investigations, the results will be admissible at trial as they were collected by the prosecutor, in accordance with Article 391-*octies* and Article 391-*decies* CCP.[24] It means that the outcome of defence investigations have the same probative value as information collected by the prosecutor, therefore the 'dossier of the lawyer' will be included, at the end of preliminary investigations, in the investigative dossier.[25]

II. Legal Framework on Admissibility of E-Evidence

A. The Definition of E-Evidence

With regard to electronic evidence ('e-evidence'), the Italian legal system has not been updated appropriately. There is no definition of 'electronic evidence' nor specific rules on its admissibility or evidentiary exclusionary rules. Therefore, judicial practice and case law play a crucial role in this field, but there are still many unclear issues, and some of the solutions adopted are questionable from a human rights perspective.

As mentioned already, the Italian CCP does not define the concept of e-evidence, but following the definition contained in the Budapest Convention[26] it is usually understood as being information that comes from data – data stored, transmitted and processed by computers or electronic devices. In brief, we are referring to data codified by means of the 'binary code'. Such concept is very broad, and may include, for example, computer files, emails, instant messages, digital photographs, audio recordings and 'metadata' (data stored by a service provider).[27]

Moreover, the gathering of e-data may cover, from a theoretical point of view, two types of activities: (i) *ex post* searches or access to stored data (data stored in personal devices or data held by service providers); and (ii) *real-time* monitoring of individuals by law enforcement authorities. Legal requirements are quite different in these two situations and depend on the type of intervention, since *ex post* searches and access to stored data are short-term measures and persons are aware of them, while real-time monitoring consists of covert investigative techniques

[24] See Mancuso (n 21) 217.
[25] See Art 391-*octies*, para 3 and Article 391-*decies* CCP.
[26] Council of Europe Convention on Cybercrime (adopted 23 November 2001) ETS No 185.
[27] G Illuminati, 'Digital evidence and admissibility' (2020) 2 *Revue internationale de droit penal* 273, 274.

that can imply a long-term intervention, and thus are considered more intrusive into fundamental rights and are subject to higher requirements.

Of relevance is that in the academic literature and in the case law, e-evidence is understood mainly in a strict sense as stored data and is treated in the proceedings as 'documentary evidence'.[28] Real-time monitoring, even if executed by means of electronic devices, is not within the scope of documentary evidence, because this concept is related to items already existing outside the criminal proceedings.

B. The Multilevel Legal Framework

As in other European countries, Italy has a multilevel legal framework.[29] At the upper level there is the Constitution, which dates back to 1948, granting protection to 'traditional' rights and freedoms: personal liberty, domicile, the right to free and secret communication. It has not been amended to include 'new rights'. Therefore, the Constitutional Court, as well as legal scholars, has tried to adapt the 'old notions' to the digital context: for example, expanding the protection established for the home to include the 'virtual home', and referring increasingly to European law and the European Convention on Human Rights (ECHR) 'to grant constitutional footing to the more flexible principles such as proportionality and privacy'.[30]

With regard to secondary sources, besides the rules in the CCP, there are some relevant provisions on data retention and access to communication-stored data held by providers (non-content information about telecommunications) in the Privacy Code of 2003,[31] recently amended[32] to ensure compliance with European Union (EU) law on data protection and the case law of the Court of Justice of the European Union (CJEU).[33]

[28] ibid 273.

[29] V Manes and M Caianiello, *Introduzione al diritto penale europeo* (Giappichelli, 2020) 3 ff, 125 ff; M Daniele, 'La norma processuale penale' in A Camon et al, *Fondamenti di procedura penale* (Cedam-Wolters Kluwer, 2019) 63, 64 ff.

[30] Bartoli and Lasagni (n 20) 88. The reference is of course to Art 8 of the European Convention for the Protection of Human Rights and Fundamental Freedoms (ECHR) and Art 52 of the Charter of Fundamental Rights of the European Union (2000/C364/01) OJ C364/1.

[31] See Art 123 (traffic data), Art 126 (location data) and in particular Art 132 (retention of data on traffic for other purposes of the Privacy Code (Legislative Decree no 163/2003)).

[32] Art 132 of the Privacy Code was recently modified by Law Decree no 132 of 30 September 2021, and converted to law, with modifications, by Law no 178 of 23 November 2021. For an in-depth analysis of the subject, see S Marcolini and R Flor, *Dalla data retention alle indagini ad alto contenuto tecnologico* (Giappichelli, 2022) chs 1 and 3.

[33] Mainly to adapt to the rulings in Cases C-293/12 and C-594/12 *Digital Rights Ireland Ltd* (CJEU (GC), 8 April 2014), and C-746/18 *Criminal Proceedings v HK (Prokuratuur)* (CJEU (GC), 2 March 2021). The arguments put forward by the *Prokuratuur* decision are the development of a series of rulings by the Grand Chamber: Joint Cases C-203/15 and C-698/15 *Tele2-Watson* (CJEU (GC), 21 December 2016); Case C-207/16 *Ministerio Fiscal* (CJEU (GC), 2 October 2018); Case C-623/17 *La Quadrature Du Net and Others* (CJEU (GC), 6 October 2020) and Case C-623/17 *Privacy International* (CJEU (GC), 6 October 2020).

i. Code of Criminal Procedure

As previously mentioned, the types of evidence that can be produced under Italian criminal procedure are not '*numerus clausus*', as the CCP contains a general clause admitting evidence not regulated specifically by the law (Article 189 CCP).[34] This clause is very often used by courts to admit new technological investigative measures, mainly when the measure is not intrusive, because interferences with the rights protected by the Constitution (ie the inviolability of the home or the secrecy of communications) require a specific legal provision and are subject to judicial warrant, as provided for in the Constitution.

For example, on the basis of this general clause, law enforcement bodies are entitled to carry out 'electronic tailing' by means of GPS or covert video surveillance in public spaces, measures which are still lacking specific regulation in Italy.[35]

By contrast, the higher courts denied the possibility to adopt more intrusive measures, such as covert video surveillance within the home,[36] or the use of malware to carry out online searches (still lacking specific regulation)[37] or surveillance of communications,[38] at least until 2017. With the reform on interceptions adopted in 2017 and in 2019,[39] the use of 'State Trojans' for communication surveillance has a specific legal basis in the Italian Code,[40] and thus the doubts as to its admissibility have come to an end.[41]

With regard to e-evidence, the first reference to digitally stored data was introduced in 2008, by the law that implemented the Budapest Convention on cyber-crime,[42] seeking to modernise the rules on inspections, searches and methods of seizure. However, in the end it consisted in applying the same rules of the

[34] See section I.

[35] For an overview, see G Di Paolo, 'Judicial investigations and gathering of evidence in a digital, online context' (2009) 1–2 *Revue internationale de droit penal* 201, 219 ff.

[36] Cass, Sez Un, 28 March 2006, no 26795, Prisco, in *CED*, no 234267.

[37] Online searches still lack specific legislation, and thus the lawfulness of this type of measure is widely debated. Legal scholars have been critical to its use, although courts have accepted the use of malware in online searches in some cases (eg, Cass, sez V, 14 October 2009, Virruso, in *CED*, no 246954; Cass, sez V, 30 May 2017, Occhionero, in *CED*, no 271412). See EM Mancuso, 'Le acquisizioni mediante captatore non disciplinate dalla legge' in A Giarda, F Giunta and G Varraso (eds), *Dai decreti attuativi della legge 'Orlando' alle novelle di fine legislatura* (Wolters Kluwer & Cedam, 2018) 193; S Signorato, *Le indagini digitali* (Giappichelli, 2018) 3, 291 ff; D Foti, 'Digital privacy and cyber-interception of communications' in L Bachmaier Winter and S Ruggeri (eds), *Investigating and preventing crime in the digital era* (Springer, 2022) 151.

[38] Cass, Sez Un., 1 July 2016, no 26889, Scurato, in *CED*, no 266905.

[39] Legislative Decree no 216/2017 (*Riforma Orlando*) as amended by Law Decree no 161/2019, later Law no 7/2020.

[40] See G Di Paolo, 'Le intercettazioni mediante captatore informatico' in Giarda, Giunta and Varraso (eds) (n 37) 165.

[41] A recent ruling by the Court of Cassation (Cass, sez I, 1 February 2022, no 3591, Romeo) has launched an interpretative trend that allows all the online surveillance activities that a trojan is available to perform, as they are considered digital or electronic interception, thereby going beyond the previous restrictive interpretations. In the specific case that was ruled to be an 'interception', an Excel file containing a financial statement was extracted at the same time as it was being created on a computer, using screenshots taken by a trojan that had been previously installed on the device.

[42] Law 18 March 2008, no 48.

'physical world' on search and seizure to a digital environment (computers, smartphones, etc).[43] The only additional provision for digital investigations is that the original data shall be preserved by adopting technical measures preventing their alteration,[44] ensuring that the duplicate (the so-called 'clone copy') is obtained following a procedure that guarantees that the copies are identical to the original and cannot be modified.[45]

It is clear that Italian legislator has acknowledged the 'volatility' of e-evidence, that is the risk of its alteration, and the need to ensure data integrity. But legal provisions do not go into any further technical details, and leave to the police and the IT forensic experts the choice of the devices, methods and procedures to be used. This approach allows flexibility, which is positive, but also entails insecurity, since there are no common standards and guidelines for law enforcement in digital investigations. Only the *Guardia di finanza* have their own guidelines,[46] but these are not binding, and thus practitioners and the courts do not always follow them.[47]

In practice, the most commonly adopted measure is search and seizure of computers and other electronic devices, producing and analysing a mirror copy of all the data stored in the device. This measure is implemented in the following way: (i) after seizure of the device and the cloning of data, the device is returned to its owner; (ii) the subsequent analysis and acquisition of the relevant data are carried out on the clone copy, by technically qualified personnel; (iii) to ensure the chain of custody, a written report and video recording should explain in detail all operations undertaken on the device and the electronic files.[48]

Given the huge amount of data stored in computers or electronic devices, the main problem that presents in the searches of computers is to limit its scope and avoid exploratory searches, in order to ensure compliance with the principles of specificity and proportionality granted by the Constitution and European sources.

In this regard, important guidance is to be found in the case law:

(a) *Time* is a relevant factor in establishing proportionality. The seizure of a device may be necessary, but for no longer than it takes to copy it.[49] If the owner is a third party, the judicial warrant should explain this person's connection to the facts under investigation, and there is an obligation to return the device as soon as possible.[50]
(b) The public prosecutor cannot seize any data beyond those that are strictly necessary, therefore he or she can keep the mirror copy only as long as is necessary to carry out the selection of data; and after the search for and

[43] Bartoli and Lasagni (n 20) 90.
[44] See Art 244 para 2, Art 247 para 1-bis, Art 352 para1-bis CCP.
[45] See Article 254-bis and Article 354 para 2 CCP.
[46] Bartoli and Lasagni (n 20) 91.
[47] ibid 92.
[48] Signorato (n 37) 140.
[49] For example, Cass, sez VI, 11 November 2016, no 53168.
[50] Cass, sez VI, 13 March 2019, no 37639; Cass, sez VI, 9 December 2020, no 6623, Pessotto, in *CED* no 280838.

identification of the relevant data, the mirror image of the device must be returned to the owner.[51]

(c) Thirdly, and most importantly, courts have also stated that there is a violation of the proportionality principle when the prosecutor orders the seizure of an electronic device containing different types of data without specifying the selection criteria for the filtering of data.[52]

Despite the important role the courts are playing in delineating the digital investigative measures and providing for guiding rules complementing the lack of specific legal provisions in the field of digital investigations and search and seizure of digital data, there are still many open questions.

First, the decisions are inconsistent with regard to the issue of the nature of the cloning process, whether it is repeatable or unrepeatable, while this can be a crucial aspect to ensure the defence rights.

Second, infringements of the best practices and guidelines rarely lead to the inadmissibility of evidence but are considered as irregularities that are taken into account when assessing the evidence, impacting only the weight and reliability of the evidence. This approach is questionable: if one of the main safeguards regarding e-evidence is to ensure its authenticity and its integrity, an intrinsic exclusionary rule based on the violation of best practices could be seen as appropriate to prevent abuses in the handling of the data, although it is doubtful that such an exclusionary rule would be accepted, at either the domestic or the European level.

Finally, it is still unclear what the consequences are of the violation of the proportionality principle in the search of devices. For the moment, the Italian criminal procedure does not follow the 'fruit of the poisonous tree' doctrine. In this context, the Italian Constitutional Court has held that the derivative effect of the illegally obtained evidence is not a constitutional mandate, and thus the legislator has wide discretion in adopting such a rule or not.[53] The possibility for the courts to exclude the evidence on the basis of the 'nullity' principle might be also considered, at least in the case of violation of defence rights. As can be seen, these issues require further analysis and development.[54]

ii. Privacy Code

Important provisions on e-evidence can be found in the Privacy Code, in particular in Article 132, which sets out rules on meta data, non-content information of communications and data retention.[55] As mentioned, the Code was recently

[51] Cass, sez VI, 22 September 2020, no 34265, Aleotti, in *CED* no 279949.

[52] Cass, sez VI, 9 December 2020, no 6623, Pessotto, in *CED* no 280838; Cass, sez VI, 24 February 2015, Rizzo, no 24617, in *CED* no 264092.

[53] C Cost, judgment no 219/2019 and C Cost ord n 116/2022 (n 18).

[54] Casiraghi (n 18) para 3.

[55] With reference to information concerning communications, there is a fundamental distinction between content information (of communications) and non-content (the data about those

amended to bring national legislation into line with the case law of the CJEU.[56] In a nutshell, the 2021 reform introduced a specific framework for acquiring non-content information of communications (known as 'traffic data'), based on the interception system, albeit with a few significant differences.

First of all, the public prosecutor was denied the power to access such data, since authorisation from the judge is now required. The idea was to leave the final say to a neutral body with no interest in the proceedings.

The second major change is that the power to access non-content data is limited for the investigation of certain offences, which are determined by a quantitative criterion (offences for which the law establishes the penalty of life imprisonment or imprisonment of not less than a maximum of three years) and by a qualitative criterion (with reference to specific types of offence, such as threats, abuse or harassment by phone).

As in the case of interceptions for Mafia or terrorism, the evidentiary threshold that justifies the investigative measure is the existence of 'sufficient suspicion of offence'; also, access to such data may be authorised if it is 'relevant to establishing the facts'.

A central element of the new framework is the provision of a final rule, according to which data acquired in violation of the said requirements 'may not be used' as evidence.

C. Transnational Gathering of E-Evidence

To conclude, it is important to mention some features concerning the transnational gathering of e-evidence in the light of the recent case law in Italy. As in other countries, mutual legal assistance (MLA)[57] instruments have been the main way for obtaining evidence located abroad, and there are no specific rules for e-evidence. Since the MLA process is complex, slow and unpredictable, many states have come up with different approaches based on unilateral action, to obtain access and avoid some of the hurdles of judicial cooperation with foreign authorities altogether.[58]

For example, consolidated case law tends to bypass the MLA mechanisms when the technical assistance of another country is not necessary, as in the case of

communications). Non-content data include transactional data, such as whom a communication was to or from, the time it was transmitted, and the duration or size of the communication.

[56] See section II.B.

[57] Within the EU, cooperation is simplified by the brand-new European Investigation Order (EIO), but it does not contain any specific provision on digital evidence, focusing only on spot operations such as the identification of the person 'holding a subscription of a specified … IP address' (Art 10(e) of the Directive 2014/41/EU of the European Parliament and of the Council of 3 April 2014 regarding the European Investigation Order in criminal matters, OJ L 130/1); the Italian transposition added to this list the identification of the person behind an email address: Art 9(e) Legislative Decree of 21 June 2017, no 108).

[58] See L Bartoli, 'Digital evidence for the criminal trial: limitless cloud and state boundaries' (2019) *Eurojus* 99.

information held by service providers in the cloud[59] or in the case of interceptions of communications, in particular when the target is outside Italy but access to his or her communications is possible through technical systems located in Italy (so called '*instradamento*').[60]

It should be noted that the recent case law also applies this reasoning to communication surveillance by means of 'State trojans' (malware). The Supreme Court of Cassation has ruled that MLA is not necessary for intercepting face-to-face communication that took place in Canada, if the device used for the communication surveillance was 'infected' in Italy. Thus if the virus (the malware) was implanted in Italy, the law enforcement bodies are entitled to carry out interceptions of communication face-to-face all over the world.[61]

This approach is not only risky, but also in clear violation of international law and bilateral agreements between Italy and Canada. This is not a case of surveillance of telecommunications by means of a device (so-called telecommunication surveillance at the source, prior to encryption) but results in conducting a measure within the territory of another state, without MLA and any communication to the other state.

It might be questioned whether an intrinsic exclusionary rule based on the violation of international law could be useful to tackle cases like this, in order to avoid an 'international Wild West' and to ensure better protection of human rights.

Finally, another strategy put in place in order to obtain information directly by service providers, bypassing MLA, is shown by the consolidated case law concerning access to Blackberry chat (pin-to-pin encrypted system).[62] The Court of Cassation has ruled that the concept of 'interception of communication' is applicable only in case of real-time monitoring, therefore *ex post* access to messages exchanged in Blackberry chats and their decryption are outside the scope of the interceptions regime. Thus, chat messages are admitted as 'digital documentary evidence' under Article 234-*bis CPP*[63] and MLA is not necessary if the Blackberry

[59] ibid 100.

[60] See L Giordano, Intercettazioni: è al tramonto la stagione dell'instradamento? in *Il Penalista* (2017) at https://ilpenalista.it/articoli/focus/intercettazioni-al-tramonto-la-stagione-dellinstradamento accessed 20 July 2020.

For different strategies put in place by France, Germany and Italy in order to obtain information directly from providers, see Bartoli (n 58) 100 ff.

[61] Cass, Sez II, 22 July 2022, no 29362, CD, in [2021] *Diritto penale e processo* 1352, with comments by F Demartis, 'La Cassazione rifiuta la rogatoria per le intercettazioni all'estero col captatore informatico', ibid.

[62] See Cass, Sez VI, 13 May 2023, no 18907, Civale, in *CED* 281819–01. See also, Cass, Sez III., 13 May 2020, no 1472 at www.altalex.com/documents/2020/06/11/non-serve-rogatoria-per-decriptare-le-chat-blackberry-se-le-comunicazioni-sono-avvenute-in-italia accessed 20 July 2022.

[63] Article 234-*bis* – Access to digital documents and data. 1. The acquisition of digital documents and data stored abroad is always permitted, even if documents and data are different from those available to the public, in the latter case subject to the prior consent of the owner. [234-*bis –Acquisizione di documenti e dati informatici. 1. E' sempre consentita l'acquisizione di documenti e dati informatici conservati all'estero, anche diversi da quelli disponibili al pubblico, previo consenso, in quest'ultimo caso, del legittimo titolare.*].

device is located in Italy (or the access to chat messages is possible through technical systems located in Italy) and the foreign company is willing to collaborate and supplies only the decryption algorithms.[64]

This interpretation has been confirmed in recent decisions by the Court of Cassation in the *Encrochat* case, dealing with the issue of access to encrypted messages exchanged by means of SKY Ecc and Encrochat (end-to-end encrypted systems). Also in this case, the Court of Cassation ruled that *ex post* access to chat messages (held and decrypted by French authorities) can be obtained – issuing an EIO – under Article 234-*bis* CPP, since these messages can be treated as 'digital documentary evidence' and the decryption of their content is outside the scope of interceptions of communication.[65] Regarding the possibility to use evidence obtained and transferred by foreign authorities, these decisions follow the 'non inquiry principle', since the Court ruled that there is a presumption that activities carried out abroad were fair. Thus the Italian judge is not required to carry out an assessment on the correctness of the methods of evidence gathering used by foreign authorities.[66]

[64] By contrast, MLA is necessary in case of refusal of collaboration by the service provider or by the company producer of the device.

[65] Cass, Sez I, 13 October 2022 no 6364/2023, Calderon Raul Esteban, in *CED* Cass, no 283998–01. See also Cass, Sez I, 15 Febr 2023, no 6363 at www.processopenaleegiustizia.it/Tool/Evidenza/Single/view_html?id_evidenza=2765 accessed 25 May 2023.

[66] Cass, Sez I, 15 Febr 2023, no 6363, §. 1.7, 13.

6

Admissibility of Evidence, Transnational E-Evidence and Fair-Trial Rights in Luxembourg

KATALIN LIGETI AND STANISŁAW TOSZA*

I. Introduction

Luxembourg criminal procedure is characterised by limited formal rules as regards admissibility of evidence. Its practice is shaped by two components of the legal system that define the approach to and discussion of evidence in criminal proceedings.

The main principle is freedom of proof (*la liberté de la preuve*), according to which any type of evidence is admissible and violations of rules on the gathering of proof do not automatically render the evidence inadmissible. The impact of those violations has to be assessed in concrete cases. The liberty of judges to make this assessment is, however, limited by the guiding principles elaborated in the case law, in particular the duty of fairness ('*loyauté*') in the administration of evidence. It is in view of those principles that the competent judicial authorities evaluate the evidence.

In that context, a second key feature of the Luxembourg legal system is the monist approach to international law instruments.[1] As treaties and conventions binding Luxembourg are directly applicable, their provisions may be used to question the validity of evidence gathered in violation of fundamental rights, in particular as enshrined in the European Convention of Human Rights (ECHR).

* In Luxembourg, virtually all legislation, case law and scholarly writing are in French. All translations in this report are the authors' own. This chapter is partially based on previous publications of one of the co-authors: K Ligeti, 'Luxembourg' in F Giuffrida and K Ligeti (eds), *Admissibility of OLAF Final Reports as Evidence in Criminal Proceedings* (University of Luxembourg, 2019) 191 at https://orbilu.uni.lu/handle/10993/40141 and K Ligeti and G Robinson, 'The Handling of Digital Evidence in Luxembourg' in M Caianiello and A Camon (eds), *Digital Forensic Evidence. Towards Common European Standards in Antifraud Administrative and Criminal Investigations* (Wolters Kluwer-CEDAM, 2021) 123.

[1] V Covolo, 'Luxembourg' in S Allegrezza and V Covolo (eds), *Effective Defence Rights in Criminal Proceedings* (Wolters Kluwer-CEDAM, 2018) 329, 330–31.

This chapter will sketch the main possibilities for gathering evidence, in particular electronic evidence ('e-evidence' – section II), before explaining the understanding of the principle of freedom of proof and its limitations in Luxembourg law (section III), as well as the limited impact of exclusionary rules of evidence in the Luxembourg criminal procedure (section IV). Finally, the chapter will provide an explanation of the particular problem of admissibility of evidence obtained in administrative proceedings (section V) and during internal investigations (section VI), which will be followed by brief concluding remarks (section VII).

II. The Gathering of Evidence in Luxembourg

In Luxembourg in principle, a pre-trial investigation (*instruction préparatoire*) is mandatory for felonies (*crimes*) and optional for crimes (*délits*).[2] The investigating judge (*juge d'instruction*) plays a prominent role in the criminal procedure and is legally empowered to carry out any investigative measure he or she deems useful for the discovery of the truth.[3] As such, the investigating judge 'plays a central role in the Luxembourgish preliminary criminal procedure',[4] and has wide discretion as to which measures to take. The only exception to the investigating judge's broad prerogatives is the *mini-instruction* procedure, applicable to crimes. In this procedure, the public prosecutor requests the investigating judge to carry out certain acts without opening a pre-trial investigation.[5] In such a case, the investigating judge can either execute the requested act or continue the investigation himself or herself.[6]

The investigating judge gathers and verifies, with equal care, both inculpatory and exculpatory (*à charge ou à décharge*) facts and circumstances.[7] The investigative measures at the disposal of an investigating judge are enshrined in Luxembourg's Code of Criminal Procedure (*Code de procédure pénale*, CCP).

[2] Code of Criminal Procedure (*Code de procédure pénale*, CCP), as amended, at https://legilux.public.lu/eli/etat/leg/code/procedure_penale/20201221 accessed 20 September 2022, Art 49. Under Luxembourg law, 'felonies' are the most serious criminal offences and are subject to a criminal sanction (*peine criminelle*), such as imprisonment for a minimum of five years to life imprisonment, financial penalty (*amende*) of a minimum €250, or confiscation (Arts 1(1), 7, 8(1) and 9 of Luxembourg's Penal Code (*Code pénal*, as amended). Crimes (*délits*) are less serious than felonies and are subject to a correctional sanction (*peine correctionnelle*), such as imprisonment for between eight days and five years, a financial penalty (*amende*) of a minimum €250 or confiscation (Arts 1(2), 14, 15(1) and 16 of Luxembourg's Penal Code). Finally, misdemeanours (*contraventions*) are the least serious offences and are subject to a police sanction (*peine de police*), which includes a financial penalty of between €25 and €250 or confiscation (Arts 1(3), 25 and 26 of Luxembourg's Penal Code).

[3] CCP, Art 51(1).

[4] M Petschko, M Schiltz and S Tosza, 'Luxembourg' in Katalin Ligeti (ed), *Toward a Prosecutor for the European Union*, vol 1 (Hart Publishing, 2013) 449, 452.

[5] CCP, Art 24-1(1).

[6] CCP, Art 24-1(2).

[7] CCP, Art 51(1).

These include common investigative measures such as search and seizure,[8] the hearing of witnesses,[9] the use of expert witnesses[10] and interception measures.[11]

Pursuant to Article 65(1) CCP, searches can be carried out in any place where objects may be found that could be useful for the discovery of the truth.[12] The investigating judge can seize objects, documents, effects, and data stored, processed or transmitted in an automated data processing or transmission system.[13] Pursuant to Article 66(3) CCP, data can be seized in two ways: by taking possession of the device (*support physique*) or by making a copy of the data in the presence of the persons attending the search.[14] The possibility to make a copy of the data avoids having to seize an object belonging to a third party, which would, in turn, require the opening of a new investigation.[15] If a copy is made, the investigating judge may order the permanent erasure of the data from the device, when it is located in Luxembourg and has not been placed in the hands of the courts, and where possession or use of the data is illegal or dangerous for the safety of persons or property.[16] In this way, the commission of other cybercrime offences (eg hacking) is prevented.[17] In urgent cases of flagrant offences (ie when an offence is being committed or has just been committed, etc),[18] an officer of the judicial police may seize stored content data, just as he or she would regarding any object or document, and in accordance with the same procedural steps in relation to a seizure ordered by the investigating judge.[19] This power is applicable in all cases where the law provides for the sanction of imprisonment.[20]

Besides search and seizure, the investigating judge has several other investigative measures at his or her disposal. For instance, an investigating judge may also order interception measures, laid down in Articles 88-1 to 88-4 CCP. This includes: (i) the interception of telecommunications and postal correspondence; (ii) audio and visual surveillance in places and vehicles; and (iii) the capture of IT data.[21] However, the use of the two last measures is available only in relation to certain serious terrorism-related offences.[22] Another investigative measure is the

[8] CCP, Arts 65–66.
[9] CCP, Arts 69–80.
[10] CCP, Arts 87–88.
[11] CCP, Arts 88-1 to 88-4.
[12] CCP, Art 65.
[13] CCP, Art 66(1).
[14] CCP, Art 66(3).
[15] K Ligeti and G Robinson, 'The Handling of Digital Evidence in Luxembourg' in M Caianiello and A Camon (eds), *Digital Forensic Evidence. Towards Common European Standards in Antifraud Administrative and Criminal Investigations* (Wolters Kluwer-CEDAM, 2021) 123, 131.
[16] CCP, Art 66(3); Ligeti and Robinson (n 15) 131.
[17] Ligeti and Robinson (n 15) 131; M Braun, 'La ratification de la Convention de Budapest sur la cybercriminalité par le Luxembourg' (2014) 35 *Journal des Tribunaux Luxembourg* 121, 132.
[18] CCP, Art 30.
[19] CCP, Arts 31 and 33; Ligeti and Robinson (n 15) 137.
[20] CCP, Art 40.
[21] CCP, Art 88-1(1).
[22] CCP, Art 88-2(2).

power to track and localise telecommunications.[23] The use of this measure is also circumscribed by certain procedural conditions, including the obligation for the investigating judge to indicate the factual circumstances that justify the measure, in a reasoned decision communicated to the State Prosecutor (*procureur d'Etat*).[24]

The gathering of e-evidence is regulated in the same way(s) as that of any other type of evidence.[25] Indeed, '[d]igital forensic procedures are carried out on the basis of horizontal, technology-neutral provisions in legislation',[26] as well as according to more general rules not specific to technology. For instance, until 2014, the seizure of electronic data was carried out on the basis of general seizure provisions,[27] despite the latter's emphasis on physical objects.[28] The Law of 18 July 2014,[29] implementing the Budapest Convention[30] in Luxembourg, updated the CCP to the specificities of e-evidence. For instance, the implementing legislation introduced the possibility to make copies of data instead of seizing the physical electronic devices, and the enlisting of decryption experts.[31] Furthermore, the implementing legislation introduced for the first time an express reference to data,[32] but also the so-called 'quick freeze' mechanism for the rapid preservation of data whenever such data are susceptible to loss or modification.[33]

In terms of transnational evidence gathering, Luxembourg authorities have three main courses of action, depending on where the evidence is located. For the gathering of evidence in another EU Member State, Luxembourg authorities make use of the European Investigation Order (EIO)[34] – transposed in Luxembourg in 2018[35] – with the exception of Denmark and Ireland, which have their respective opt-out regimes from the measures adopted in the Area of Freedom, Security, and Justice (AFSJ).[36] However, it should be noted that the EIO does not specifically target e-evidence but evidence more generally.[37] For the gathering of evidence in

[23] CCP, Art 67-1.
[24] CCP, Art 67-1(1).
[25] Ligeti and Robinson (n 15) 123.
[26] ibid.
[27] CCP, Arts 31 and 33.
[28] Braun (n 17) 132.
[29] Loi du 18 juillet 2014 portant 1) approbation de la Convention du Conseil de l'Europe sur la cybercriminalité ouverte à la signature à Budapest le 23 novembre 2001 (…), Mémorial A133.
[30] Council of Europe Convention on Cybercrime (adopted 23 November 2001) ETS No 185 ('Budapest Convention').
[31] CCP, Art 66.
[32] Ligeti and Robinson (n 15) 130.
[33] CCP, Art 48-25.
[34] Directive 2014/41/EU of the European Parliament and of the Council of 3 April 2014 regarding the European Investigation Order in criminal matters [2014] OJ L130/1.
[35] Loi du 1er août 2018 portant 1° transposition de la directive 2014/41/UE du Parlement européen et du Conseil du 3 avril 2014 concernant la décision d'enquête européenne en matière pénale (…), Mémorial A787.
[36] S Tosza, 'All evidence is equal, but electronic evidence is more equal than any other: The relationship between the European Investigation Order and the European Production Order' (2020) 11 *New Journal of European Criminal Law* 161, 163–67.
[37] S Tosza, 'Cross-border gathering of electronic evidence: Mutual legal assistance, its shortcomings and remedies' in D Flore and V Franssen (eds), *Société numérique et droit pénal* (Bruylant 2019) 269, 277. On the use of the EIO for gathering e-evidence, see Tosza (n 36) 161–83.

Denmark, Ireland and third countries, Luxembourg law enforcement authorities (LEAs) have two options: the use of mutual legal assistance (MLA) instruments or treaties (MLAT), or direct voluntary cooperation with foreign Internet service providers.[38] Such cooperation is voluntary in nature, because usually service providers are not legally obliged to provide data to foreign LEAs.

While the nature of the investigative measure and the type of the ensuing evidence bind the hands of Luxembourg's investigative authorities, they might have limited impact as to the question of admissibility of evidence, since Luxembourg's criminal procedure system follows the principle of freedom of proof (*la liberté de la preuve*) under which any type of evidence is, in principle, admissible.[39] Hence, the impact of potential violations of the above-mentioned rules is assessed each time in concrete cases, but the proof is not 'automatically' excluded. However, a set of principles regarding the impact of potential violations limit the freedom to admit evidence gathered in violation of the rights of suspects and defendants.

III. Legal Framework of Admissibility of Criminal Evidence

A. Rules of Admissibility of Evidence

In accordance with the principle of freedom of proof, Luxembourg's criminal procedure law does not impose any specific rules on the admissibility of evidence – including e-evidence[40] – in criminal proceedings. Luxembourg 'trial courts assess freely the admissibility and probative value of evidence'.[41] In this regard, Luxembourg jurisprudence has developed a series of guiding principles such as 'fairness' (*loyauté*) in the administration of evidence and respect for the adversarial principle (*contradictoire*). For instance, evidence obtained as a result of police provocation (*provocation policière*), which dominated a person's will and led that person to commit an offence, was found inadmissible because it was not obtained in a fair manner.[42] In another instance, unilateral expert reports were deemed

[38] On this topic, see K Ligeti and G Robinson, 'Sword, Shield and Cloud: Toward a European System of Public-Private Orders for Electronic Evidence in Criminal Matters?' in V Mitsilegas and N Vavoula (eds), *Surveillance and Privacy in the Digital Age: European, Transatlantic and Global Perspectives* (Hart Publishing 2021) 27.

[39] V Bolard, 'Preuve et vérité' (2013) 23 *Annales du droit luxembourgeois* 37, 75.

[40] Confirmed in Council of the European Union, 'Rapport d'évaluation sur le septième série d'évaluations mutuelles "Mise en œuvre pratique et fonctionnement des politiques européennes en matière de prévention de la cybercriminalité et de lutte contre celle-ci" – Rapport sur le Luxembourg' (May 2017) 51: 'Il n'y a pas de conditions d'admissibilité particulières pour les preuves électroniques.' (Author's translation: 'There are no specific admissibility conditions for electronic evidence.') See at https://data.consilium.europa.eu/doc/document/ST-7162-2017-REV-1-DCL-1/fr/pdf accessed 16 September 2022.

[41] Covolo (n 1) 366.

[42] Court of Cassation (*Cour de cassation*), 12 June 2007, n° 304/07. For similar instances, see Court of Cassation, 26 February 2008, n° 106/08; District Court of Luxembourg (*Tribunal d'arrondissement de Luxembourg*), 2 July 2014, n° 1872/2014.

admissible as long as the parties were able to freely discuss them.[43] In accordance with this approach, evidence legally obtained in another Member State or a third country is admissible[44] if it has been duly communicated to the defence.[45]

In relation to unlawfully obtained evidence, Luxembourg's Court of Cassation established the rule that the trial courts may discard such evidence if: (i) the lack of respect for certain formal requirements is sanctioned by nullity; or (ii) the irregularity committed has tainted the credibility of the evidence; or (iii) the use of the evidence is contrary to the defendant's right to a fair trial.[46] The discarding of unlawfully obtained evidence is not limited to these criteria. Indeed, in evaluating the admissibility of unlawfully obtained evidence, judges examine whether there has been overall legality (*légalité*) in the administration of evidence.[47] To do so, judges look at the case as a whole, including the way(s) in which the evidence was obtained and the context of the illegality committed. In this regard, Luxembourg's Court of Appeal has held that the mere adversarial discussion of evidence at trial is not enough to redress irregularities in the gathering of evidence.[48]

The application of the three criteria has led to the exclusion of illegally obtained evidence. For instance, in a case of alleged theft by a cleaner of lunch vouchers and gift vouchers from a bank, the public prosecutor sought to rely on CCTV footage of the vouchers' being spent at a supermarket.[49] However, the supermarket committed an offence, since the CCTV system lacked authorisation by the national data protection authority. The District Court of Luxembourg rejected the public prosecutor's argument that the gravity of the offence outweighed that of the illegality committed in obtaining the CCTV footage. It held that the violation of rules designed to protect individuals' fundamental rights (eg the right to privacy) was more serious than the property offence.[50] In reaching its decision to discard the evidence, the District Court emphasised the public prosecutor's duty of fairness in the administration of evidence, which is essential to ensure a fair trial.

Regarding e-evidence, desk research and contacts with legal practitioners uncovered no court rulings in Luxembourg with immediate relevance to the issue

[43] Pre-trial Chamber of the Court of Appeal (*Chambre du conseil de la cour d'appel*), 6 December 2013, n° 699/13; see also Court of Appeal (*Cour d'appel*), 28 February 2017, n° 9/17.

[44] Petschko, Schiltz and Tosza (n 4) 467.

[45] See, eg, Court of Cassation, 7 July 2000, n° 235/00. In this case, despite the differences between United States and Luxembourg law in the field of evidence gathering, the Court declared admissible the witness testimony given before United States federal courts, and which was duly communicated to the defence.

[46] Court of Cassation, 22 November 2007, n° 57/2007; this judgment is often mentioned in Luxembourg decisions where the issue of admissibility of evidence comes up (see, eg, Court of Cassation, 20 December 2017, n° 493/17). Noting the strength of the Court's position in favour of the inadmissibility of illegally obtained evidence compared to its counterparts in Belgium and in France, see M Marty, *La légalité de la preuve dans l'espace pénal européen* (Larcier Brussels, 2016) 274–313.

[47] Court of Appeal, 26 February 2008, n° 106/08.

[48] ibid.

[49] District Court of Luxembourg, 2 July 2014, n° 1872/14.

[50] Ligeti and Robinson (n 15) 159.

of admissibility of such evidence.[51] Nor did our exchanges with an investigating judge and the Luxembourg police on the topic of cross-border judicial cooperation detect any case law regarding the use of electronic data accessed cross-border as evidence in criminal proceedings in Luxembourg.

B. Legal Remedies

Luxembourg's criminal procedure allows interested parties to challenge investigative acts carried out illegally and the admissibility of evidence resulting from such acts. If the challenge is successful, the investigative act is declared null and void and the evidence resulting from that act is discarded as inadmissible.[52] In this regard, a significant feature of Luxembourg's system is its monist approach, whereby international fundamental rights are directly (ie without the need to adopt implementing legislation) incorporated into Luxembourg law and prevail over national law.[53] For instance, the rights enshrined in the ECHR are given direct effect before Luxembourg courts and can be relied upon to challenge the admissibility of evidence obtained in violation of such rights.[54]

The CCP lays down the rules and procedures that must be followed to request the invalidity (or nullity, '*nullité*') of pre-trial acts carried out by the public prosecutor (*nullités de la procedure d'enquête*)[55] or the investigating judge (*nullités de la procedure d'instruction*),[56] and – by extension – the inadmissibility of evidence collected via those investigations. There are two types of nullities: formal (ie provided by law)[57] and substantive (ie developed in case law to sanction violations of substantive procedural requirements – in particular, defence rights).[58] In accordance with Luxembourg's monist approach, the violation of rights enshrined in international treaties, such as the ECHR, could result in the nullity of a procedural act.[59]

[51] A highly discussed case concerning Skype involved Luxembourg, where Skype was located, but the legal proceeding took place before the Belgian courts. For more on this case, see V Franssen, 'The Belgian Internet Investigatory Powers Act – A Model to Pursue at European Level?' (2017) 3 *European Data Protection Law Review* 534.

[52] Covolo (n 1) 337.

[53] ibid 330–31.

[54] Covolo further notes that 'Luxembourg judges give direct effect to the fundamental rights guaranteed under the Convention as well as to EU Directives harmonising defence rights in criminal proceedings, which prevail over national legal provisions': ibid.

[55] CCP, Art 48-2.

[56] CCP, Art 126.

[57] The CCP provides that some formalities shall be respected – vis-à-vis investigative acts – under penalty of nullity (*à peine de nullité*). For instance, if the investigative judge fails to inform the suspected person of the right to be assisted by a lawyer before questioning him or her, such questioning is invalid: CCP, Art 81(2) and (12). See Petschko, Schiltz and Tosza (n 4) 469.

[58] Covolo (n 1) 366.

[59] See, eg, Pre-trial Chamber of the Court of Appeal, 16 May 2012, n° 301/12; Court of Cassation, 31 January 2013, n° 7/2013; Pre-trial Chamber of the Court of Appeal, 12 February 2014, n° 102/14; Pre-trial Chamber of the Court of Appeal, 24 December 2015, n° 1017/15.

If the pre-trial investigation was carried out by the investigating judge (*procédure d'instruction*), 'the public prosecutor, the accused, the party incurring civil liability and any third party with a legitimate interest' can request the pre-trial chamber of the District Court (*chambre du conseil du tribunal d'arrondissement*) to declare 'the nullity of the pre-trial investigation or of any act thereof' (*requête en nullité*).[60] In addition, the public prosecutor or any person with a legitimate interest can request the nullity of the preliminary inquiry (*enquête préliminiraire*) carried out by the public prosecutor or of any act thereof.[61] If a pre-trial investigation is not opened at the end of the preliminary inquiry, the defendant (*prévenu*) shall ask the District Court to rule on the invalidity of acts of the preliminary inquiry before raising any other argument (with the exception of incompetence).[62] If the request for nullity is well-founded, the act in question – as well as any linked subsequent acts – is declared null and void and any evidence resulting from the acts becomes inadmissible.

Any request for the nullity of an investigative act must specify the act(s) challenged and be filed within the five days when the defendant becomes aware[63] of the act (the investigative order or the act relating to the retention or processing of the defendant's data).[64] Beyond the five-day period the action is foreclosed, and the defendant will not be able to challenge the measure. The strict interpretation of Article 126(3) CCP, especially regarding the deadline for filing such a request on the nullity of the act challenged, is very well established in Luxembourg case law. The courts have particularly held that this time limit starts with the knowledge of the act itself by the applicant, and not by his or her lawyer, and the starting of this deadline is not delayed by the absence of knowledge of the content of the investigative order.[65] Luxembourg courts may review if such a time limit complies with the right of access to a tribunal, enshrined in Article 6 ECHR, although the

[60] CCP, Art 126(1).

[61] CCP, Art 48-2(1).

[62] CCP, Art 48-2(3); See further in Covolo (n 1) 365–66; the same rule applies to acts of the *mini-instruction*, if no investigation is eventually opened (CCP, Art 24-2(3)). As explained in section II, the term '*mini-instruction*' refers to the procedure in which the public prosecutor is 'entitled to ask the investigative judge to perform certain acts without formally opening an investigation … This procedure is generally used for cases which appear to be clear and may be sent directly to the *chambre du conseil* or the Court (for crimes (*délits*)) without a formal investigation being open, but the public prosecutor needs a piece of evidence that only the investigative judge may obtain (eg the video recording from a CCTV camera).': Petschko, Schiltz and Tosza (n 4) 463–64; See also J Nies, 'Detecting Economic and Financial Crime: A Special Toolkit of Investigation Techniques in Luxembourg' in K Ligeti and V Franssen (eds), *Challenges in the Field of Economic and Financial Crime in Europe and the US* (Hart Publishing, 2017) 83, 88–89.

[63] According to Arts 48-26, 65, 88-4 and 182-1 CCP, for those cases where the interception, seizure or processing of data leads to a trial, the accused or his or her lawyer shall receive the information about the execution of those measures at the end of the investigation that led to the charges. The precise content of the data shall also be communicated within a reasonable period of time before the day of the trial. In the event of the dismissal of a case without trial, the information is sent at the same time as the decision to dismiss.

[64] CPP, Art 126(3); It is worth clarifying that the time limit applies to requests based both on domestic or EU and international norms and is not altered by the seriousness of the alleged illegality.

[65] Judgment of the Court of Appeal of 16 December 2011, n° 913/11 and 194/11.

applicant must demonstrate 'a concrete infringement of a guaranteed right in the context of a specific investigation procedure'.[66] While the time limit of five days applies to any ground for nullity and does not depend on the gravity of the alleged violation, one court decision has admitted an exception that could be relevant for the annulment of acts pertaining to personal data. This exception does not concern the gravity of the violation of applicable provisions but rather the gravity of the limitation of rights. More specifically, if a ground for nullity is 'based on facts and circumstances that substantially vitiate the investigative procedure proceedings in that they seriously undermine the essential rights of the parties, in particular the rights of the defence', the five-day limit can be lifted.[67] By analogy, Luxembourg courts might well lift the five-day limit in the event of a request to annul an investigative act claiming a disproportionate infringement of particularly sensitive data, such as stored content data.[68]

A similar regime to the one concerning investigative acts is applicable to the measures that are authorised by the investigating judge during the *mini-instruction*.[69] The time limit to challenge such measures is two months starting from the execution of the contested act.[70] Yet, in the event that the measure in question has led to the opening of an investigation, the request must be filed in the five days of being charged with a criminal offence.[71] If no judicial investigation was opened, the request to annul specific investigative acts relating to personal data needs to be raised prior to any defence on the merits of the case.[72]

In principle, judicial review of decisions on admissibility is not possible.[73] Nevertheless, Article 133 CCP provides for the possibility to appeal the decisions of the pre-trial chamber of the District Court, including those on the nullity of pre-trial investigative measures, before the pre-trial chamber of the Court of Appeal (*chambre du conseil de la cour d'appel*).[74] If the District Court issues a decision on a case, the latter can be appealed before the Court of Appeal and it is the last opportunity to challenge the admissibility of evidence.[75] Indeed, if illegally or improperly obtained evidence is not challenged at that stage, it cannot be further challenged before the Court of Cassation.[76]

Two conclusions may be drawn from the aforementioned rules: (i) if no request for the annulment of illegally or improperly obtained evidence is launched on time

[66] Judgment of the Court of Appeal of 22 October 2012, n° 674/12.
[67] G Vogel, *Lexique de procédure pénale de droit luxembourgeois* (Larcier, 2009) 125 with reference to Judgment of the District Court of 10 March 2003, n°588/2003.
[68] See further in Covolo (n 1) 336–37.
[69] CCP, Art 24-1.
[70] CCO, Art 24-2(2).
[71] CCP, Art 24-2(3)1.
[72] CCP, Art 24-2(3)2.
[73] Covolo (n 1) 370.
[74] Ibid 338; CCP, Art 133.
[75] F Giuffrida and K Ligeti, 'Luxembourg' in F Giuffrida and K Ligeti (eds), *Admissibility of OLAF Final Reports as Evidence in Criminal Proceedings* (University of Luxembourg, 2019) 191 at https://orbilu.uni.lu/handle/10993/40141 accessed 16 September 2022.
[76] Covolo (n 1) 374.

(or at all), such evidence becomes valid (*purge de nullité*);[77] and (ii) Luxembourg's criminal procedure confines objections to the admissibility of evidence to the pre-trial phase of a case.[78] The fact that the request for annulment cannot – save for exceptional circumstances – be lodged before the trial court aims to ensure the timely administration of justice, since pre-trial decisions cannot be called into question again during the trial.[79]

Overall, Luxembourg's criminal procedure rules on admissibility of evidence are intended to safeguard the rights of the parties involved in the proceedings and the overall fairness of the procedure, by preventing courts from reaching a decision based on illegal investigating acts.[80] For instance, the testimony of persons who are legally incapable of testifying is not admissible.[81]

IV. Exclusionary Rules of Evidence at EU Level

As explained in section III, the freedom of proof principle entails that Luxembourg law does not impose any specific exclusionary rules of evidence. Exclusionary rules have instead been formulated in case law, as previously explained. One of the most important exclusionary rules is that evidence resulting from investigating acts carried out in violation of fundamental rights, such as those enshrined in the ECHR, will be declared inadmissible. Drawing inspiration from Luxembourg's criminal procedure system, exclusionary rules of evidence at EU level could target evidence obtained in violation of fundamental rights, or in violation of other principles elaborated in Luxembourg case law, such as fairness and legality in the overall administration of evidence.

V. Admissibility of Evidence Obtained in an Administrative Procedure

In accordance with the freedom of proof principle, evidence gathered in an administrative procedure may be admissible as evidence in criminal proceedings. However, the key principles that must be respected remain applicable, and their violation can lead to the exclusion of evidence obtained in an administrative procedure. Therefore, to be admitted, evidence obtained in an administrative procedure should be useful to the discovery of the truth, gathered in a fair manner and debated in an adversarial manner.[82] It should be noted that, in principle, evidence

[77] ibid 366; Petschko, Schiltz and Tosza (n 4) 466–67.
[78] Giuffrida and Ligeti (n 73) 189.
[79] ibid; Court of Appeal, 28 February 2017, n° 9/17; see also Court of Cassation, 28 April 2016, n° 17/2016.
[80] See, in that respect, Court of Cassation, 28 April 2015, n° 158/15; Giuffrida and Ligeti (n 73) 187.
[81] CCP, Arts 156-1 and 189.
[82] Giuffrida and Ligeti (n 73) 194.

that has been declared inadmissible in administrative proceedings can be used in criminal proceedings pursuant to the principle of the autonomy of criminal law.

One of the potential sources of such evidence is Luxembourg's VAT Administration, which is obliged to transmit information to the judicial authorities that may be used in criminal proceedings.[83] Furthermore, any authority, public officer or civil servant, etc that becomes aware in the course of their duties of facts that are liable to constitute a criminal offence, must inform the public prosecutor.[84]

The case law shows that Luxembourg courts take a strict approach vis-à-vis evidence obtained in an administrative procedure. For instance, in proceedings before the correctional chamber (*chambre correctionnelle*) of the District Court, the public prosecutor sought to rely on mobile phone screenshots that had been obtained first by the customs authority in the course of an inspection.[85] Taking a literal interpretation of Article 23(2) CCP, the court held that whereas the CCP required agents to transmit all information (*renseignements*), reports (*procès-verbaux*) and related acts to the public prosecutor, Article 23(2) CCP did not extend to the obtaining of evidence governed exclusively by the CCP. According to the court, the evidence was obtained illegally because the public prosecutor had not executed seizure in accordance with the relevant CCP provisions. Relying on a strict interpretation of the principle of legality in the administration of evidence, the court concluded that the illegally obtained screenshots violated the right to a fair trial and had to be discarded. Finally, the court did not exclude other aspects of the customs agents' report since it had been transferred lawfully.

Our research did not reveal any case law dealing with the proprietary nature of software used to perform digital investigations, or to open/access digital data.[86] In Luxembourg, almost all digital investigations (except for decryption operations) are carried out in-house by Luxembourg's 'New Technologies unit' (*section Nouvelles Technologies*) of the judicial police, whose agents use – as far as possible – open source tools.[87]

VI. Admissibility of the Results of Internal Investigations Carried Out in the Field of Compliance Programmes – Where Corporate Criminal Liability Exists

A Luxembourg framework on admissibility of results of internal investigations is not expressly mentioned in the case law, literature or in Luxembourg law.

[83] Loi du 19 décembre 2008 ayant pour objet la coopération interadministrative et judiciaire (...), Mémorial A206, Art 16(1).

[84] CCP, Art 23(2).

[85] District Court of Luxembourg (*Tribunal d'arrondissement de Luxembourg*), 20 December 2017, n° 493/17 X.

[86] Ligeti and Robinson (n 15) 162.

[87] ibid. This 'New Technologies unit' is called upon to provide operational support to criminal investigators in all matters of digital evidence requiring technical expertise.

As is the case with evidence obtained in an administrative procedure (see section V), the results of internal investigations carried out in the field of compliance programmes may – in principle – be admissible in criminal proceedings pursuant to the freedom of proof principle.[88] The general guiding principles for assessing the admissibility and probative value remain applicable and such evidence can be excluded on a case-by-case basis.

In particular, the principle of fairness will be applicable, according to which judges cannot base their reasoning on evidence acquired in an illicit way.[89] Such illicitness may in general stem from three sources: violations of formal conditions rendering the evidence void or inadmissible; an irregularity that tainted the credibility of the piece of evidence; or a violation of the right to a fair trial.[90] It will be the second and third sources that will be applicable as regards evidence resulting from internal investigations. While more detailed rules are scarce, we may find some in connection with two problems: video surveillance of employees and access to their correspondence.

Under Luxembourg law, the setting up of video-camera surveillance within company premises is regulated under the Labour Code and includes – in particular – conditions as to employees' being informed about the presence of surveillance.[91] Employees or their representatives may require an opinion from the National Commission for Data Protection, and surveillance cannot commence before the opinion is given.[92] In cases when video surveillance has been set up to detect criminal activities within the premises in breach of these provisions, the courts tend to consider evidence thus gathered to be inadmissible due to violation of the fairness principle.[93] However, the courts demonstrate more flexibility if the video recordings do not constitute the sole proof demonstrating guilt (they may be admissible as subsidiary means),[94] or if the employees were aware of the surveillance by the employer signalling it.[95] The main criterion for the proof to be admissible thus rests on the employees' awareness of being under video surveillance.[96]

[88] The authors are very grateful to Jean-Luc Putz for his valuable remarks and suggestions, and to Théo Antunes for additional research on this section of the chapter.

[89] G Vogel, *Traité de procédure pénale* (Larcier, 2018) 314.

[90] Court of Cassation, 22 November 2007, n° 57/2007.

[91] Labour Code (*Code du Travail*) as amended at https://data.legilux.public.lu/filestore/eli/etat/leg/code/travail/20220416/fr/pdf/eli-etat-leg-code-travail-20220416-fr-pdf.pdf accessed 13 November 2022, Art L.261-1.

[92] Labour Code, Art L.261-1 (4).

[93] District Court of Luxembourg, 16 October 2008, n° 2925/2008; in this instance, it was to detect thieving within the company.

[94] Court of Cassation (*Cour de cassation*), 2 March 2021, 60/21 V.

[95] District Court of Luxembourg, 8 July 2008, n° 2400/2008.

[96] District Court of Luxembourg, 16 October 2008, 2925/2008; in this context, the employer had directly sent to the police fragments of the video surveillance, which was not accepted as evidence because the original copy was not retrieved by the police.

Moreover, Luxembourg courts have transposed the requirements of Article 6 ECHR into internal investigative measures concerning disciplinary procedures. First, any procedure must precisely state the reasons for it to be undertaken,[97] entailing that a person targeted by such a procedure is aware of the charges against him or her and why certain measures are being taken.[98] Second, the persons concerned must have the right to a defence lawyer.[99] One could theorise that for such a right to be effective, the defence lawyer would need to have access to the proof or other evidence on which the charges are being based.[100] Hence, the right to a defence lawyer could be the point of origin for the setting up of linked defence rights such as the equality of arms. Third, the body deciding on the result of the procedure must present an impartial aspect.[101] Article 6 ECHR is thus a source for framing both the procedure and the decision-making process during investigative measures in Luxembourg law. As regards the correspondence of employees (in particular emails), it can be accessed on suspicion of activities that are infringing the company's interests.[102] Luxembourg courts have admitted such evidence in a labour law cases if they related to professional activities and when access was made under the scrutiny of a third party.[103] However, the limits of such access lie with purely personal data.[104] The employer cannot access purely private information and use it as evidence against an employee during investigative measures. Such evidence may be deemed to be inadmissible because of an illegitimate and disproportionate interference with the right to respect for private life.[105]

VII. Concluding Remarks

As can be seen from the preceding analysis, Luxembourg law does not provide for rigid rules on admissibility of evidence in criminal proceedings, instead offering limited discretion to the judicial authorities in concrete cases. This discretion is limited, however, by general principles demanding fairness in the administration

[97] Court of Appeal, 25 March 2021, n° CAL-2020-00659.

[98] District Court of Luxembourg, 30 January 2019, n°0 TAL 20190130-5.

[99] ibid.

[100] Especially in the context where rights of the Convention must be 'practical and effective and not theoretical and illusory': *Airey v Ireland* App no 6289/73 (1979) 2 EHRR 305, para 24.

[101] District Court of Luxembourg, 30 January 2019, n°0 TAL 20190130-5.

[102] M Thewes, 'La surveillance des salariés sur le lieu du travail et les nouvelles technologies de l'information au Grand-Duché du Luxembourg' (2012) 21 *Journal des Tribunaux Luxembourg* 69, 72–73.

[103] Court of Appeal, 3 March 2011, n° 35462 (in this context, the retrieval of the correspondence was made by a computer expert under the monitoring of a bailiff).

[104] Court of Appeal, 7 April 2011, n° 35507 and 35651.

[105] Court of Appeal, 12 November 2015, n° 41245. See also Court of Appeal, 31 May 2018, n° 43972.

of evidence and respect for the adversarial principle, with the possibility to invoke international law instruments protecting fundamental rights. Further limitation is provided by the rules of procedure (in particular, the *purge de nullité*).

Thanks to the principle of freedom of proof, Luxembourg is relatively easily able to accommodate new types of evidence or deal with transfers of administrative evidence to criminal procedure. It also offers measures to defend one's rights in that context. They rely, however, on active defence in order to question their validity.

7

Admissibility of Evidence in EU Cross-Border Criminal Proceedings: Electronic Evidence, Efficiency and Fair-Trial Rights in the Netherlands

JOEP LINDEMAN, MICHIEL LUCHTMAN
AND DAVE VAN TOOR*

I. Introduction

This chapter presents an analysis of the current Dutch legal system with respect to the admissibility of electronic evidence (e-evidence). The current Code of Criminal Procedure (CCP) originates from 1926. A large-scale revision of the Code is currently underway (hereafter: the proposed CCP). A comprehensive legislative proposal was submitted in March 2023.[1] However, consecutive Ministers of Justice and Security have made it clear that the revisions will not lead to a complete overhaul of the Code or the principles underlying the choices made in the past (for example, no juries, prosecutorial freedom). Many of the distinctive features of the current system, which are analysed in this chapter, will return in one way or another in the revised Code.

This chapter starts with a short presentation of the main features of admissibility rules in Dutch criminal procedure (section II). What follows is a specification of these rules in relation to the admissibility of e-evidence in criminal proceedings (section III) and the framework for exclusionary rules in Dutch practice, also in relation to possible interventions by the European Union (EU) legislator (section IV). Section V deals with the framework for transnational e-evidence and

* This contribution was concluded in September 2022. The proposal for a new Code of Criminal Procedure of March 2023 and the Encrochat/SkyECC judgment of the Court of Cassation of 13 June 2023 were also taken into account.

[1] For more information, see 'Inhoud nieuwe wetboek van strafvordering' at www.rijksoverheid.nl/onderwerpen/nieuwe-wetboek-van-strafvordering/inhoud-nieuwe-wetboek-van-strafvordering and also www.moderniseringstrafvordering.nl/ (both sites in Dutch, last visited on 17 August 2022).

its admissibility in criminal proceedings. Section VI then discusses the admissibility of administrative (e-)evidence in criminal procedures, while section VII deals with the use of evidence obtained in compliance programmes.

II. The Legal Framework on Admissibility of Criminal Evidence

A key provision in the Dutch evidentiary system is Article 338 CCP, which stipulates that a judge can only establish the defendant's guilt for the charged crime if the judge has become convinced of the defendant's guilt on the basis of *statutory* accepted evidence, presented to him or her during the trial.[2] This provision defines a number of characteristics of the Dutch legal system, which is qualified as a negative statutory system, based on the principle of immediacy.

Such a negative system implies, first of all, that the presentation of any given number of evidentiary materials as such is not enough to convict (as in a positive system). Rather, a judge may not declare the charge proven if he or she is not convinced, on the basis of the statutory evidence, that the accused has committed the offence.[3] On occasion, there are evidentiary minima. Convictions may not, for instance, be based on the testimony of a single witness,[4] though this rule relates to the entire statement of proof (*bewezenverklaring*) and not to specific elements of it.[5]

The adjective 'statutory' in the qualification of the Dutch system brings to the fore that it only recognises certain types of evidence that are designated as such by law. This is laid down in the Article 339 CCP, which provides that only (i) the judge's own observations; (ii) the statements of the accused; (iii) the statements of a witness; (iv) the statements of an expert; and (v) written documents are recognised as means of evidence. That same article provides that facts or circumstances that are general knowledge do not require proof.

The current Dutch Code came into effect almost a century before e-evidence was first introduced in criminal procedures. This does not seem to have had a serious impact on legal practice. Until recently, for instance, video or audio recordings could be admitted as evidence because they were shown to the judge and thus constituted the judge's own observations,[6] or because they were described in police

[2] Art 338 CCP: 'Het bewijs dat de verdachte het telastegelegde feit heeft begaan, kan door den rechter slechts worden aangenomen, indien hij daarvan uit het onderzoek op de terechtzitting door den inhoud van wettige bewijsmiddelen de overtuiging heeft bekomen.'

[3] GJM Corstens, MJ Borgers and T Kooijmans, *Het Nederlands strafprocesrecht* (Wolters Kluwer, 2021) 797. See also the Explanatory Memorandum to the proposed Code of Criminal Procedure (n 2) 835.

[4] Art 341(2) CCP. Other examples are Art 341(2) CCP (no conviction solely on the basis of an admission of guilt by the defendant), Art 344a(1) CCP (no conviction solely on the basis of an anonymous witness).

[5] At all times, the statement of the defendant needs to be sufficiently supported by other means of evidence; HR, 30 June 2009, ECLI:NL:HR:BG7746.

[6] Corstens, Borgers and Kooijmans (n 3) 798, 805.

reports and introduced as such in criminal proceedings. This is not to say that the qualification of certain types of e-evidence as, for example, a police report or the judge's own observations cannot be artificial or even impractical.[7] The observations of a judge, for instance, will usually take place in court, in the presence of all other parties. That is why audio-visual recordings have very recently been introduced as a separate category of legal evidence under Article 576 CCP.[8] This change anticipates the new CCP, which also – at least in its current version – includes audio and video recordings as autonomous means of statutory evidence.[9]

The aforementioned fifth category – written documents – is broad and allows for all sorts of materials to be used as evidence in criminal proceedings. Further rules on this may be found in Article 344 CCP. This category includes, inter alia, expert reports and police reports (*processen-verbaal*), both of which may refer to electronic data. Police reports have a special evidentiary status. Article 344(2) CCP provides that the proof that the accused has committed the offence may be accepted solely on the report of an investigating officer. However, as police reports may, for instance, also include witness statements, we should emphasise that this special evidentiary status relates only to what the police officer has directly witnessed himself or herself; the rule cannot and should not be used to bypass evidentiary minima with respect to, for instance, witness statements (see below).[10] The (contested) background of this rule lies, inter alia, in the fact that these reports are drafted by professionals who – as police officers – have been trained to report on their work.[11] Reports that have been drawn up by foreign officials or officials of EU or international organisations can also qualify as evidence. Those sources are referred to as 'documents drawn up by a person in the public service of a foreign State or an international organisation'.[12] However, the rule under Article 344(2) CCP does not apply to this category of documents.

The principle of immediacy in Dutch evidentiary law is as important as it is contested.[13] It entails that all evidence must be presented to the judge at a public hearing.[14] Yet – although the risks inherent in the use of hearsay evidence are certainly not disregarded in legal practice – for the requirement of immediacy to have been fulfilled, a witness statement may also be laid down in a police report, the

[7] B de Wilde, A de Hingh and A Lodder, *Digitale informatie in het strafproces – De noodzaak van aanpassing van strafvorderlijke wetgeving* (Free University/WODC, 2019) 93–106.

[8] The so-called *Innovatiewet strafvordering, Staatsblad* 2022, 276. That same Act has made it possible to replace, under certain conditions, the often-laborious process of drafting official records with reliable and accessible audio-visual recordings. In light of the new evidentiary status of audio-visual recordings, some additions to (the later discussed) Art 301 CCP were also inserted.

[9] See also the Explanatory Memorandum to the proposed Code of Criminal Procedure (n 2) 841.

[10] Corstens, Borgers and Kooijmans (n 3) 863.

[11] ibid.

[12] Art 344(1)(3) CCP; HR, 7 October 2008, ECLI:NL:HR:BC3741.

[13] See, eg, DAG van Toor, 'The Dutch pre-trial procedure' in E Johnston, R Erbas and D Jasinksi (eds), *A Comparative Analysis of Pre-Trial Procedure in Europe: The Search for an Ideal Model* (Istanbul University Press, 2020) 41.

[14] Corstens, Borgers and Kooijmans (n 3) 57–58.

core content of which is then read out in court.[15] Current practice, therefore, does not adhere to the position that evidence that is presented in open court is inherently better than written versions of statements that were made during preliminary investigations. This so-called *de auditu* practice was made possible shortly after the introduction of the current CCP in 1926 and has not been changed considerably since.[16] The proposed CCP does not change the Dutch approach to hearsay evidence. In fact, this legal practice will be codified[17] and fits well with the ambition of the Government to ensure that criminal cases are better prepared for the trial hearing, in order to improve the quality of justice and to reduce the lead time (the so-called '*beweging naar voren*').[18] The Dutch *de auditu* approach, however, is an important reason why Dutch cases are omnipresent in the Strasbourg case law on the right to interrogate witnesses, as defined by Article 6 of the European Convention on Human Rights (ECHR).[19]

Despite its qualification as a negative statutory system, the law on evidence does not pose significant limitations on the admissibility of evidence. Foreign evidence is also generally accepted as evidence in criminal procedures. On occasion, depending on the specifics of the applicable legal regimes, additional rules are in place. Article 5.2.3 CCP, for instance, holds that documents drawn up by foreign members of a joint investigation team (JIT) concerning official acts relating to investigations and prosecutions that they have performed abroad as part of the investigation team's activities shall have the evidential value in the Netherlands of documents concerning corresponding acts performed by Dutch officials in the Netherlands, though their evidential value cannot exceed the value of the law of the state of origin.[20] Clearly, this provision is relevant to the many recent Encrochat cases, in which data were transferred from the French to the Dutch authorities within the framework of such a JIT. Another special characteristic of JITs in Dutch law is that public prosecutors are required by law to make sure that a JIT agreement specifies, inter alia, the obligation of foreign investigators to comply with a summons to be heard as witness, as referred to in Article 210 CCP, or a summons as referred to in Article 260 CCP.

[15] Art 301 CCP. This provision was recently supplemented by additional rules for audio-visual sources of evidence; see the new Art 565 CCP, introduced by the aforementioned *Innovatiewet Strafvordering* (n 8).

[16] HR, 20 December 1926, ECLI:NL:HR:1926:BG9435, NJ 1927, 85 (*de auditu*). The *de auditu* judgment of the court covered both oral (eg a police officer's declaration of what another person has told him or her) and written versions (including declarations by a person made to a police officer) of hearsay evidence.

[17] Art. 4.3.9. (4) of the proposed CCP (n 2) provides that a statement made by the accused, a witness or an expert and made elsewhere than at the hearing may be admitted as evidence if it is incorporated into legal evidence.

[18] See the Explanatory Memorandum to the proposed CCP (n 2), sections 4.8 and 6.2.

[19] See again the Explanatory Memorandum to the proposed CCP (n 2), section 4.8, referring inter alia to *Keskin v the Netherlands* App no 2205/16 (ECtHR, 19 January 2021). This is why Art 4.3.11 of the proposed CCP provides that '[e]vidence that the accused has committed the offence cannot be conclusively based on statements made by a person who has not had the opportunity to question the suspected person, unless the right to a fair trial is not violated.'

[20] A similar provision is found in Art 5.3.15, dealing with the instrument of a transfer of criminal proceedings.

Dutch courts are free in the choice of which means of evidence they use and how they assess the evidence put before them. This is a core rule of Dutch criminal procedure. It implies that these judicial processes are generally outside the range of control of the higher courts, particularly the Dutch Supreme Court, the *Hoge Raad* (HR). That is not to say that courts do not need to give reasons for their decisions. If a court arrives at a guilty verdict, under Article 359(3) CCP it must indicate the means of evidence used and the relevant facts and circumstances that follow from it. In accordance with Article 359(2) CCP, second sentence, Courts must also give reasons in cases where they have disregarded certain pieces of evidence, in spite of an express request for their use by the prosecutor or defendant. This feature of Dutch criminal procedure is again maintained, with some minor modifications, under the proposed CCP.

Regarding the issue of evidence that has been unlawfully obtained or transferred, the core provision is Article 359a CCP, which in itself is a codification of the relevant case law of Dutch courts. In very broad strokes, Dutch legal practice follows the case law of the Strasbourg Court in these matters. Unlawfully obtained or transferred evidence is not inadmissible as such. Though we will come back to Article 359a in the following sections, one important characteristic of the Dutch legal system is already worth mentioning. Dutch courts are not required to test the lawful gathering or transfer of evidentiary materials under foreign law or under Article 8 ECHR, if those materials were collected under the responsibility of foreign authorities of a State Party to the ECHR. The task of the Dutch criminal court is limited to ensuring that the manner in which the results of this investigation are used in the criminal case does not violate one's right to a fair trial under Article 6 of the Convention.[21] This is a clear application of the so-called *Trennungsprinzip* in international criminal law.[22]

III. The Admissibility of E-Evidence in Criminal Proceedings

After the introduction of the evidence law of the Dutch CCP in the section above, we take a step back and describe which rules apply to the gathering of evidence and, in more detail, how the gathered evidence is used to create the case file. Prosecutors are tasked with the supervision of criminal investigations (Article 132a CCP), and their decision to prosecute a suspect should be based on the results of

[21] HR, 5 October 2010, ECLI:NL:HR:2010:BL5629, 4.4.1; confirmed recently in HR, 13 June 2023, ECLI:NL:HR:2023:913 (Encrochat).

[22] On this concept, see M Böse, M Bröcker and A Schneider, 'Introduction' in M Böse, M Bröcker and A Schneider (eds), *Judicial Protection in Transnational Criminal Proceedings* (Springer, 2021); M Luchtman, 'Pertinent Issues of Punitive – Enforcement in a Composite Legal Order' in M Luchtman, K Ligeti and J Vervaele (eds), *EU Enforcement Authorities: Punitive Law Enforcement in a Composite Legal Order* (Hart Publishing, 2023) 273 (281 et seq).

the criminal investigation (Article 167 CCP). The results of the investigation are laid down in procedural documents (also known as the case file). The public prosecutor is responsible for the compilation of the case file, which should contain all materials that can reasonably be of interest to any decision by a judge at the trial hearing (Article 149a CCP). As the judge is bound by the indictment, which is also formulated by the prosecutor,[23] the prosecutor's decision on the indictment is a very determinative factor in the compilation of the case file. In general, the case file will hold the reports that result from the criminal investigation carried out by the police. As demonstrated in the section II, virtually all written documents are admissible as evidence.

For e-evidence, this generally means that the nature, the contents and/or an analysis of the data that have been collected throughout the investigation are described in reports that are part of the case file. In some cases, a sole description may not be enough and further analysis and interpretation are necessary. For example, images allegedly containing child pornography may require specialised analysis of physical features to ascertain the age of the persons shown in the images. The descriptions may then need to be made by specialised police officers. Therefore, the 'e-evidence' presented to a court is likely to comprise a written report, considering the selection, analysis and interpretation of whatever data the authorities have obtained. It is also possible that appointed experts will write an expert report, following which the experts may be called to give additional oral testimonies at a trial hearing to further explain their findings. As already noted, new legislation will allow audio or audio-visual recordings to be admitted as evidence as well, but we do not expect that this will change the practice that descriptions of incriminating evidence will be part of the case file – and will thus be used as evidence.

It is common practice that criminal investigation officers (often the police) collect the evidence. If they use powers that cause more than minor breaches of fundamental rights and/or are likely to breach the integrity and reliability of the criminal investigations, these powers should have a concrete basis in statutory law. As such, most means of collecting evidence in criminal cases are regulated by statutory law. Traditional means of gathering evidence (such as a house search, seizure of objects) often lead to the confiscation of data-carriers (such as smartphones, personal computers, tablets, external hard drives and similar devices). In addition to that, so-called Special Investigative Police Powers (*Bijzondere Opsporingsbevoegdheden*),[24] aimed at tackling organised crime by dramatically expanding the statutory law, came into force in 2000 and have been altered and supplemented since then. Undercover policing (keeping people under observation, infiltrating criminal organisations, undercover purchasing of drugs), the use

[23] S Brinkhoff, J Bemelmans and M Kuipers, 'Criminal procedure Law' in PH van Kempen, M Krabbe and S Brinkhoff (eds), *The Criminal Justice System of the Netherlands* (Intersentia Ltd, 2019) 97, 123.

[24] The proposed new Code uses a different terminology and speaks of 'covert investigative powers' (*heimelijke opsporingsbevoegdheden*).

of covert methods (wiretaps on phones, bugging a house) and/or data production and preservation orders have been regulated extensively in Dutch law. As this legislation was mostly designed in the late 1990s and early 2000s, it has been amended to make it more suitable for the gathering of e-evidence: for example, powers to perform 'network searches' (Article 125j CCP) and to order the production or preservation of data (inter alia Articles 126na, 126nd, 126ne CCP) have been updated. Also, some more specific powers have been introduced, such as the power that allows the police to gain access to (to 'hack') a computerised device under Article 126nba/126uba CCP.

In general, the police need prior written authorisation by the public prosecutor to carry out the aforementioned powers. The most far-reaching methods require additional authorisation by an investigative judge, or even additional review by the Central Review Committee of the Public Prosecutor's Service, again prior to the use of the method. There are also rules and regulations regarding the contents of the reports (Article 126aa CCP) and the equipment that the police use (Article 126ee CCP). The power to covertly enter (hack) automated devices under Article 126nba CCP is furthermore subject to general supervision and evaluation by the Inspectorate of Justice and Security. All this, as said, is to guarantee a process of evidence-gathering that meets the demands of proportionality, subsidiarity, integrity and reliability.[25] In addition to this legislation that deals with the *gathering* of the evidence, in the past years there has been extensive legislation on the *storing* and *processing* of evidence, especially when the evidence contains personal data (the Police Data Act). Again, the safeguards that stem from international instruments such as the ECHR and CFR play an important role in this legislation.[26]

Still, there are lacunae in the legislation. There is, for example, no specific legislation regarding the search of electronic devices.[27] It has long been considered that the confiscation of, for example, a smartphone or a personal computer would allow the police to perform extensive research and analysis on the contents of the device, but the Supreme Court ruled that a search that is bound to lead to more than a minor interference with civil rights (such as the right to privacy) needs to be supervised by a public prosecutor or (when using very intrusive measures) an investigative judge.[28] This reasoning is in line with the legislation discussed above, which offers procedural safeguards. Under the proposed CCP, a new Article 2.1.7 CCP will allow the public prosecutor to seek an authorisation from the magistrate judge also in cases where the statutory provision in which that power is vested does not require this, as an additional, precautionary measure to protect the right to

[25] Compare Art 8(2) ECHR and Art 52 of the Charter of Fundamental Rights of the European Union [2016] OJ C202/02 ('CFR').

[26] JJ Oerlemans and M Galič, 'Cybercrime investigations' in W van der Wagen, JJ Oerlemans and M Weulen Kranenbarg, *Essentials in cybercrime* (Boom, 2022) 199, 202.

[27] Provisions for this are, however, included in the proposed Title 7.3 of the Second Book of the CCP, entitled '*onderzoek van gegevens*' (examination of data); see also sections 6.4, 9.2 and 9.3 of the Explanatory Memorandum of the proposed CCP (n 2).

[28] HR, 4 April 2017, ECLI:NL:HR:2017:592.

privacy. This will also help legal practice to quickly implement new legal requirements that may follow from, for instance, the case law of the Court of Justice of the European Union (CJEU).[29]

The existence of detailed legislation and case law might suggest that evidence that has been obtained and/or processed in breach of this legislation is not admissible in a criminal case. However, as will be explained in section IV, this is not common practice. There is no strict exclusionary rule: unlawfully obtained evidence is usually admissible as long as the right to a fair trial is guaranteed. In this regard, Dutch law makes an important distinction between unlawful (or improper) acquisition of evidence and the unreliability of such evidence as reasons for its exclusion. A judge who finds that evidence is unreliable (or that the reliability cannot be properly tested), should exclude this evidence.[30]

While unlawfully obtained evidence is not unreliable evidence per se, sometimes the doubts as to the reliability of the evidence arise because the formal rules have not been followed. The main rule remains, though: the judge is free in assessing the quality of the evidence and with regard to the selection of the evidence. However, the Supreme Court has defined situations in which a court has an obligation to specifically explain the decision to reject the defence's claim that evidence is unreliable. If such a claim has been thoroughly substantiated and specifically concerns the adequacy or the suitability of an investigatory method, or the reliability of an expert, the court will have to explain why it still considers the evidence to be reliable.[31]

It follows from the foregoing that e-evidence is generally admissible, unless there are grounds to question its reliability or the reliability of the inferences made from the e-evidence. In order to allow the defence to test and challenge e-evidence and/or the inferences made from it, equality of arms is an important notion. Debates as to the extent of disclosure that would be necessary to assess the reliability of e-evidence are not uncommon, especially in cases in which the e-evidence has been (partly) gathered in other countries. If, for example, the police made use of crawlers or scrapers when collecting data from the Internet, what were the settings? If the police have performed research on datasets, what were the exact contents of the initial datasets that were used? What is the exact design of specifically developed software that has been used to analyse datasets? Can the defence have access to the same datasets to perform their own analysis or to reproduce the analysis the police have made? In the so-called *Tandem II* case, the court provided the defence with opportunities to assess the reliability and verifiability of the data and the software that was used to access the data. However, the court did not allow full disclosure of the so-called primary or secondary dataset, and also did not allow the defence individual and unsupervised access to the software that

[29] Explanatory Memorandum of the proposed CCP (n 2) 283–84.

[30] Corstens, Borgers and Kooijmans (n 3) 874.

[31] ibid 913–15; AJA van Dorst and MJ Borgers, 'Cassatie in strafzaken' in J Boksem et al (eds), *Handboek Strafzaken* (Wolters Kluwer, 2022) 45.7.4.2 (online).

had been used to access and analyse the data. The court found that the defence had not sufficiently specified the need for such far-reaching and time-consuming research.[32] This approach is in line with existing case law regarding the disclosure of police data: requests that essentially are based on the mere assumption that it *might* be possible to find something that puts the incriminating evidence into another light, are likely to be dismissed as *fishing expeditions*.

IV. Exclusionary Rules in Dutch Practice and at the EU Level

In the section above, exclusionary rules are already described in short. Dutch legal practice, as previously indicated, resembles the approach of the Strasbourg Court when it comes to unlawfully obtained/transferred evidence. Article 359a CCP codifies the relevant case law and has in turn become the object of extensive case law. It is relevant to note that it was introduced, among other things, to meet social dissatisfaction with the functioning of the criminal process. Its purpose was 'to make a contribution to reducing the undesirable consequences of procedural errors in the criminal process'.[33]

Article 359a CCP gives courts the discretionary power to attach consequences to irregularities (*vormverzuimen*) that can no longer be repaired, in cases where the law itself does not define the consequences of such a finding of irregularity. In those cases, the court may decide to reduce the sentence, to exclude the evidence or even to dismiss the prosecutor's case altogether (*niet-ontvankelijkheid Openbaar Ministerie*). In its case law, the *Hoge Raad* has accepted that courts may also respond by a mere recognition of the irregularity, without further consequences. If courts apply these procedural sanctions, they have to give reasons for doing so, taking account of the interest served by the rule infringed, the seriousness of the omission and the disadvantage caused by it. Incidentally, irregularities that affect the reliability of investigative results are outside the scope of this provision. In those cases, exclusion follows directly from the rule that the judge only uses the evidence he or she finds reliable and useful (see section III).[34]

The Supreme Court (HR) has made it very clear that, as a matter of principle, the task of a criminal court is to judge, with due regard for the rules of due process, on the substance of the accusation against the accused. It is not the task and responsibility of the criminal court to monitor the lawfulness and integrity

[32] District Court Amsterdam, 19 April 2018, ECLI:NL:RBAMS:2018:2504; see also MM Egberts, 'De reikwijdte van het inzagerecht en "equality of arms" in het licht van grote datasets, Hansken en toekomstige ontwikkelingen' (2022) (2) *Tijdschrift Bijzonder Strafrecht & Handhaving* 119.

[33] HR, 20 March 2015, ECLI:NL:HR:2015:643, 2.4.1, referring to the Explanatory Memorandum to the Bill, Parliamentary Papers (*Kamerstukken*) II, 1993/94, 23 705, no 3, p 1.

[34] HR, 30 March 2004, ECLI:NL:HR:2004:AM2533, 3.6.4; HR, 1 December 2020, ECLI:NL:HR:2020:1890, 2.4.5.

of the actions of the police and the judiciary as a whole, nor is the criminal court able to do so. However, although disciplining the police can thus not be said to be the dominant principle guiding Dutch courts' decisions,[35] it is certainly not totally absent from its case law either.

A core question is what rationale guides the interpretation of the Supreme Court's reference to due process or fair trial in the above. As has been noted by others, 'the way in which fairness is construed and exclusionary discretion is exercised inevitably depends on the theoretical rationale for exclusion of evidence one adopts'.[36] Indeed, it makes a difference if fairness is approached as, for instance, a vindication-of-rights approach or as a principle guaranteeing the reliability of the contested evidence. Traces of any of these and other rationales recur in the Supreme Court's case law. Indeed, criminal courts are required to carry out a balancing exercise, taking account of all relevant factors.[37]

In the case law of the Court, which has recently been slightly readjusted, the three measures clearly serve as an interdependent whole, in which reduction of the sentence is perceived as a less intrusive response than the dismissal of the case. Courts, by implication, are required to establish via the principles of proportionality and subsidiarity which measure best reconciles all the interests involved:

- For reduction of the sentence, it is required that the accused has suffered actual damage as a result of the procedural error, and that the reduction of the sentence is also justified in view of the importance of the rule that was violated and the seriousness of the error. It must therefore concern a sufficiently serious procedural error that has specifically affected the interests of the defendant – for instance his or her right to liberty or privacy – in the case.
- Regarding the exclusion of evidence, there are, first of all, cases in which the exclusion of certain results of the investigation from use as evidence is necessary to prevent a violation of Article 6 ECHR. Yet the Supreme Court has made very clear that a procedural irregularity of *another* legal provision or principle of criminal procedure does not in principle preclude those results from being used. Only in certain exceptional circumstances (bad faith, etc) may the exclusion of evidence be considered necessary as a safeguard of the rule of law and as a means of preventing investigating and prosecuting officials from acting unlawfully, and therefore as a means of preventing similar formal violations from occurring in the future. Courts must assess whether the procedural error is so serious that a reduction of the sentence will not suffice but exclusion of evidence is justified. A rare example in Dutch case law is the situation in which conversations between a lawyer and his client have been recorded: the lawyer–

[35] On other potential mechanisms to monitor police work, see *in extenso*, M Somadi, *Normering en toezicht in de opsporing* (Boom. 2020).

[36] M Panzavolta, E Maes and A Mosna, *Streamlining the exclusion of illegally obtained evidence in criminal justice* (KU Leuven. 2022) 105.

[37] HR, 1 December 2020, ECLI:NL:HR:2020:1890, 2.1.3.

client privilege is of such an absolute nature that these conversations must be excluded from evidence.[38]

- For the dismissal of the entire case, finally, there must be an irreparable breach of the right to a fair trial that has not been or cannot be compensated for in a way that meets the requirements of a proper and effective defence.[39] Obviously, this sanction can only be applied in very exceptional circumstances.

In the Supreme Court's case law, there is an important role for the defence. The defence must clearly indicate, based on the factors in Article 359a CCP, what the legal consequence of an irregularity should be. Only on the basis of such an argument is the court obliged to give a reasoned decision. The court must assess whether the facts and circumstances on which that defence is based have become *plausible* (*aannemelijk*).[40]

We have already indicated that the approach of the Dutch courts in transnational cases is partly different. The Supreme Court makes a twofold distinction between, on the one hand, issues relating to the lawfulness of investigations abroad and, on the other, issues relating to their reliability. Moreover, it is relevant whether or not investigations were carried out under the auspices of Dutch prosecutors or not. The Supreme Court recently clarified that the latter situation may also cover situations in which such close cooperation exists between Dutch and foreign authorities that the authority over the investigation actually belongs entirely or predominantly to the (Dutch) public prosecutor.[41]

Regarding questions of lawfulness, Dutch courts – as is also stressed in the case law[42] – are responsible for guaranteeing the fairness of the trial, which includes the use of materials that were obtained outside the scope of the Dutch (part of the) criminal proceedings. But what is meant precisely with this reference to Article 6 ECHR is not entirely clear. We can assume, however, that a vindication-of-rights approach is not what the Supreme Court has in mind when it refers to the fairness of the trial. As was noted before and under the conditions specified there, Dutch courts are after all not required to check for compliance with foreign law or for conformity with Article 8 ECHR if investigations were conducted under the auspices of foreign authorities. The rationale behind this is that, at least for State Parties to the ECHR, effective remedies will/must then be offered in the gathering/transferring state. Recently, the Supreme Court added in its Encrochat judgment that if Dutch courts were to review the manner in which the investigation was conducted under the responsibility of foreign authorities under their own law, Dutch courts would also infringe upon the sovereignty of that other country.[43]

[38] HR, 19 February 2013, ECLI:NL:HR:2013:BY5321, 2.4.5.

[39] HR, 1 December 2020, ECLI:NL:HR:2020:1890.

[40] HR, 30 March 2004, ECLI:NL:HR:2004:AM2533, 3.7; HR, 1 December 2020, ECLI:NL:HR:2020:1890, 2.6.1.

[41] HR, 13 June 2023, ECLI:NL:HR:2023:913, 6.18.

[42] HR, 1 December 2020, ECLI:NL:HR:2020:1890, 2.2.2.

[43] HR, 13 June 2023, ECLI:NL:HR:2023:913, 6.5.2. This is different only if it has been irrevocably established in the country in question that the investigation was not carried out in accordance with the applicable rules of law: ibid.

Moreover, one could argue that it is at the least very doubtful that the exclusion of evidence by a Dutch court will have any impact as regards disciplining foreign police action. Even less so than in the national context, this is not a task for Dutch criminal courts.

On the other hand, however, one might wonder how effective any remedy can be if it cannot lead to the exclusion of evidence or any other sanction for violations of foreign law or Article 8 ECHR, because Dutch authorities are not formally tasked with supervising those parts of the investigation. Particularly given that the number of transnational cases or data exchanges is steadily increasing, it may become a bit arbitrary that some police actions do fall within the full scope of control of Dutch courts, while others do not and the materials are used as evidence without further scrutiny.

When it comes to the reliability of evidence, the Supreme Court has meanwhile clarified that there may be grounds for exclusion of evidence if irregularities have occurred that have substantially affected the reliability and accuracy of investigation results. It makes no difference, in principle, whether those investigation results were obtained under the responsibility of foreign authorities or in a Dutch criminal investigation. Still, criminal courts may take as their starting point that investigations conducted under the responsibility of foreign authorities were conducted in such a way that the results obtained by that investigation are reliable. This is different only in cases where there are concrete indications to the contrary. Then, courts must examine the reliability of those results.[44]

As regards the issue of whether there is, in light of Dutch practice, a need for EU rules, it may be a good thing to differentiate between, on the one hand, the role of (Dutch) courts in the assessment of the lawfulness of foreign acts and, on the other, the criteria for the procedural consequences attached to such a finding. Regarding the latter, we are not so convinced that Dutch practice is in need of change,[45] nor does this follow from the case law of the CJEU, although the latter court has also suggested that this may change when specific EU legislation is introduced.[46] At the least, it would have to be very clear what overriding interest of EU law would merit such further harmonisation.

Regarding the former issue (the scope of control exercised by Dutch courts in transnational cases), it is currently unclear whether the CJEU and the Dutch Supreme Court have the same understanding of how violations of law, other than those covered by Article 6 ECHR or Articles 47 and 48 CFR, relate to the notion of a fair trial in transnational procedures. Clearly, the Dutch Supreme Court sees no role for Dutch courts when it comes to violations of the right to privacy by foreign agents. Its reasoning is strongly based on notions of state sovereignty and certainly

[44] HR, 13 June 2023, ECLI:NL:HR:2023:913, 6.6.

[45] HR, 5 April 2022, ECLI:NL:HR:2022:475, 6.12.3-6.12.5, as well as the Opinion of the Council of State (*Raad van State*) on the proposed CCP of 6 April 2022, Part E, sub 3.

[46] See, inter alia, Case C-746/18 *Prokuratuur (Conditions d'accès aux données relatives aux communications électroniques)* ECLI:EU:C:2021:152, para. 42–43.

not framed in light of the goals of the EU's Area of Freedom, Security and Justice, with hardly any references to the EU Charter. On the other hand, we do not yet know how the Luxembourg Court will approach questions relating to evidence in transnational criminal proceedings in light of, for instance, Articles 6, 7, 47, 48 and 52 of the Charter. It has ruled in national data retention cases that

> [i]n deciding whether to exclude information and evidence obtained in contravention of the requirements of EU law, regard must be had, in particular, to the risk of breach of the adversarial principle and, therefore, of the right to a fair trial entailed by the admissibility of such information and evidence. If a court takes the view that a party is not in a position to comment effectively on evidence pertaining to a field of which the judges have no knowledge and that is likely to have a preponderant influence on the findings of fact, it must find an infringement of the right to a fair trial and exclude that evidence in order to avoid such an infringement.[47]

That, in our view, sounds very much like a vindication-of-rights approach, comprising not only issues of reliability but also a review of the legality of the contested investigative measure. Yet whether the CJEU will also apply this logic in transnational cases remains, of course, to be seen. Such a position would not be without merit, and not necessarily in contradiction to the principle of mutual trust in cases where no effective remedies would be open to the defendant in the gathering/transferring jurisdiction. At any rate, the principle of effectiveness does raise the question of how, under a strict application of the transnational *Trennungsprinzip*, a violation of EU rights can effectively be remedied; and if not, how a trial can then still be considered 'fair'.[48] This is a particularly urgent matter in cases where legal remedies are hampered by considerations of operational secrecy in the gathering/transferring jurisdiction in the investigative stage.

V. Transnational E-Evidence and its Admissibility

Due to the large-scale introduction of e-evidence in recent decades, it is now much more common for judges to be confronted with e-evidence collected abroad. Despite the fact that no special rules apply to it (as mentioned in section II on the Dutch evidence law), in recent years courts have seen an influx of such e-evidence, which has led to a stream of case law on the topic. This is mainly due to the criminal investigations conducted into crypto communication providers, especially Ennetcom and EncroChat.[49]

[47] ibid para 44.

[48] For a similar argument in the (different) context of punitive enforcement by EU authorities, see Luchtman (n 22).

[49] See, for more detail about EncroChat and proceedings based on EncroChat-data, JJ Oerlemans and DAG van Toor, 'Legal aspects of the EncroChat operation: a human rights perspective' 30 (2022) *European Journal of Crime, Criminal Law and Criminal Justice* (309).

These companies offer specially prepared smartphones with all functions removed or blocked, except for applications for sending and receiving encrypted messages and files, storing encrypted notes and Internet-based encrypted phone calls. By using these smartphones, criminals thought to stay out of the grasp of the police, because no user data are registered, the smartphones and subscriptions are paid for in cash or with cryptocurrency, and because all content communication is encrypted. Indeed, despite some successes in hacking a seized device in a specific case,[50] for a long time it was impossible to obtain data in bulk (as is possible with registered users based on the mandatory data retention of Internet service providers and telecommunications providers). As a result, the Dutch police, often in collaboration with authorities from other countries, have shifted their focus to dismantling the crypto communication providers (rather than investigating the users of these services). Because of the seizure of the Canadian server Ennetcom and the digital intrusion of, amongst others, the French-based server EncroChat, e-evidence obtained abroad is admitted in many cases.[51] For example, the acquisition of the EncroChat server in 2019 has resulted in more than 150 judgments to date (August 2022).[52] The Dutch case law on this subject – especially on the admissibility and use of transnational e-evidence – is presented and analysed below, focusing in particular on the problems judges face and how they are resolved within the nationally applicable evidence laws.

A. International Cooperation in Criminal Matters Regarding the Gathering of E-Evidence

As briefly mentioned the High Tech Crime Unit (HTCU) of the Dutch police is a leading digital intrusion team, which was involved in several police hacks. It is involved in many criminal investigations against dark web markets, crypto communication providers and other cybercriminal activities, such as botnets.[53]

[50] For example, *Tandem II*, District Court, 19 April 2018, ECLI:NL:RBAMS:2018:2504.

[51] The first case that can be found about the EncroChat operation is of the Court of Amsterdam, 10 September 2020, ECLI:NL:RBAMS:2020:4495. The number of judgments is estimated, based on the search term 'EncroChat' in the register of published judgments on the website rechtspraak.nl. The search results are filtered to first-instance judgments of criminal courts until 12 May 2022. See also, for an analysis of Dutch case law following the EncroChat operation, BW Schermer and JJ Oerlemans, 'De EncroChat-jurisprudentie: teleurstelling voor advocaten, overwinning voor justitie' 2 (2022) *Tijdschrift Bijzonder Strafrecht & Handhaving* 82 (in Dutch); Oerlemans and van Toor (n 49).

[52] Oerlemans and van Toor (n 49) 1.

[53] A Bannister, 'Dutch police shut down 15 DDoS-for-hire platforms' Portswigger (14 April 2020) at https://portswigger.net/daily-swig/dutch-police-shut-down-15-ddos-for-hire-platforms accessed 9 August 2022; Europol, 'Massive blow to criminal Dark Web activities after globally coordinated operation' Europol (20 July 2017) at www.europol.europa.eu/media-press/newsroom/news/massive-blow-to-criminal-dark-web-activities-after-globally-coordinated-operation accessed 9 August 2022; Europol, 'World's most dangerous malware EMOTET disrupted through global action' *Europol* (27 January 2021) at www.europol.europa.eu/media-press/newsroom/news/world's-most-dangerous-malware-emotet-disrupted-through-global-action accessed 9 August 2022.

The HTCU was also involved in the digital intrusion of the EncroChat servers. Due to the technical complexities and transnational character of the use of cryptophones, the decision to cooperate with law enforcement agencies of other countries appears to be necessary in such investigations.[54] For example, the seizure of EncroChat phones in 2017[55] led law enforcement officers to a server in Rouen, France. This server was located at the end of 2018 by French and Dutch law enforcement agencies, and they started a JIT in 2020.[56] So, as is often the case with e-evidence, the seizure of hardware can start a trip 'around the world', and the increased use of hardware and complex software leads to an influx of e-evidence gathered abroad in criminal proceedings.

Back to EncroChat, French law enforcement authorities took the lead in the investigation, due to the fact that the servers of EncroChat were based in their territory. As a result, under the EU Convention on Mutual Assistance, the activities took place under French criminal procedure law.[57] French law enforcement authorities are authorised to share data with JIT members (in this case Dutch law enforcement authorities) under the following conditions: (i) only for the purposes for which the team has been set up; (ii) subject to the prior consent of the Member State where the information became available, for the purposes of detecting, investigating and prosecuting other criminal offences; (iii) for preventing an immediate and serious threat to public security; or (iv) for other purposes to the extent that this is agreed between Member States setting up a JIT.[58]

To conclude this section: after the seizure of EncroChat smartphones by Dutch and French law enforcement agencies separately, the server of EncroChat was traced back to Rouen, France. Both law enforcement agencies started a JIT to digitally intrude into the servers, seize all data and gather all communication in real time. Because of the popularity of EncroChat among members of organised crime, the members of the JIT gathered millions and millions of messages. Although the French law enforcement agency took the lead, as the server was located in its territory, information on 60,000 users led law enforcement to 140 countries,[59] with

[54] See Art 13(1) of the EU Convention on Mutual Assistance, 12 July 2000 ([2000] OJ L123/1): '… A joint investigation team may, in particular, be set up where: (a) a Member State's investigations into criminal offences require difficult and demanding investigations having links with other Member States; (b) a number of Member States are conducting investigations into criminal offences in which the circumstances of the case necessitate coordinated, concerted action in the Member States involved.'

[55] 'The masterstroke of French cybercriminals who hacked the "traffickers' WhatsApp"' at https://tricksfast.com/france/the-masterstroke-of-french-cybercriminals-who-hacked-the-traffickers-whatsapp/ accessed 9 August 2022.

[56] 'Dismantling of an encrypted network sends shockwaves through organised crime groups across Europe' *Europol* (2 July 2020) at www.europol.europa.eu/media-press/newsroom/news/dismantling-of-encrypted-network-sends-shockwaves-through-organised-crime-groups-across-europe accessed 9 August 2022.

[57] See Art 13(a)(b) EU Convention on Mutual Assistance.

[58] Art 13(10) EU Convention on Mutual Assistance; see also the Council Framework Decision of 13 June 2002 on joint investigation teams [2002] OJ L162/1.

[59] 'EncroChat: The shadowy Dutch "tech firm" that sold "encrypted phones" for "worry free communications" about "murder, buying kilos, guns and millions of pills" before disappearing without trace'

one-quarter of the users located in the Netherlands.[60] Most importantly for this chapter, the EncroChat investigation (in combination with other dismantling of crypto communication providers) led to the introduction of e-evidence gathered abroad on a large scale.

In section V.B., we discuss two major issues that have recently been addressed in Dutch case law. First, we examine how Dutch judges rule on the admission of e-evidence obtained abroad, after which we describe Dutch case law on the transfer of seized e-evidence from the original investigation to other cases.

B. Legality of Investigative Police Methods in Other Countries

The EncroChat case is a perfect example of the issues that can arise when e-evidence is gathered abroad and without the supervision of Dutch judicial authorities. The defence are understandably interested in the state of affairs surrounding the EncroChat investigation, not least because parts of the digital intrusion were declared to be a French state secret. More specifically, the defence wanted to be able to investigate whether the investigation was carried out lawfully,[61] in view of the potential consequences under Dutch law, particularly Article 359a CCP.

For the time being, however, the courts in the Netherlands have been unanimous in their opinions on requests by the defence about possible human rights violations during the digital infiltration of EncroChat: a substantive review of the lawfulness of the French investigation – that is, the investigation carried out in France under the auspices of the French authorities – is not possible. This, as said, was recently confirmed by the Court of Cassation (see section IV).[62]

Two arguments were brought forward by the defence to substantiate that, in Dutch criminal cases, the legality of the use of digital intrusion as an investigate power should be scrutinised in detail. The first is that the Dutch police were *actively* involved in the digital intrusion, that is, the French law enforcement agency was not solely responsible for the digital intrusion.[63] Dutch courts accepted that French and Dutch law enforcement agencies cooperated closely, in accordance with the JIT agreement, but also emphasised that judicial authorisation for and supervision

Daily Mail (2 July 2020) at www.dailymail.co.uk/news/article-8484673/EncroChat-shadowy-Dutch-tech-firm-sold-encrypted-phones.html accessed on 15 August 2022.

[60] 'Aardschok voor georganiseerde misdaad' *OM* (2 July 2020) at www.om.nl/actueel/nieuws/2020/07/02/aardschok-voor-georganiseerde-misdaad accessed on 15 August 2022.

[61] For example, District Court Rotterdam, 11 October 2021, ECLI:NL:RBROT:2021:9906; District Court Amsterdam, 16 July 2021, ECLI:NL:RBAMS:2021:3707.

[62] See extensively on this in the context of EncroChat, SGAM Adams, 'Vertrouwen is goed, maar controle is beter. De interpretatie van het interstatelijke vertrouwensbeginsel door Nederlandse feitenrechter bij samenwerking tussen EVRM-lidstaten in het kader van internationale digitale rechtshulp in strafzaken en het beginsel van equality of arms' (2021) 10 *Delikt en Delinkwent* 959.

[63] For example, District Court Midden-Nederland, 17 June 2021, ECLI:NL:RBMNE:2021:2570.

of the digital intrusion of the server took place in France. Moreover, there was no evidence that Dutch law enforcement officers intruded into the EncroChat server, only that the Dutch law enforcement agency co-developed the software that was being used. The latter was, however, insufficient to claim that the investigations were conducted under the authority of the Dutch prosecution service.[64]

Second, defence attorneys argued that the French law enforcement agencies disregarded EU law because they stored location data of EncroChat users during the operation[65] and should have requested the permission of Dutch agencies to investigate users on Dutch territory.[66] This argument also did not convince the courts before which the defence was raised.[67] For example, on 21 June 2021, the District Court of Rotterdam considered that there was no evidence of any, let alone decisive, intervention by Dutch authorities at individual user level.[68] After all, at the time of installation of the malware on EncroChat phones by the French authorities, the location of the devices concerned was not yet known. So neither point led to any other judgments regarding the legality of the digital intrusion, mainly because Dutch courts trusted the French judicial supervision the investigation regarding EncroChat.

Although the Supreme Court – like all other Dutch courts – did not see a significant role for Dutch courts in assessing the French part of the interception in Encrochat, it did nevertheless emphasise that the CCP does not *preclude* the (Dutch) public prosecutor from seeking prior judicial authorisation to issue an order to enter and search automated work and/or record (tele)communications, even in cases where the authorisation is not sought by the Dutch authorities with a view to obtaining data. In the sphere of large-scale collections of (crypto)communications, the reasons for requesting such an authorisation may be that

> (i) foreign authorities, on their own initiative, have already used or will use similar powers under their responsibility, (ii) while in so doing large amounts of data have been or will be obtained which, on the one hand, may be of great value not only to the investigation in which the authorization is sought but also with a view to other (future) investigations and, on the other hand, (may) include data relating to persons who, at the time of their obtaining, are not (yet) concretely known to the investigative authorities as suspects, and (iii) where it is agreed that the data thus obtained will be shared on that broad scale with the Dutch authorities for the purpose of processing such data for the purposes of the current investigation and any other investigations[translated from Dutch].'[69]

[64] HR, 13 June 2023, ECLI:NL:HR:2023:913, 6.18.

[65] Again, District Court Midden-Nederland, 17 June 2021, ECLI:NL:RBMNE:2021:2570.

[66] Art 31 Directive 2014/41/EU regarding the European Investigation Order in criminal matters [2014] OJ L130/1. On the basis of this argument, a German District Court ruled the digital intrusion illegal: LG Berlin, Beschl v 1.7.2021 (525 KLs) 254 Js 592/20 (10/21). However, this ruling was overturned upon appeal: KG, Beschl v 30.08.2021–2 Ws 79/21.

[67] See also HR, 13 June 2023, ECLI:NL:HR:2023:913, 6.23.

[68] District Court Rotterdam, 25 June 2021, ECLI:NL:RBROT:2021:6113, 3.2.4.

[69] HR, 13 June 2023, ECLI:NL:HR:2023:913, 6.24.2.

In this way, the Supreme Court does give way to the deployment of additional safeguards to protect the right to privacy, by allowing examining magistrates to add additional criteria to ensure the possibility of verifying the authenticity and reliability of data, and/or relating to the method of selection of data before they are used in a specific investigation, also with a view to protecting the interests of third parties (including, in particular, persons against whom there is not yet a suspicion of involvement in a criminal offence), as well interests associated with the right to refuse to give evidence.[70]

C. The Transfer of E-Evidence from One Case to Another

That being said, the e-evidence gathered in the cases against crypto communication providers is, of course, not only valuable for those cases. It also gives an insight into worldwide organised crime due to the communication between individual users of the phones. However, as the target of the investigations are the crypto communication providers, it is not *ipso facto* the case that the gathered evidence can be used against individual users of those crypto communication services. So, potential discussion about the use of data seized from crypto communication servers can arise, because the seizure is part of one investigation – in the case of EncroChat, the company itself was the target of the investigation; in the case of Ennetcom, four individual users of Ennetcom's Blackberries were targeted, but the complete server of Ennetcom was seized after a legal assistance request – but further analysis of the data can lead to thousands of suspects.

In the case of Ennetcom, the Superior Court of Justice in Toronto allowed such a transfer of data after additional judicial supervision, and the Dutch Supreme Court ruled that such a system of an additional judicial warrant is in line with Dutch law.[71] The Superior Court of Justice in Toronto further limited the transfer to certain offences, namely participation in criminal originations, murder and manslaughter, arson and money laundering.[72] The request can be based on the data retention provisions under Article 126ng CCP, and should include specific search terms (for example, IMEI numbers, email addresses, nicknames).[73]

This system of checks and balances is copied regarding the EncroChat data, but the criteria used for the transfer are different.[74] A Dutch investigative judge has to decide, upon a request from the public prosecutor, whether (certain pieces of)

[70] HR, 13 June 2023, ECLI:NL:HR:2023:913, 6.24.

[71] Supreme Court of the Netherlands, 28 June 2022, ECLI:NL:HR:2022:900, 3.5.2.

[72] Court of Appeal Amsterdam, 3 March 2021, ECLI:NL:GHARL:2021:1917.

[73] ibid.

[74] The details of warrant became known in a judgment of the Court of Gelderland, 8 December 2021, ECLI:NL:RBGEL:2021:6584, 2.1. The exact text of the warrant remains classified to avoid revealing the personal data of the judges and public prosecutors involved, or naming or providing the technical description of what kind of software is used in the operation (Court of Rotterdam, 11 October 2021, ECLI:NL:RBROT:2021:10412).

data can be transferred to be used against a suspect who was not targeted during the initial digital intrusion (in the case against EncroChat). The investigative judge who authorised the initial investigation against EncroChat decided that in only one of the following two circumstances might e-evidence from the full dataset be transferred to another investigation: (i) it might be transferred to criminal cases that were already pending during the investigation against EncroChat and for which the investigative judge has given separate authorisation (in the initial warrant against EncroChat); or (ii) it mightbe transferred to investigations that resulted from searching the EncroChat data with search keys from a pre-defined list of search terms.[75] The request of the public prosecutor must be based on the digital intrusions paragraph (Article 126uba CCP), as that paragraph was used for the initial digital intrusion.

D. Conclusion

All in all, the finding that there are no specific rules for the introduction of e-evidence in Dutch criminal cases applies *mutatis mutandis* to (e-)evidence gathered abroad. However, because the evidence is gathered abroad without the judicial supervision of Dutch magistrates, discussions at Dutch trials focus on the legality of the evidence gathering and the transfer of the evidence from one case to another. Dutch courts conclude that they cannot rule upon the legality of investigative methods authorised abroad, because the principle of trust prohibits that. In addition, as a main protocol in the cases of Ennetcom and EncroChat, a system of checks and balances has been developed for investigative judges to review requests to transfer the obtained e-evidence to other cases.

VI. Admissibility of Administrative Evidence in Criminal Procedures

There are not many additional remarks to be made regarding the admissibility of administrative evidence in criminal procedures. As is also apparent from our analysis in section II, written administrative evidence is admissible if it qualifies under any of the evidentiary sources that have been mentioned in Article 344 CCP. The relevant legal source is mentioned in Article 344 (1) (3) CCP, which holds that written documents shall be understood to mean documents drawn up by public bodies or officials, relating to matters falling within the scope of the service under their authority.

There is case law dealing with how materials that have been obtained in breach of rules of one area of law may be used in another. Most cases deal with the use

[75] Court of Gelderland, 8 December 2021, ECLI:NL:RBGEL:2021:6584, 2.1.

of evidence that was obtained unlawfully in criminal procedures in subsequent administrative procedures. As a matter of principle, Article 359a CCP does not apply to evidence obtained during administrative proceedings. That article is confined to procedural faults that are committed during 'the preparatory [criminal] investigation' against the suspect. However, in certain circumstances, legal consequences may be attached to procedural errors that were not committed during the preliminary investigation. The latter may be appropriate if the procedural error or unlawful act in question has had a decisive influence on the course of the investigation into and/or (further) prosecution of the suspect for the offence charged. Article 359a CCP is then applied analogously.[76]

The criterion that will then most likely be applied for violations other than violations of Article 6 ECHR or Articles 47 and 48 CFR, is whether or not the materials have been gathered in a way that is so contrary to what may be expected from a government acting properly that this use must be considered inadmissible in all circumstances (the so-called *zozeer indruist* criterion).[77] If that is not the case, criminal courts are in no way precluded from using the materials. This will most likely not even be different in cases where an administrative court has already declared the investigative measure to be unlawful under administrative law. This approach follows from the viewpoint that both areas of law serve different goals and follow different procedures.[78]

VII. The Use of Evidence Obtained in Compliance Programmes

In section III, we explained that the public prosecutor is responsible for the compilation of the case file. It is possible to add pieces of evidence (mostly reports) to the case file that have *not* been drawn up under the supervision of the public prosecutor, when the prosecutor assesses that the material is of any relevance (be it for or against the accused). In past years, it has been discussed whether it would be possible that a criminal trial would be based to a decisive extent on such reports. Scarce case law in this regard seems to indicate that judges exercise restraint if evidence has been produced without the supervision of the prosecution (so outside the realm of the criminal investigation). The legitimacy and, most of all,

[76] HR, 1 December 2020, ECLI:NL:HR:2020:1890, 2.2.2.

[77] HR, 1 July 1992, nr. 26331, BNB 1992/306; HR, 20 March 2015, ECLI:NL:HR:2015:643, 2.5.3. In both cases, the criterion was applied to the use of unlawfully obtained criminal evidence in administrative (tax) procedures. We assume the same applies in the reverse situation, ie the use of unlawfully obtained administrative evidence in criminal procedures; cf APW Duijkersloot, AJ de Vries and RJGM Widdershoven, 'The Netherlands' in F Giuffrida and K Ligeti (eds), *Admissibility of OLAF Final Reports as Evidence in Criminal Proceedings* (University of Luxembourg, 2019) 202, 209–11.

[78] See NGH Verschaeren and VL Meijerman, 'Uitzonderingen op de ongebondenheid van de strafen Belastingrechter – Over onrechtmatig verkregen bewijs, onschuld en onverbindendverklaring' (2019) 18 *Delikt en Delinkwent* 252.

the reliability of such evidence is scrutinised carefully.[79] This means that a report that has been drawn up by a private party, containing evidence that a criminal offence has been committed, can in itself be important evidence, but only if the prosecutor has demonstrated that he or she has scrutinised the report and has found that the report does indeed represent the facts, holds enough objective information to start a criminal investigation, and that additional research to check and verify the contents of the report has been undertaken under the supervision of the prosecutor.[80] Recent reports on out-of-court settlements between the Public Prosecution Service (PPS) and companies have led to debate, because these settlements allegedly relied too heavily on reports that had been drawn up by the suspect or commissioned by the suspect, suggesting a conflict of interests. Scholars argue that additional legislation is required in order to improve the transparency of these settlements and/or to elucidate the potential benefits for the suspects when they come forward with self-incriminating reports.[81]

That said, self-reporting and notification obligations are common in certain business sectors, and these reports are often made to so-called autonomous administrative authorities,[82] which in turn often have agreements (*convenanten*) with the police (or specialised criminal investigation services) and the PPS on the processing of these reports. Prosecution as a consequence of these reports is not uncommon.

In the Netherlands, legal entities can be the subject of criminal prosecution under Article 51 of the Criminal Code (CC). As such, not only natural persons but also legal entities enjoy fundamental procedural rights in criminal proceedings, such as the right to remain silent. This means that natural persons who act in the capacity of spokespersons of a legal entity may also invoke the legal entity's right to remain silent. A grey area in this regard is the situation in which the spokesperson could be liable for individual prosecution as a responsible individual:[83] the obligation for the legal entity to disclose certain information could incriminate the individual. Another point of discussion in this regard is the situation in which a legal entity asks a law firm to perform an investigation that could disclose criminal offences and subsequently 'buries' the results of that research under the client–attorney privilege.[84]

The use of evidence that has been assembled through legal obligations to report on specific topics can conflict with the privilege against self-incrimination (Article 6 ECHR). The case law of the European Court of Human Rights has, of course,

[79] S Brinkhoff, 'Strafvorderlijke kaders voor burgeropsporing' (2020) 19 (2-3) *Tijdschrift voor Veiligheid* 99.

[80] ibid 102.

[81] T Beekhuis, 'Het gebruik van zelfonderzoek door het openbaar ministerie behoeft nadere normering' (2020) (3/4) *Tijdschrift voor Sanctierecht &Onderneming* 131.

[82] *Zelfstandig Bestuursorgaan* (ZBO).

[83] Under certain conditions, these individuals can be prosecuted for their role in the criminal offences committed by the legal entity (Art 51 CC).

[84] M van der Horst and R Klein, 'Het verschoningsrecht, de toekomst met vertrouwen tegemoet?' (2019) (4) *Tijdschrift voor Sanctierecht & Onderneming* 150.

been of major importance in the Netherlands in this regard (especially because the Netherlands does not have a Constitutional Court). Within the limited space of this chapter, it is not possible to reflect on the Dutch approach in detail. Dutch law does not hold a general rule that the use in a criminal trial of evidence that has come to light as a consequence of legal duties to provide information is in breach of the privilege against self-incrimination. There is an important exception, however, regarding information existing in dependence on the will of the accused. In most cases, existing files (such as bookkeeping records, correspondence that has been stored, administration) are considered to hold information that exists independently of the will of the accused, even when the accused has been forced to disclose the files against his or her will. Van Toor refers to this as a 'material based' approach; the nature of the evidence – the material – decides the extent of the protection offered under the privilege against self-incrimination.[85] In that light, a lot of e-evidence is likely to be considered as information that exists independently of the will of the accused as well. While the general rule in the CCP is that suspects cannot be ordered to hand over evidence, a lot of sector-specific legislation (regarding, inter alia, 'economic offences',[86] tax evasion, weapons and/or drugs) specifically determines that suspects can be required to hand over objects that are liable to seizure and/or to provide certain information. The obligation to hand over e-evidence, then, will not be in breach of the privilege against self-incrimination. Also, suspects can be ordered to give access to e-evidence that has already been confiscated. The Supreme Court held, for example, that suspects can be forced to unlock their smartphones with a fingerprint.[87]

E-evidence that has been gathered in the course of internal investigations or within compliance programmes is therefore admissible as evidence in criminal proceedings. Again, the major test is that of reliability: if judges are satisfied that it is safe to use the evidence (and that the defence have had a proper opportunity to assess its reliability – see section III), they can choose to use it. So far, specific legislation is not available, but this may change in the near future.

VIII. Conclusion

The Dutch legal system on evidence in criminal cases qualifies as a 'negative statutory' system, which means that (i) only means of evidence that have been qualified as such by law may be used, and (ii) legal proof alone is not enough: judges must be convinced that the suspect has indeed committed the offence as charged. That only statutory means of evidence are accepted does not pose a significant hurdle for

[85] Corstens, Borgers and Kooijmans (n 3) 367, with reference to DAG Van Toor, *Het schuldige geheugen* (Wolters Kluwer, 2017) 422.

[86] The Economic Offences Act (*Wet Economische Delicten*, WED) is a framework Act that covers dozens of Acts that deal with activities in socio-economic and environmental law.

[87] HR, 9 February 2021, ECLI:NL:HR:2021:202.

courts to use the materials they deem fit. All written documents can, for instance, be used as evidence, including documents describing the contents of data carriers. In the very near future, audio(-visual) recordings will also be allowed as means of evidence. Admitting e-evidence through written reports or in other ways is, therefore, not problematic.

Dutch legislation allows for a wide variety of powers to collect evidence, including powers that are specifically aimed at collecting e-evidence. This legislation is mostly defined in detail and contains safeguards aimed at assuring the proper and secure collection of evidence to guarantee the integrity of the (chain of) evidence and to allow for a sufficient degree of transparency of the procedure.

Even so, unlawful collection of evidence very rarely leads to the exclusion of that evidence. The case law of the Supreme Court usually precludes the exclusion of evidence as a consequence of unlawfulness, save for irreparable violations of the right to a fair trial. Effective remedies are more often sought (and found) in procedural guarantees and/or sentence reduction. Unlawfully obtained evidence must be distinguished from unreliable evidence, though. Judges are free in the selection and assessment of the evidence. The main reason for judges to dismiss evidence is the unreliability of the evidence, regardless of the fact of whether it was obtained lawfully or not. As a consequence, 'the right to a fair trial' as a reason to exclude evidence after unlawful police action seems to be a residual category for cases in which the evidence in itself is deemed reliable (despite having been obtained unlawfully), whereas using it would still be in breach of the right to a fair trial. These cases are very rare.

So, the bottom line is that it is mostly evidence that has been demonstrated to be unreliable that gets excluded by the judge. This puts the burden on the defence, who will have to demonstrate that there are indeed circumstances that cast doubt on the reliability of evidence. Proper disclosure of all relevant material and *equality of arms* are important notions in this regard. However, if the defence claim that there has not been full disclosure, or that the defendant has not been able to fully enjoy his or her rights, judges will expect a proper substantiation of these claims. This is sometimes viewed as a *probatio diabolica:* the defence, after all, cannot give the required substantiation *unless* they get access to more material. In cases with e-evidence, doubts regarding, inter alia, the use of improper or invalid algorithms or opaque compilation of datasets have led to requests for extensive research from the defence (eg for unlimited access to datasets or software). These requests were commonly granted only in part, with judges claiming that, indeed, the need for farther-reaching investigation was not substantiated.

The problem of *probatio diabolica* is all the more palpable in cases with transnational dimensions. The principle of trust has a very broad scope in Dutch case law, and virtually all evidence (again mostly reports) will be admissible, with very little room for the defence to demonstrate that evidence has been obtained unlawfully and/or that there are circumstances that could prejudice the reliability of the evidence. While evidence that has been collected within the national jurisdiction may be the object of significant procedural scrutiny and judicial review, such scrutiny is mostly not available when evidence comes from another jurisdiction. This leads to the question whether an 'effective remedy' is left for the defence, especially when the other jurisdiction does not offer an effective remedy either, for example because of reasons of operational secrecy or state security. Can Dutch judges really maintain that they admit reliable evidence when there is no actual possibility to verify it? There is concern among Dutch scholars that the current Dutch approach could lead to the defence's falling between two stools.[88]

In the meantime, it remains rather a puzzling question whether the application of the *Trennungsprinzip*, which we consider to be leading in Dutch criminal procedures, can be upheld: after all, many of the statutory procedural safeguards have been introduced to guarantee the integrity (and thus reliability) of the process of acquiring evidence. Separating the legality and the reliability of evidence is not always as easy as it seems, which we find to be all the more true for e-evidence.

[88] MJJP Luchtman, 'Het Europees Openbaar Ministerie in Nederland. Over zijn ondeelbaarheid en de verhouding tot de Nederlandse strafrechter' (2021) (10) *Delikt en Delinkwent* 806.

8

Admissibility of Evidence, Transnational E-Evidence and Fair-Trial Rights in Portugal

VÂNIA COSTA RAMOS

I. Introduction

This chapter focuses on Portuguese domestic law, covering statutory law and case law and including, where applicable, my opinion on the matters described. The first sections address the legal framework on admissibility of criminal evidence in Portugal and cross-border evidence, outlining the main principle (section II), the existence of constitutional exclusionary rules and further explicit exclusionary rules provided in the Code of Criminal Procedure (CCP) (section III), and the law on cross-border evidence and exclusionary rules, including case law (section IV). The chapter then goes on to outline that the same rules are in principle applicable to electronic evidence ('e-evidence'), also addressing some precise issues of admissibility of e-evidence (section V), including certain cross-border aspects (section VI). At the end of these sections, I will discuss on the possible exclusionary rules of evidence that could be agreed at the level of the European Union (EU), taking into account the Portuguese legal framework (section VII). The last section addresses the gathering of evidence in administrative proceedings and in internal investigations in the field of compliance programmes and its use in criminal cases, focusing on the right against self-incrimination (section VIII).

II. The Legal Framework on Admissibility of Criminal Evidence in Portugal

A. General Principle

Under Article 125 CCP, the governing principle in Portuguese criminal proceedings is that any evidence that is not prohibited by law is admissible;[1] and under

[1] This is reiterated in Art 292 CCP for the judicial investigative stage.

Article 127 CCP, admissible evidence is subject to 'free evaluation' by the court, that is, '[u]nless the law provides otherwise, evidence is assessed according to the rules of experience and the free assessment of the competent body'. Thus, the relevant question is what evidence is prohibited by law? And, where evidence is prohibited, what are the consequences in the event of a violation? Are there 'exclusionary rules'? And what are their features?

B. Evidence Prohibited by Law – Exclusionary Rules in Portugal

The most prominent feature of the Portuguese legal system in this respect is that Portugal has a constitutional exclusionary rule[2] and several exclusionary rules laid down in the CCP and other laws.[3] The constitutional exclusionary rule under Article 32 was introduced in 1976 and provides that 'All evidence obtained by torture, coercion, infringement of personal physical or moral integrity, or improper intrusion into personal life, the home, correspondence or telecommunications is null and void.'[4] At the time it was introduced, it was argued by Andrade, Member of the Constituent Assembly, that this was one of the requirements to overcome the inquisitorial police models of criminal procedure that tended to forget the human rights dimension in the gathering of evidence.[5] This was already argued

[2] See Art 32, para 8, Portuguese Constitution.

[3] For a summary in English by other authors, see PS Mendes, 'Comparative exclusionary rules, Portuguese and Brazilian perspective' (2013) at http://carlospintodeabreu.com/wp-content/uploads/2019/03/comparative_exclusionary_rules.pdf; P Caeiro and MJ Costa, 'The Portuguese System' in K Ligeti (ed), *Toward a Prosecutor for the European Union*, vol 1 (Hart Publishing, 2013) 540, 573–77. For more details on the Portuguese system, see MC Andrade, *Sobre as proibições de prova em processo penal* (Coimbra Editora, 1992); GM Silva, 'Produção e Valoração da Prova em Processo Penal' (2006) 4 *Revista do Centro de Estudos Judiciários* 37; JC Correia, 'A distinção entre prova proibida por violação dos direitos fundamentas e a prova nula numa perspectiva essencialmente jurisprudencial' (2006) 4 *Revista do Centro de Estudos Judiciários* 175; H Morão, 'O efeito-à-distância das proibições de prova no direito processual penal português' (2006) 16 *Revista Portuguesa de Ciência Criminal* 575; MC Andrade, 'Proibições de prova em processo penal (conceitos e princípios fundamentais)' (2008) 10 *Revista Jurídica da Universidade Portucalense* 143; SO Silva, 'Legalidade da prova e prova proibida' (2011) 21 *Revista Portuguesa de Ciência Criminal* 545; PS Mendes, 'O efeito-à-distância das proibições de prova' (2013) 74 *Revista do Ministério Público do Rio Grande do Sul* 219; JF Dias, 'Revisitação de algumas ideias-mestras da teoria das proibições de prova em processo penal (também à luz da jurisprudência constitucional portuguesa)' (2016) 4000 *Revista de Legislação e Jurisprudência* 3; MF Mata-Mouros, 'Sistemas de prova: da irracionalidade à dimensão constitucional das proibições de prova em processo penal' in ML Amaral (ed.), *Estudos em Homenagem ao Conselheiro Presidente Rui Moura Ramos* (Almedina, 2016) 413; JC Correia, 'A proibição de valoração decorrente da violação das formalidades relativas à constituição como arguido' (2016) at https://cej.justica.gov.pt/LinkClick.aspx?fileticket=tbmuUugvKrM%3D&portalid=30, 85.

[4] Constituição da República Portuguesa de 1976, DR I S 10 April 1976. English translation available at www.parlamento.pt/sites/EN/Parliament/Documents/Constitution7th.pdf.

[5] Diário da Assembleia Constituinte, no 18 of 17 July 1975, 408. See at https://debates.parlamento.pt/catalogo/r3/dac/01. JG Canotilho and N Brandão, 'Colaboração premiada e auxílio judiciário em matéria penal: a ordem pública como obstáculo à cooperação, com a operação, Lava Jato' (2016) 4000

by Dias in his handbook on criminal procedure, published before the Constitution was in force.[6]

The CCP has a corresponding rule in Article 126:

Forbidden methods of evidence:

1 – Evidence obtained by torture, coercion, or, as a general matter, infringement of personal physical or moral integrity, is null and void and may not be used.

2 – Evidence obtained by the following methods infringes the physical or moral integrity of the persons, irrespective of their consent:

a) Disturbance of freedom of will or of decision making through ill-treatment, bodily harm, administration of means of any nature, hypnosis or use of cruel or deceptive methods;
b) Disturbance, by any means, of the capacity of remembrance or judgement;
c) Use of force outside the cases and limits permitted by law;
d) Threat with a legally inadmissible measure or with the denial or constraint of the enjoyment of a legally established benefit;
e) Promise of legally inadmissible advantage.

3 – Subject to the cases permitted by law, evidence obtained by interference in the private life, the home, the correspondence or telecommunications without the consent of the right holder is equally null and void and may not be used.

4 – If the use of the methods of gathering of evidence foreseen in this article constitutes a punishable offence, the evidence may be used with the exclusive aim of prosecution against the authors of said offence.

Scholars have distinguished – along the lines of the characterisation by Beling[7] – between prohibitions on gathering evidence (eg by torture), prohibitions on assessing evidence (either associated with the former, or independently, eg a prohibition on using chance findings or *Zuffalsfunden* through lawful intercept evidence in

Revista de Legislação e Jurisprudência 16, 37–38 argue that Art 32, para 8, Constitution, as a fundamental right which has to be protected as a consequence of the principle of the rule of law, belongs to the Portuguese *ordre public*.

[6] JF Dias, *Direito Processual Penal*, vol I (Coimbra Editora, 1974) 75 (referring to the establishment of a 'prohibition of evidence' obtained by a violation of the ethical autonomy of the person, irrespective of their consent, as one of the corollaries of a criminal procedure as foundation of a rule-of-law state and of the establishment of regulation of the problems of criminal procedure that is in conformity with the Constitution), 197 (stating that the legality of the evidence and the rules of production of evidence and the prohibitions of evidence – narco-analysis, lie-detectors, etc – are preconditions for the procedural validity of the evidence, and thus criteria of the 'material truth' itself) and in particular 453–63 (arguing in favour of the existence of 'prohibitions of evidence' in respect of the interrogation of the accused, in light of the Constitution then in force, which established the 'necessary safeguards of defence' and the absolute right to 'life and personal integrity', including moral integrity, in Arts 8, para 1 and 8, para 10, and referring to the provisions in respect thereof as not being mere formalities or 'rules of production of evidence' but rather protections of the accused's right to defence and of the right to personal integrity). The author called upon the legislator to regulate these matters in the CCP, and the proposals made are akin to Art 126 CCP in force today. In Dias (n 3) 3, the author states he believes he was the first scholar to bring the topic up for debate in the Portuguese language literature.

[7] E Beling, *Die Beweisverbote als Grenzen der Wahrheitserforschung im Strafprozess* (Wissenschaftliche Buchgesellschaft, 1903).

relation to offences for which the intercept could not have been ordered; or prohibitions on using witness evidence gathered in previous stages, eg if the witness invokes a privilege) and prohibitions on the subject matter of evidence (eg state secrecy). In my opinion, this distinction does not help much in terms of understanding the exclusionary rules at stake. It is much more important to understand whether the exclusionary rules are 'intrinsic' or 'extrinsic', following Wigmore's classification.[8] As noted by Damaška, despite the use of different labels, exclusionary rules (which would be the equivalent of prohibitions on the use, admission or assessment of evidence) exist both in Continental and common law systems, although in the former they are mostly limited to extrinsic exclusionary rules.[9] Portugal is not an exception: even without studying all of the Portuguese exclusionary rules in detail (which would be outside the scope of this chapter), I would risk saying that the exclusionary rules in force in Portugal are mostly extrinsic exclusionary rules, that is those established to protect an interest that is different from the interest in the 'search for the truth'. However, there are a few cases of intrinsic exclusionary rules, established to protect the accuracy of the fact-finding process.

Although I prefer to use the term 'exclusionary rule', Portuguese scholars and courts tend to use the term 'prohibitions of evidence' (*proibições de prova*[10]) and, in order to refer to the exclusionary rules (prohibitions of the use, admission or assessment of evidence), 'prohibitions of assessing evidence' (*proibições de valoração da prova*), undoubtedly because of the influence of the work published by Andrade in 1992 on this subject, following Beling's classification.[11] It should be noted that, save for a few exceptions,[12] Portuguese exclusionary rules apply throughout all procedural stages, that is, the use of the evidence is excluded not only in respect of the final decision of the trial court but also during earlier stages and for all types of decisions (eg for the indictment, ordering pre-trial detention, etc), and also vis-à-vis police authorities and prosecutors (the former of course are

[8] JH Wigmore, *A treatise on the system of evidence in trials at common law: including the statutes and judicial decisions of all jurisdictions of the United States* (Little Brown, 1904).

[9] MR Damaška, *Evidence Law Adrift* (Yale University Press, 1997) 12–17. The author follows the classification, which he considers useful for a perfunctory overview, although it is not without ambiguities, proposed by Wigmore (n 8).

[10] Divided into 'prohibitions of themes of evidence', 'prohibitions of means evidence' and 'prohibition of methods of evidence'; see, eg, PS Mendes, *Lições de Direito Processual Penal* (Almedina, 2013) 177–78.

[11] Andrade, *Sobre as proibições de prova* (n 3). See, eg, Mendes (n 10) 177–78. See, however, Judgment of the Supreme Court of 16 June 2004, case 04P721 at www.dgsi.pt, cited by Correia, 'A distinção' (n 3) 192, fn 32, explicitly using the term 'exclusionary regime': '[T]he regime of null and void evidence which is translated into disregarding the evidence affected by the defect which produces the nullity or into the impossibility of producing or weighing evidence affected thereby is, in reality, an exclusionary regime; the particular evidence affected thereby is excluded from the case and thus cannot be regarded or weighed in by the court. It is a regime coined by the influence of the doctrine of the "exclusionary rule" of the Anglo-Saxon model of criminal process.'

[12] Eg, the police may use witness evidence they gathered, even where they are not allowed to make a statement on the content of that testimony in court and even if the court cannot use the written records on the witness statements at the trial stage – see Arts 355 and 356 CCP.

not required to 'rule' on the existence of the exclusionary rule but should refrain from using evidence that cannot be admitted).[13]

Another important feature of the Portuguese system of exclusionary rules is that case law and literature have not always been unanimous, either in the classification of the procedural infringements as 'prohibitions of evidence' or other 'merely procedural breaches' (nullities and irregularities), or in the definition of the regime applicable in terms of standing and deadlines to invoke the breaches. Although scholars have long argued that the regime of exclusionary rules is autonomous and different from the regime covering procedural nullities and irregularities, the connection to nullities stems from the Constitution (Article 32, para 8 of which uses the wording 'null and void', an expression that replaced 'prohibitions of evidence' in the original proposal), tying this new institution to the system of nullities that was more familiar to the Portuguese procedural system.[14] This is one of the sources of conflict and misunderstandings in the interpretation of the regime of exclusionary rules versus nullities.[15]

The distinction is not merely academic, since the procedural regime on 'prohibitions of evidence' established in Article 126 CCP (and Article 32, para 8 of the Constitution) is much more robust: for example, exclusionary rules may be raised at any time during the proceedings – there is no deadline within which to raise them. Also, if a conviction is final and it comes to light that it was based on such

[13] GM Silva, *Curso de Processo Penal*, vol II (5th edn, Verbo 2011) 178; Mendes (n 10) 178, fn 372, 180–81; JF Dias and N Brandão, 'O controlo pelo juiz de instrução das invalidades e proibições de prova durante a fase de inquérito' in JL Moutinho et al (eds.), *Homenagem ao Professor Doutor Germano Marques da Silva* (Universidade Católica, 2020) 1155, 1170–72.

[14] Dias (n 3) 8, who presided over the Commission drafting the new CCP, affirms that Portugal belonged to the French tradition, which sanctioned any violation of the rules on evidence that would taint the act of gathering, producing or weighing that evidence with a nullity, which could be of different types, or with an irregularity. Thus, when the new CCP was drafted, it was intended to create an autonomous regime for the prohibition of evidence, which was unanimously approved. However, there was no agreement on the limitation of evidentiary nullities to those concerning mere evidentiary procedural rules. Some members found that the theory on evidentiary nullities would be consequent and dependent on the theory of nullities in civil law, and due to its historical and legal importance, it would be better to maintain a 'dual' character within the general category of criminal procedural nullities.

[15] In addition to that, although the CCP states that the provisions regulating nullities and irregularities (Arts 118 to 123) are 'without prejudice' to the rules on 'prohibitions of evidence', which is interpreted by most scholars as meaning that these have an autonomous nature and regime, some of the rules applicable to procedural defects are applied to exclusionary rules or 'prohibitions of evidence', namely that in Art 122 on the consequences of the violation of procedural breaches (see sectionII.C). See, however, Mendes (n 10) 196–97, changing his opinion in the name of coherence with the autonomy of 'prohibitions of evidence' versus 'mere nullities', and adhering to the thesis that the *fruit-of-the-poisonous-tree doctrine* in respect of the 'prohibitions of evidence' derives directly from Art 32, para 1 and 32, para 8, Constitution, in line with the position of the Constitutional Court (see section II.C) and Morão (n 3). See also Caeiro and Costa (n 3) 574; PP Albuquerque, *Comentário do Código de Processo Penal à luz da Constituição da República e da Convenção Europeia dos Direitos do Homem*, 4th edn (UCP, 2011) Art 126, 4;. Silva (n 13) 178–80; SO Silva (n 3) 587, fn 81 (arguing that the amendment to Art 126, para 3 CCP in 2007, adding 'and may not be used', made this clear and almost led to unanimity in the literature); Mendes (n 10) 188, 190; Correia, 'A distinção' (n 3) 180, fn 7, 187, 191; Correia, 'A proibição' (n 3) 89–91; SO Silva (n 3) 555 (noting that there is no correspondence between the clarity of the conceptual distinction and the ease to identify such rules in practice); Mendes (n 10) 182 (the violation of formalities does not fall within the remit of 'prohibitions of evidence' unless it violates rights to liberty).

'prohibited evidence', this will constitute grounds for an extraordinary appeal against the conviction under Article 449, para 1, *lit* d) CCP. Even where the investigative judge has ruled on a prohibition of evidence, under Article 310, para 2 CCP this does not preclude the trial court from deciding the matter again. On the other hand, 'incurable' nullities may be invoked until the case becomes final (Article 119 CCP), but cannot be invoked as a ground for an extraordinary appeal against a final conviction. Under Article 120 CCP, 'nullities subject to remedy' have to be invoked within specific deadlines during the process, and any other procedural defects (which are not considered as prohibitions of evidence or nullities) are deemed to be irregularities and have to be invoked immediately, or within three days after the person has become aware of the defect (subject to certain exceptions).

This chapter should be read bearing in mind that the topic of exclusionary rules or 'prohibitions of evidence' is contentious, in particular in terms of its application in individual cases, and to this day, scholars affirm that there is no general theory on 'prohibitions of evidence', albeit that such a theory is necessary.[16]

C. Fruit of the Poisonous Tree?

The fruit-of-the-poisonous-tree doctrine applies in Portugal, with limitations regarding the 'attenuation of the taint', 'inevitable discovery' and 'independent source'.[17] The Constitutional Court has explicitly recognised the doctrine in its judgment no 198/2004, of 24 March 2004.[18] The decision dealt with the constitutionality of Article 122, para 1 CCP.[19]

The first-instance court had decided that, given the nullity of the telephone tapping conducted, the records and transcripts of the conversations could not be used, in accordance with Article 126, para 1 CCP and Article 32, para 8 of the Constitution. Furthermore, the Court had ruled, derivative evidence, including the drugs seized, was to be excluded in accordance with Article 122, para 1 CCP. Despite the suppression of such evidence, the defendants had been convicted based on further evidence, including a confession they made during the main trial hearing.

The defendants appealed the decision, claiming that the derivative effect ('*efeito à distância*') laid down in Article 122, para 1 CCP applied to any evidence causally linked to evidence declared null and void and did not allow for any limitations. The Coimbra Court of Appeal ruled that, notwithstanding the nullity of the intercept, not all derivative evidence had to be excluded,[20] and the Supreme Court affirmed its decision.

[16] Dias, 'Revisitação' (n 3) 4; Andrade, 'Proibições de prova' (n 3) 143.

[17] On this topic, see Mendes, 'Comparative exclusionary rules' (n 3); Caeiro and Costa (n 3) 573–76.

[18] Judgment of the Constitutional Court no 198/2004 of 24 March 2004, case 39/04 at www.tribunalconstitucional.pt/tc/acordaos/20040198.html.

[19] Art 122, para 1 CCP states that nullities render invalid the act in which they occurred, as well as the acts that depend on the former act and may be affected by those nullities.

[20] Namely: (i) it was not prohibited to use derived evidence for the mere verification of emerging information (eg the identification of the defendants, if this identification had been confirmed by

The Constitutional Court limited its ruling to the constitutionality of the interpretation of Article 122, para 1 CCP, according to which the use of derivative evidence other than the intercept itself was permitted when the subsequent evidence was the statement given by the defendants themselves in form of a confession. According to the Court, although the Constitution has a specific provision laying down a right to obtain the suppression of evidence obtained unlawfully by a violation of constitutionally protected values, the general statement contained in Article 32, para 1 of the Constitution ('criminal procedure shall ensure the broadest safeguards of the defence, including the right to appeal') would in itself suffice to affirm the existence of a constitutional right to have such evidence suppressed (invalidated, declared null and void or ineffective). According to the Court, the right to exclusion of unconstitutionally obtained evidence is no more than 'a particular and inextricable dimension of the right to a criminal process with the widest guarantees of defence'.[21] Thus, the Court adhered to principle of *Justizförmigkeit des Verfahrens*, according to which the judgment on culpability will only be in conformity with the procedural legal system if no procedural safeguards have been violated to the detriment of the defendant, quoting Roxin's statement that in a rule-of-law state, this principle has as much value as a conviction of a guilty man and the re-establishment of legal peace.[22]

The issue at stake was then to decide whether the 'broadest safeguards of defence' also included, beyond the nullity of the unconstitutionally obtained evidence itself, the derivative effect of the nullity on otherwise valid evidence, leading to its suppression, which would amount to an extension of the unlawfulness of the former evidence. The Constitutional Court considered that the derivative effect was certainly one of the right-protective dimensions of the criminal process, and therefore it would be permissible to verify, on a case-by-case basis, whether the naturalistic link between the unlawfulness and the otherwise lawfully obtained evidence also established an 'unlawfulness link' (*nexo de antijuridicidade*) that generated a derivative effect; or whether, on the other hand, a degree of autonomy existed between the subsequent evidence and the unlawfully obtained evidence, such that it would substantially break the link. The Constitutional Court underlined that the principle of the fruit-of-the-poisonous-tree doctrine is not more than the analysis of the circumstances of the case in order to determine the existence of a link of unlawfulness between the unlawfully obtained evidence and the subsequent evidence, which requires dealing with the latter in the same manner as the former from a legal point of view.

themselves, by witnesses, during searches, even if conducted after the intercept; the travel of the defendants and seizure of the drugs in the vehicle driven by one of the defendants); (ii) it was not prohibited to use conclusive data (for example, affirming that evidence could have been obtained by alternative investigation processes, since the causal link between the unlawfulness and the evidence had to be proved by the defendants); (iii) it was not prohibited to use real evidence that was 'persistent' (such as the instruments/objects of the crime, the vehicle, the drugs), even where its seizure was affected by the nullity; (iv) the confession made by the defendants by their free will, because it was not entirely a result of the intercept.

[21] Judgment of the Constitutional Court no 198/2004 (n 18) para 2.2.1.

[22] C Roxin, *Strafverfahrensrecht*, 25th ed. (C.H. Beck, 1998) 2.

The Constitutional Court underlined that the doctrine had been developed within a legal system completely different from the Portuguese one, and that some of the solutions adopted in the United States (US) legal system accordingly would have absolutely no correspondence with our law, but it had nonetheless had an influence upon our legal system.[23] Nonetheless, the definitive argument was that, even in the system where it was developed, the doctrine never implied the automatic 'dominoes-exclusion' of all evidence subsequent to and somehow related to the unlawfully obtained evidence.[24] The Constitutional Court also summarised the position of other European legal systems on this issue (Germany, Spain, Italy), underlining that there was a tendency to recognise the derivative effect of the exclusion of evidence (although not without dispute and not in a general manner).[25]

Reading Article 122, para 1 CCP in the light of the US Supreme Court case law, the Constitutional Court stated that

> this rule makes interpretative room for searching for relationships of dependency or production of effects (art 122, para 1 CCP refers to acts that depend on the invalid act or may be affected thereby), which, based upon rational criteria, require projection [on the derivative evidence] of the same negative value that affects the preceding act.[26]

In the case at hand, the Constitutional Court concluded that the unlawfulness of the primary evidence did not affect the later confession, provided that the latter was made knowingly and voluntarily, thus constituting an independent act of free will – which was the case, as it could not be accepted that the defendants had only confessed because they thought the evidence obtained by means of interception of telephone communications was valid, as their lawyers had invoked the unlawfulness of that evidence prior to the trial hearing.[27] The Constitutional Court considered that a confession has such an autonomous nature that it enables the judge to have access to the facts by means of evidence that is totally detachable from any other piece of evidence that was affected by a negative value and that might have emerged at an earlier stage.[28]

Consequently, the Constitutional Court concluded that 'the understanding of art 122, para 1 CCP underlying the appealed decision, according to which this article provides for the possibility to weigh the meaning of subsequent evidence,

[23] Judgment of the Constitutional Court no 198/2004 (n 18) para 2.2.4.

[24] The Constitutional Court summarised the development of the fruit-of-the-poisonous-tree doctrine in the case law of the US Supreme Court with reference to *Silverthorne Lumber Co v United States*, 251 US 385 (1920), *Nardone v United States*, 308 US 338 (1939), *Weeks v United States*, 232 US 383 (1914) and *Mapp v Ohio*, 367 US 643 (1961). The Constitutional Court mentioned that, in the US, this doctrine had always been adopted with limitations, and reviewed the case law of the US Supreme Court concerning the 'independent source limitation' (*Silverthorne Lumber Co v United States* and *Segura v United States*, 468 US 796, 1983), the 'inevitable discovery limitation' (*Nix v Williams*, 467 US 430 (1983)) and the 'purged taint limitation' (*Wong Sun v United States*, 371 US.471 (1962); *Michigan vTucker*, 417 US 433 (1971); *Oregon v Elstad*, 470 US 298 (1985)).

[25] Judgment of the Constitutional Court no 198/2004 (n 18) para 2.2.5.

[26] ibid para 2.2.4.

[27] ibid para 2.3.1.

[28] ibid para 2.3.1.

without declaring its invalidity, when a confession is at issue, is in accordance with the Constitution' and does not infringe Articles 32 and 34 of the Portuguese Constitution.[29]

This doctrine is applied to exclusionary rules in a general manner. However, as with the issues pertaining to exclusionary rules in respect of primary evidence, there is no unanimity in the application of the doctrine to the factual situations that come about in different cases.

III. Examples of Exclusionary Rules in Portuguese Law

Portuguese law establishes several exclusionary rules.[30] However, it is not always clear whether these are actual exclusionary rules ('prohibitions of assessing evidence', attached or not to a 'prohibition to gather evidence' or 'prohibition to produce evidence') or merely procedural irregularities that could be deemed cured if not raised. Therefore, there is often conflicting case law on the nature and procedural regime of the exclusionary rules in force in the Portuguese legal system. As it is not possible to list the existing exclusionary rules exhaustively in this chapter, I will refer to some of them, to give the reader an overview of the type of rules in force.

In respect of the rights of the accused, the CCP established that the lack of compliance with the formal procedures for charging a suspect (namely, informing him that he is a suspect and has certain rights and duties) implies that his statements 'may not be used as evidence' (see Article 58, para 6).[31] Equally, a violation of the rules on the duration (eight hours, with one break of 60 minutes) and time of the interrogation of the accused (between 7am and midnight, except if there was an arrest *in flagrante*) implies that the statements obtained thereby 'are null and void and may not be used as evidence' (Article 103, para 5). The violation of the duty of professional secrecy by an interpreter in relation to the conversations between the accused and his defence counsel will also imply that the evidence 'may not be used', under Article 92, para 5 CCP. Concerning the right to legal assistance, a violation thereof will taint the relevant acts with an incurable nullity (Article 119, *lit* c) CCP), meaning that the acts are not valid, which will affect the evidence obtained thereby (Article 122 CCP). There is no reference to a 'prohibition of evidence', but one can state that the invalidity of the act and the ensuing prohibition on using the evidence is indeed an 'exclusionary rule'.[32]

[29] ibid para 2.3.1.

[30] For further details, see the literature listed in n 3, eg Correia, 'A proibição' (n 3) 91–93, identifying 'exclusionary rules' that are considered 'prohibitions of evidence' and not only procedural defects.

[31] On this particular provision, see Correia, 'A proibição' (n 3).

[32] Whether it would fall within the stricter regime of nullities, in terms of being 'cured' by the res judicata of the case and not permitting an extraordinary appeal in the event that a violation is found only after the case has been finally disposed of, or within the regime of 'prohibitions of evidence' is disputed.

Most scholars argue that serious violations of procedural rights (such as the right to legal assistance, enshrined in Article 32, para 3 of the Constitution[33]) should also be considered as 'prohibitions of evidence' falling under Article 32, para 8 of the Constitution.[34] The accused has the right to silence, but if he decides to make a statement during the pre-trial stages, under Article 357 CCP this statement can be used in court at the request of the accused, or if the statements were made during an interrogation by a prosecutor or a judge, in the presence of a defence lawyer, and the accused was informed that the statements could be used in court against him, even if he were to remain silent at the trial stage. This means that statements the accused makes to the police cannot be used in court unless the accused requests it. This bar is established in Articles 355 and 357 CCP, and the expression used in Article 355 is 'prohibition of assessing evidence'.[35] Albeit that the Portuguese Constitution does not explicitly foresee the right against self-incrimination, and the CCP only regulates explicitly the right to silence, the former has long been recognised as an implicit right included in the right to a fair trial, and also (at least indirectly) as connected to the right to moral integrity of the person and human dignity, and its violation falls within the provision in Article 32, para 8 of the Constitution, as well as under Article 126, para 1 CCP. Law 109/2009 of 31 August (the 'PT-Cybercrime Law'[36]) explicitly establishes a prohibition on issuing production orders against the suspect or accused (see Article 14, para 5).

In respect of witness statements, Article 129 CCP establishes that hearsay evidence[37] is admissible only if the person who has direct knowledge of the facts, or source of knowledge about the facts, is identified by the indirect witness and is then called to testify, except when the direct witness is unavailable due to death or supervening psychic anomaly or could not be located. However, Article 356 CCP does exceptionally allow for the reading and weighing in evidence of documents

[33] For further reading on the right to legal assistance in Portugal, see VC Ramos and B Churro, 'Report on Portugal' in S Quattrocolo and S Ruggeri (eds), *Personal Participation in Criminal Proceedings, A Comparative Study of Participatory Safeguards and in absentia Trials in Europe* (Springer, 2019) 305, 309–17; VC Ramos, CP Abreu and JV Cordeiro, 'Confidentiality of Correspondence with Counsel as a Requirement of a Fair Trial in Portugal' in L Bachmaier Winter, SC Thaman and V Lynn (eds), *The Right to Counsel and the Protection of Attorney-Client Privilege in Criminal Proceedings* (Springer, 2020) 235.

[34] eg Mendes, 'O efeito-à-distância' (n 3) 225, citing the Judgment of the Constitutional Court no 198/2004 of 28 March 2004 (n 18), where the Court states that the reference to the guarantees of defence in Art 32, para 1 of the Constitution 'would be enough for the rights of defence to include the right to have unlawful evidence related to constitutionally relevant values excluded from the proceedings (rendered ineffective, invalid or null and void)'; Correia, 'A distinção' (n 3) 189–91.

[35] Under the heading 'prohibition of assessing evidence', Art 355 CCP states that during a trial, the court may not use evidence that was not produced or examined at the hearing, except for the use of such evidence as is included in procedural acts that may be read out, viewed or heard in court in accordance with Arts 356 and 357.

[36] Law 109/2009 of 31 August at www.pgdlisboa.pt/leis/lei_mostra_articulado.php?nid=1137&tabela=leis. There is an outdated English translation available at https://cibercrime.ministeriopublico.pt/sites/default/files/documentos/pdf/portuguesecybercrime_law.pdf.

[37] The heading of the provision is 'indirect testimony' and refers both to hearsay about the content of what another person has said and about what the content is of a document produced by another person.

that are 'procedural acts' containing witness statements. This applies, for example, if the statements were obtained by means of a letter rogatory executed abroad, or if the witness cannot appear in court due to death, supervening psychic anomaly or long-term impossibility of appearing (ie in those cases in which all attempts to locate the person have been to no avail) and the statements were made before a prosecutor or judge (see Article 356, para 1, *lit* b), 2, *lit* c) and 4 CCP). If statements were made before a police officer, such statements may only be read out and weighed in evidence if all parties agree thereto (prosecutor, accused and a victim who is acting as an 'assistant'[38]). Where the reading of a statement is prohibited, viewing a recording of such statement is also prohibited, as is hearing the interviewing police officers about the content of such statement (Article 356, para 7 and 8 CCP). And once a witness validly invokes the privilege, earlier statements may equally not be used, under Article 356, para 6 CCP.[39] The expression adopted in this realm is 'prohibition of assessing evidence', as in respect of Article 355 CCP (above). Provisions establishing testimonial privileges will give rise to exclusion of evidence if violated (ie if the witness is not informed of his rights – Article 134, para 2 CCP). But the classification of this breach is controversial, with some viewing it as a 'nullity subject to remedy', others as a 'prohibition of evidence'.[40] Articles 136 and 137 CCP establish that witnesses may not be interviewed in relation to subject matter covered by official secrecy or state secrecy. The use of evidence obtained in violation thereof is not permitted.[41] While in these cases, and in the case of professional secrecy, this prohibition extends to intercept evidence under Article 188, para 6, *lit* b) CCP,[42] the testimonial privileges (due to close familial relationships, or belonging to the organs of an accused corporate body) do not extend to intercept evidence. A breach of professional secrecy in respect of lawyers, bankers, journalists or medical doctors may be ordered, in which case the ensuing evidence may be used and weighed in the case. This does not apply to religious secrecy. State secrecy is subject to a special regime and may only be lifted upon authorisation by the Prime Minister; while in respect of crimes against state security, documents may be communicated to the competent authorities for investigation.[43] Articles 14, para 6 and 7, 15, para 6, 16, para 5 and 6 of the PT-Cybercrime Law also established rules on production orders and the search and seizure of electronic systems and data, in accordance with the rules on secrecy established in the CCP.

[38] See Ramos and Churro (n 33) 331–36 on the different roles of victims in Portuguese criminal proceedings.

[39] See, inter alia, Art 356, para 6 CCP, 'The reading of a statement made during an inquiry or instruction by a witness who has validly refused to testify during a hearing is prohibited in any case.'

[40] JS Cabral, 'Commentary to article 134' in AH Gaspar et al, *Código de Processo Penal Comentado* (Almedina, 2014) 6, with further references; Mendes (n 10) 190 (arguing this is a mere violation of a formality of the evidence classified as a curable nullity).

[41] Correia, 'A proibição' (n 3) 100, *in fine*.

[42] See Art 188, para 6, *lit* b) CCP, determining that the judge will order the elimination of recordings touching upon those matters.

[43] See Arts 32 et seq, Law 30/84 of 5 September at www.pgdlisboa.pt/leis/lei_mostra_articulado.php?nid=764&tabela=leis.

In respect of eyewitness recognition of persons (line-ups), Portuguese law establishes several formalities to gather such evidence and sanctions their violation for a 'lack of value as evidence'. This also applies to recognition of objects under Articles 147, para 7 and 149, para 3 CCP. It should be noted, however, that case law admits that such evidence is used as 'mere' witness evidence, which may be 'weighed freely' by the judge, as such evidence does not require such strict formalities as line-ups. In my opinion this is a completely flawed interpretation that is connected to a lack of understanding of the nature of the exclusionary rule established in Article 147, para 7 CCP, which is an 'intrinsic' rule, established because an eyewitness recognition made in violation of such formalities is inherently unreliable and therefore prejudicial to truth-seeking.

The Code also regulates to what extent recordings may be used. Article 167 CCP, under the heading 'Evidential value of mechanical reproductions', established that such recordings can only be weighed as evidence of the facts or things reproduced thereby if those recordings do not constitute a criminal offence.[44] This applies to photographic, cinematographic, phonographic or electronic reproductions and, in general, any mechanical reproduction. Article 167 CCP must be read in connection with Article 199 of the Criminal Code, which states that the making or use of audio or video recordings or photographs without consent is a criminal offence. The trend of recent case law has been to consider that when such private recordings are made without consent by the victim in respect of conversations that are criminal (threats, slander), they are admissible.[45] In respect of images gathered by CCTV systems, if these have been installed with a lawful purpose (protection of persons and goods, prevention of crime) and in public places, or in private domiciles by their inhabitants, courts tend to consider the evidence admissible, even if there is no authorisation from the data protection authority. Recordings of a crime being committed made by a smartphone or other device are also admitted.[46] Intercept evidence, gathering of live audio and visual conversations, or records of conversations or communications made in compliance with the provisions of the CCP, the PT-Cybercrime Law and other special laws also fall within the exception.[47] The rules on interception of communications established that the violation of the requirements and conditions imposed by Articles 187 to 189 regarding interception and access to stored communications data is subject to the sanction of 'nullification'. The regime

[44] On this topic, commenting on a series of decisions in respect of a case where there was unlawful intercept by private persons followed by lawful intercept by a private person under the control of the authorities, see AB Neves, '"Emprestai-me os vossos ouvidos" – comentário às decisões do caso Bragaparques' (2020) 11 *Anatomia do Crime* 221.

[45] Procuradoria-Geral da República, Gabinete Cibercrime, 'Nota prática 16/2020' (19 March 2020) 17–18 at https://cibercrime.ministeriopublico.pt/sites/default/files/documentos/pdf/nota_pratica_16_jurisprudencia_prova_digital.pdf.

[46] ibid 18–19.

[47] On these topics, in particular the right to images and the audio-visual recording of live conversations, see JG Caires, 'O registo de som e imagem e as escutas ambientais' in MF Palma et al (eds), *Direito da Investigação Criminal e da Prova* (Almedina, 2014) 273; JG Caires, 'O direito à imagem e a Prova' in PS Mendes and RS Pereira (eds.), *Prova Penal teórica e Prática* (Almedina, 2019) 115.

also applies to interception of electronic communications under Article 18, para 4 of the PT-Cybercrime Law. However, there are diverging views about whether this is the case for all formal requirements established in the CCP and PT-Cybercrime Law, or whether this applies only to the requirements for ordering the measure but not to the formalities, which would be a 'mere nullity', that is, one that could be cured if not argued in a timely fashion.[48] The law also establishes further rules in respect of the use and weighing of intercept evidence, namely, that it may only be used in a different case if it involved a conversation by the suspect, its proxy or the victim (with her consent) and the new case concerns an offence listed in Article 187, para 1, CCP (Article 187, para 7 CCP).

In respect of correspondence, Article 179, para 3 CCP establishes that if the judge who ordered the interception of correspondence considers it irrelevant to the case, it should be returned to the legitimate owner and may not be 'used as evidence'. The regime also applies to seizure of emails or records of similar conversations under Article 17 of the PT-Cybercrime Law.

Another relevant area is attorney–client privilege. Article 75, para 1 of the Law on the Bar (LB) states that searches, seizure, or equivalent evidence-gathering acts in practising lawyers' premises, as well as the interception of lawyers' communications by phone or email that are used in the discharge of the lawyers' functions and are registered at the Bar Association, may only be ordered by a competent judge. Searches and seizure in lawyers' premises, as well as the interception of lawyers' communications, may only be ordered in highly exceptional cases, and the CCP stipulates the requirements.[49] The search and seizure may only be ordered by a judge, and it must be conducted by the judge in person, in the presence of a representative of the local Bar (Article 177, para 5 and 180, para 1 CCP[50]). If during the search the lawyer or the Bar representative claims that privilege applies, the documents will be sealed and sent to the President of the Court of Appeal, who will decide on whether privilege applies and on whether a breach of privilege may be ordered, which will only be the case if the lawyer in question is accused and the documents themselves are the object or an element of a crime (see Article 180, para 2 CCP; Article 76, para 4 LB). These rules also apply to electronic searches and seizure, that is searches in computer systems used by practising lawyers, under Articles 15, para 6 and 16, para 5 of the PT-Cybercrime Law. Article 14, para 6 of the PT-Cybercrime Law likewise forbids production orders to obtain data from electronic systems used by practising lawyers. Seizure of correspondence between defence counsel and their clients is equally prohibited, unless the judge has substantiated grounds to believe that such correspondence is the object or an element of an offence (see Article 76 LB; Article 179, para 2 CCP). The same rules apply to stored electronic communications under Article 17 of the PT-Cybercrime

[48] Mendes (n 10) 190–91 (referring to a delay in delivering recordings of intercepted communications to the judge for judicial control as an example of a mere violation of a formality of the evidence classified as a curable nullity).

[49] For more detail on this topic, see Ramos, Abreu and Cordeiro (n 33).

[50] See also Art 75 LB.

Law. The procedure for search and seizure of electronic correspondence or stored communications is the same as for traditional correspondence.

However, the operational implementation of judicial control and control by the Bar representative faces additional hurdles, since it would have to be implemented both during the search and seizure (for the selection of the data to be seized) and (mostly) afterwards, since it is sometimes difficult to carry out proper filtering and selection of materials during the search. Interception of communications between the accused and his defence counsel, pursuant to Article 187, para 5 CCP (applicable to electronic communications via Article 18, para 4 of the PT-Cybercrime Law), is not permitted unless the judge has substantiated grounds to believe that such conversations are the object or element of an offence. The result may only be used in evidence concerning the offence of which the lawyer is suspected.[51] Do exclusionary rules attach to the violation of the provisions in respect of protection of attorney–client privilege? Generally, evidence obtained by means of an unlawful search or interception of the correspondence or communications, in particular as it amounts to the infringement of constitutional rights (privacy of the home and of communications, professional secrecy, etc) must be excluded pursuant to the rules outlined above (ie Article 32, para 8 of the Constitution and Articles 126, para 1 and 3 CCP), without prejudice to the exceptions to the exclusion of derivative evidence. As mentioned above, there is relevant commentary and case law considering that evidence obtained in breach of procedural fundamental rights, such as the right to a defence or to legal assistance, must also be excluded pursuant to those provisions. A search of lawyers' premises in violation of the rules of the CCP is sanctioned with a 'nullity' (Article 177, para 1 and 5 CCP).

Seizure in breach of legal privilege is sanctioned with a 'nullity' under Article 180, para 2 CCP. As regards the seizure of correspondence or stored electronic communications and the interception of communications between the client and the defence lawyer, the requirements established by the CCP and in the PT-Cybercrime Law concerning the use of these methods of gathering evidence, explicitly establish the 'nullity' as a sanction for their violation (eg Articles 179, para 1 and 190 CCP; Articles 17 and 18, para 4 PT-Cybercrime Law). These nullities are considered as 'prohibitions of evidence' in connection with the above-mentioned constitutional provisions and Article 126, para 1 and 3 CCP.[52] Furthermore, Article 92, para 5 of the Law on the Bar establishes a general exclusionary rule for any acts committed in violation of attorney–client privilege. Pursuant to this rule, acts undertaken by the lawyer in breach of legal privilege, that is outside of the legal possibilities for exemption or breach of the privilege, 'may not be used as evidence in court'. In any event, privilege concerning confidential correspondence between

[51] Caeiro and Costa (n 3) 556.

[52] As outlined above, there are disputes as to whether, in respect of intercept evidence, this is the case for all formal requirements established in the CCP and PT-Cybercrime Law or applies only to the requirement for ordering the measure but not to the formalities, which would be a 'mere nullity', ie one that could be cured if not argued in a timely manner.

lawyers is absolute, and such correspondence may never be used as evidence and is therefore not subject to an exemption or breach of privilege (Article 113, para 2 LB). Consequently, evidence obtained in breach of the rules regulating attorney–client privilege, as well as derivative evidence not covered by the exceptions mentioned above, will be considered null and void and must be excluded.

IV. The Legal Framework on Admissibility of Cross-Border Evidence in Portugal

A. Is Cross-Border Evidence Treated Differently in Positive Legislation?

There are no generally applicable explicit provisions in respect of exclusionary rules for evidence obtained abroad, and in principle admissibility follows the same rules as are applicable to evidence obtained in Portugal.[53] Despite the 'simplicity' of this theoretical equivalence, its operation in practice may raise some issues. In fact, since the law states that all evidence that is not prohibited 'by law' is admissible, one might ask what law is relevant when evidence is collected abroad? Does it suffice that such evidence would not be prohibited by the *lex loci*? Or does it mean that it is the prohibitions of the *lex fori* that apply? Or are both applicable?

Zooming in on Portugal's domestic law provisions, I can identify three explicit provisions related to the admissibility of cross-border evidence. First, Article 85 of Law 144/99 of 31 August, in respect of the transfer of criminal proceedings.[54] Under the heading 'Validation of the procedural steps taken abroad', the provision states (emphasis added):

> The judicial decision to the effect of continuing the foreign criminal proceedings automatically gives the same validity to the procedural steps taken abroad, as those taken before a Portuguese judicial authority, *save where such steps would be considered inadmissible under the terms of the Portuguese criminal procedure law.*

This clearly establishes the *lex fori* principle.

[53] See also P Caeiro and MJ Costa, 'Country Report Portugal' in M Böse et al (eds), *Judicial Protection in Transnational Criminal Proceedings* (Springer, 2021) 284 (referring to Art 125 CCP). In this regard, see MC Andrade, '*Bruscamente no Verão Passado*', *a reforma do Código de Processo Penal – Observações críticas sobre uma lei que poderia e devia ter sido diferente* (Coimbra Editora, 2009) 119, who argues that the Portuguese legislator should have already intervened and regulated this field explicitly.

[54] Law 144/99 of August 31 (Law on International Judicial Cooperation in Criminal Matters) at https://gddc.ministeriopublico.pt/sites/default/files/documentos/pdf/act_144_99_31_august_international_judicial_coop_criminal_matters.pdf. There is an outdated English translation available at https://gddc.ministeriopublico.pt/sites/default/files/documentos/pdf/act_144_99_31_august_international_judicial_coop_criminal_matters.pdf. The wording of Art 85 is up-to-date.

The provision seems to draw on Article 26(1) of the European Convention on the Transfer of Proceedings in Criminal Matters,[55] which in turn draws on Article 26(4) of the European Convention on the International Validity of Criminal Judgments.[56] The latter provision applies in the context of a 'trial', with the opposition of the sentenced person lodged in the requested state against a decision *in absentia*, and provides:

> Any step with a view to proceedings or a preliminary enquiry, taken in the sentencing State in accordance with its law and regulations, shall have the same validity in the requested State as if it had been taken by the authorities of that State, provided that assimilation does not give such steps a greater evidential weight than they have in the requesting State.

The former applies in the context of transfer of criminal proceedings and similarly establishes:

> Any act with a view to proceedings, taken in the requesting State in accordance with its law and regulations, shall have the same validity in the requested State as if it had been taken by the authorities of that State, provided that assimilation does not give such act a greater evidential weight than it has in the requesting State.

The explanatory report outlines that the provision means that there is an 'assimilation of steps' taken lawfully by the requesting state, but not of the 'effects which result from them'.[57] These are regulated by the requested state, as '[u]nder the rule laid down in the Convention, the effects prescribed by the foreign law are not equated with the effects of the national law'.[58] The sole limitation deriving from the Convention applies in respect of the probative effect or value of evidence: 'there will be a limit to the evidential weight in the national law: that weight cannot be greater than that in the foreign law'.[59] It is not entirely clear if the domestic provision in Article 85, para 1 of Law 144/99 of 31 August, sets more limitations than the Conventions or merely clarifies, for the Portuguese legal order, the limitation of the 'effects' of any evidence that would be inadmissible under Portuguese law.

A second example is Article 11, para 3 of Law 88/2017 of 21 August,[60] implementing the EU Directive on the European Investigation Order in criminal matters:[61]

> The EIO shall indicate, where appropriate, the particular formalities and procedures required in obtaining or producing the evidence, in accordance with and by reference to

[55] European Convention on the Transfer of Proceedings in Criminal Matters of 15 May 1972, ETS 073 at www.coe.int/en/web/conventions/full-list?module=treaty-detail&treatynum=073.

[56] European Convention on the International Validity of Criminal Judgments of 28 May 1970, ETS 070 at www.coe.int/en/web/conventions/full-list?module=signatures-by-treaty&treatynum=070.

[57] Explanatory report to the European Convention on the Transfer of Proceedings in Criminal Matters (n 55) Art 26 at https://rm.coe.int/16800c9312.

[58] Ibid Art 26.

[59] Ibid Art 26.

[60] Law 88/2017 of 21 August, Approving the legal framework for issuing, transmitting, recognising and enforcing European investigation orders in criminal matters, transposing Directive 2014/41/EU of the European Parliament and of the Council of 3 April 2014 and repealing Law no. 25/2009 of 5 June, at www.pgdlisboa.pt/leis/lei_mostra_articulado.php?nid=2754&tabela=leis&nversao=&so_miolo.

[61] Directive 2014/41/EU of the European Parliament and of the Council of 3 April 2014 regarding the European Investigation Order in criminal matters [2014] OJ L130/1 ('EIO Directive').

the applicable legal provisions, and shall request compliance with them by the executing authority, in order to ensure the validity and effectiveness of the evidence.

The Directive provides the issuing authority with the possibility to request the executing authority to comply with certain formalities and procedures (eg requesting the presence of a lawyer during questioning or other evidence-gathering measures). Article 9(2) of the EIO Directive states that Member States' authorities should comply with these unless otherwise provided in the Directive and provided that such formalities are not contrary to the fundamental principles of their domestic law. This establishes the possibility of applying the *lex fori* in the executing Member State. As I see it, the purpose of this provision is to guarantee the rights of the defence and thereby the admissibility of evidence, which would mean that the use of the provision by Member States' authorities would be mandatory whenever – but also only if – it is necessary for the respect of the rights of the defence and admissibility of evidence.[62]

On this point, the Portuguese rule implementing transposition in Article 11, para 3 of Law 88/2017 of 21 August, is clear: this possibility corresponds to a binding power that must be used whenever such formalities concern fundamental rights and rights of defence and, as such, are a pre-condition for the admissibility of the evidence. The expression 'where appropriate' in Article 11, para 3 should therefore be interpreted as meaning 'when the law imposes the formality to respect the rights of defence or validity of evidence', which is confirmed by the very wording of our transposition law, which states in the final part of that provision that such a request aims at 'ensuring the validity and effectiveness of the evidence'. Otherwise, the evidence in question cannot be used.[63] This means that, once again, Portuguese law clearly establishes the *lex fori* principle.[64]

[62] In this sense, see F Zimmermann, 'Die Europäische Ermittlungsanordnung: Schreckgespenst oder Zukunftsmodell für grenzüberschreitende Strafverfahren?' (2015) 127 *Zeitschrift für die gesamte Strafrechtswissenschaft* 143, 151, arguing that in the transposition in Germany, an express rule should be enshrined to the effect that it is mandatory to indicate those formalities lack of compliance with which may be sanctioned with a prohibition of valuation of evidence. However, the literal wording of the Directive leaves the gathering of evidence according to the principle of *forum regit actum* to the discretion of the issuing authorities, as pointed out by B Schünemann, 'The European Investigation Order: A Rush into the Wrong Direction' in S Ruggeri (ed), *Transnational Evidence and Multicultural Inquiries in Europe* (Springer, 2014) 29, 32. Member States' authorities may decide for tactical reasons to use or not use such a faculty in order to benefit in a concrete case from the most permissive measures, diminishing the rights of the individual concerned. In the same sense, R Belfiore, 'The European Investigation Order in Criminal Matters: Developments in Evidence-gathering across the EU' (2015) 5 *European Criminal Law Review* 312, 322; S Ruggeri, 'Introduction to the Proposal of a European Investigation Order: Due Process Concerns and Open Issues' in S Ruggeri (ed), *Transnational Evidence and Multicultural Inquiries in Europe* (Springer, 2014) 3, 16.

[63] In this sense see Caeiro and Costa (n 3) 576–77, stating in fn 175 that when obtaining evidence from another Member States' authorities, it is advisable to request them to respect the conditions set out in Portuguese law because, in the absence of such authorisation, the evidence gathered is null and void – eg, according to Article 34, para 2, of the Constitution only a judicial authority may order a house search.

[64] In the same sense, Caeiro and Costa (n 53) 290, stating that the evidence 'can only be used if it is valid in light of Portuguese law' (namely, if it would have been possible to gather it in accordance with national criminal procedure). Though the authors do not state that requiring the formalities is mandatory, but only 'sensible'.

A third example from the CCP is relevant. As outlined previously, live witnesses (including victims) should normally give live testimony, but their previous statements may also be used at a criminal trial in some cases. One of those cases is where cross-border procedures have been used in order to obtain such statements: 'if the statements have been obtained through legally permitted rogatory letter' (Article 356.2, *lit* c) CCP). Does this provision establish a principle of *lex loci*? There is some case law on point, which will be outlined in section IV.B.

Article 6 CCP establishes the applicability of Portuguese procedural law to the Portuguese territory, stating that it is only applicable in foreign territory under the limits established in international law. At first sight, it could appear that this rule points in the direction of the *lex loci* principle to determine whether evidence gathered abroad should be excluded. However, this is not the case. The problem of exclusion of evidence is a problem that will be dealt with by the Portuguese authorities as *forum* authorities, and thus they are bound to apply Portuguese law to that end. From another viewpoint, this rule is more related to the *jurisdiction to adjudicate* and to *enforce* (or 'competence'), and thus establishes the territorial limits for procedural action.[65]

Looking at the above-mentioned provisions, it does indeed seem that Portuguese law follows the *lex fori* principle.[66] However, how this principle operates, namely whether it is a principle of strict compliance or of equivalence, is not clear just from reading the above-mentioned provisions. Therefore, let us take a closer look at the case law in section IV.B.

B. Case Law Examples on Exclusionary Rules in Respect of Evidence Obtained Abroad

To gain a better overview of the treatment of cross-border evidence in practice, we should investigate how the issue arises and has been dealt with by the courts. I will refer to judgments handed down by Portuguese courts, including here decisions concerning evidence obtained in EU Member States but also in other jurisdictions.

The first area in which there is some notable case law is that of *witness testimony obtained abroad*. In a 1996 case, the question arose whether the failure of the defendants to attend in person the questioning of witnesses (with confrontation) in Spain at the trial hearing stage, as requested by the Portuguese court to the Spanish authorities, violated the right to adversarial proceedings enshrined in

[65] See Judgment of the Supreme Court of Justice of 5 July 2012, case 911/10.5TBOLH.E1.S1, Rapporteur Santos Carvalho, discussed below, text preceding fn 118.

[66] Caeiro and Costa (n 53) 284–85 (stating that evidence obtained abroad by foreign authorities by means unlawful or improper under Portuguese law will be excluded unless a treaty or international convention provides a legitimate basis for evidence to be obtained under foreign law, but admitting that there are a few 'exceptions to the exception' since such norms cannot supersede the constitutional exclusionary rule).

Article 32 of the Constitution and Article 327 CCP.[67] The statements in question had been taken in Spain, in the presence of the Court, Public Prosecutor's Office and defence lawyers from the Portuguese case, and the defendants had not participated. The questions to be put to the witnesses had been previously determined at a hearing in Portugal. The statements taken in Spain were subsequently read out at the hearing, where the defendants were able to exercise their right to comment on and to challenge that evidence. The Supreme Court of Justice (SCJ) stated that the possibility for the accused to appear in actions to be carried out in foreign territory is limited because 'the sovereignty [of the foreign state] can only be limited if the corresponding legal systems consent, by treaty or convention or on grounds of international cooperation based on reciprocity'. In the case at hand, although this possibility was provided for in the 1959 European Convention on Mutual Assistance in Criminal Matters,[68] the defendants had not requested their presence beforehand. The Court therefore considered that there had been no breach of the adversarial principle, either as provided for in domestic law or in the European Convention on Human Rights (ECHR), Article 6(3)(c) and (d), with particular emphasis on the facts that: (i) the defendants had phrased the questions to be put to the witnesses;[69] (ii) the defendants' lawyers had been present at the proceedings; (iii) even in domestic law, the right to be present was not absolute. In this case, the SCJ applied the Portuguese and international law in force in order to decide on the issue of the admissibility of the evidence obtained abroad with the participation of the Portuguese authorities. But, *in fine*, it determined that the formalities of the proceedings were governed by the *lex loci* (Spanish law), as determined by the applicable Mutual Assistance Convention, and stated that this law determined, amongst other things, whether witnesses testified under oath or not. The SCJ also decided that there was no prohibition on reading the letter rogatory at a trial hearing and that, on the contrary, such a reading was conducive to a better adversarial process.

Although the wording of Article 356, para 2, *lit* c) CCP in force at the time only referred to statements obtained by domestic letters rogatory, the SCJ held that international letters rogatory were types of communication, akin to the domestic ones, used when the act took place outside the judicial district of the trial court within Portugal. Since questioning by international letters rogatory was permitted and even, *in casu*, recommended under the terms of the provisions of the CCP then in force – Articles 318, 229 and 230 CCP – the Court concluded that the reading of international rogatory letters should be permitted under the terms of Article 358, para 1, lit *a*), in conjunction with Article 318 CCP.

[67] Judgment of the Supreme Court of Justice of 7 October 1996, case 048675, Rapporteur Lopes Rocha at www.dgsi.pt, paras V and VII.

[68] European Convention on Mutual Assistance in Criminal Matters of 20 April 1959, ETS 30 at https://rm.coe.int/16800656ce.

[69] It is not clear from the judgment whether the defendants personally phrased the questions, or whether such questions were phrased by their lawyers in the presence of the defendants.

The reading of letters rogatory in court, sent at the trial stage, was also the subject of decisions by the Oporto[70] and Coimbra[71] Courts of Appeal. Both considered it unnecessary to read them during the trial hearing since, once they were added to the case files, they had the nature of a document, the reading of which was permitted under the terms of Article 356, para 2, *lit* c) CCP but not mandatory, and which was therefore admissible evidence under the terms of Article 355, para 2 CC.

On the other hand, the Guimarães Court of Appeal ruled that witness evidence included in a letter rogatory sent out at the trial stage could not be weighed in the judgment since it had not been read and examined in open court.[72] The Court examined whether the interview by letter rogatory was admissible, concluding in the affirmative, since the witnesses called by both accused and the victim lived abroad. Applying Portuguese law, namely Articles 355 and 356, para 2, *lit* c) CCP, it ruled that since those letters rogatory included testimonies, these could not be used unless they had been read in court and subject to comment by the defence. The Court stated that the conviction had been based, even if not primarily or essentially, at least also on the said testimonies. And that 'the consequence of the violation of the principle of immediacy and its regime contained in Articles 355 to 357 CCP, consists fundamentally in the non-usability of the evidence affected thereby, which, therefore, cannot be invoked or be valid for the effect of forming the belief of the court'.[73] Thus, an exclusionary rule applied, and since the Court could not expunge or autonomously consider the evidence without taking the testimonies into account, it quashed the decision and remanded the case for a new decision by the first-instance court. Interestingly, the judgment includes *obiter dictum* to the effect that since the letter rogatory had been issued at the trial stage, it had to comply with the formalities of Portuguese law for the trial hearing (just like domestic letters rogatory); a matter that was not ruled on since the court excluded the use of the evidence.[74]

A decision of the Oporto Court of Appeal, concerning a letter rogatory sent to Germany, also ruled that the formalities provided for in Portuguese law applied to the act pursuant a letter rogatory issued at the trial stage, and that, in the instant case, these formalities had been complied with.[75] The Court applied the *lex fori*

[70] Judgment of the Porto Court of Appeal of 19 September 2007, case 0712685, Rapporteur António Eleutério at www.dgsi.pt.

[71] Judgment of the Coimbra Court of Appeal of 6 July 2011, case 2157/04.2PCCBR.C1, Rapporteur José Eduardo Martins at www.dgsi.pt.

[72] Judgment of the Guimarães Court of Appeal of 15 December 2016, case 376/11.4TACHV.G1, Rapporteur Ausenda Gonçalves at www.dgsi.pt.

[73] Judgment of the Guimarães Court of Appeal of 15 December 2016, case 376/11.4TACHV.G1, Rapporteur Ausenda Gonçalves at http:///www.dgsi.pt.

[74] The defence had argued that the statements in the international rogatory letters could not be used because the victim had waived her request to have testimony of the relevant witnesses heard in court, and because those witness statements had been gathered without the assistance of the defence counsel and therefore without being subject to cross-examination.

[75] The defendant had claimed that photographic recognition had been carried out in violation of Art 147 CCP, but the Court held that such formalities were not applicable to recognition in a hearing and that, furthermore, what the court had valued was the testimony of the people heard.

here, both on the question of obtaining evidence and on the question of whether evidence should be allowed to be weighed. The Évora Court of Appeals, in another judgment, decided that the reading in the trial of statements made by the victim in the pre-trial stage before the Public Prosecutor (without the participation of the defence) would not be permitted under Articles 355 and 356.2, *lit* c) CCP, until after the courts had sought to exhaust the possibilities to hear the witness in person, by video or by means of a letter rogatory, in particular in a case where the address abroad was known to the court, the crimes and sentences applicable were serious, and the witness evidence was the sole basis of the conviction, as this would violate the primacy of immediacy and the right to confrontation established in Portuguese domestic law.[76]

Lastly, the Oporto Court of Appeals ruled that the interrogation records of an accused given before the Spanish authorities pursuant to a letter rogatory could not be read as a witness statement under the afore-mentioned provisions in case he did not appear, even if he was no longer an accused at the time of the trial, since they had been taken in a different framework and not subject to cross-examination.[77]

In another decision, the Oporto Court of Appeal examined the reading of letters rogatory containing statements collected for future reference.[78] In this case, the Court concluded that the procedure followed in Spain upon the request by the Portuguese authorities had not complied with the adversarial principle and therefore violated Article 271, para 1 and 2 CCP and Article 32, para 5 of the Constitution, since the accused had not even been informed that such acts would be taking place. The Court concluded that the *lex fori* would apply to the completion of that act. The Court further concluded, also applying the *lex fori*, that the evidence in the letters rogatory could not be taken into account because it had not been read out in the hearing, which violated, *in casu*, the adversarial principle and Articles 327, 355, 348 and 360 CCP (on this point, the decision seems to contradict the above-mentioned decisions, although in this case the letters rogatory were not issued for the taking of testimony during the trial stage).

Finally, there is an interesting decision by the Lisbon Court of Appeal excluding witness evidence obtained by French authorities pursuant to letters rogatory sent to Morocco, in the course of an investigation not directed against the person accused in Portugal, and then sent by France to Portugal on the basis of 'spontaneous exchange of information' (following coordination meetings and 'agreements' made in EUROJUST coordination meetings).[79] The Court of Appeals of Lisbon stated that spontaneous exchange of information was admissible, but that in this case it was not 'information' or 'documentary evidence' but rather witness

[76] Judgment of the Évora Court of Appeal of 6 November 2021, case 2592/08.7PAPTM.E1, Rapporteur Sérgio Corvacho at www.dgsi.pt.

[77] Judgment of the Oporto Court of Appeal of 23 March 2013, case 423/10.7TABGC.P1, Rapporteur Neto de Moura at www.dgsi.pt.

[78] Judgment of the Oporto Court of Appeal of 22 March 2006, case 0544312, Rapporteur António Gama at www.dgsi.pt.

[79] Judgment of the Lisbon Court of Appeal of 27 November 2018, case 78/15.2JBLSB.L1-5, Rapporteur Simões de Carvalho at www.dgsi.pt.

testimony that could only be obtained by a letter rogatory. The Court affirmed the first-instance decision, which had based its ruling on the rights of the defence, namely the right to examine and cross-examine witnesses.

A second area in which there is case law of interest is the *seizure of correspondence*. The Coimbra Court of Appeal ruled on seizure of correspondence.[80] In casu, it concerned a search in compliance with a letter rogatory issued by the Portuguese authorities and executed in Guinea-Bissau, in which a seized safe was opened. The search was requested by the Public Prosecutor's Office and authorised by the Portuguese Criminal Investigation Judge, the latter being the competent authority for the decision. As for its execution, the search was executed by the competent Guinea-Bissau authorities, in accordance with Guinea-Bissau law. The safe seized was only later opened, the accused having provided the code to do so. The accused claimed that this was a prohibited method of evidence, due to intrusion into correspondence and/or private life. However, the court found that the intrusion into private life was duly authorised by a judge and that there was no question of secrecy of correspondence or telecommunications, since the safe in question was in the possession of the accused. The court therefore considered that the actions in question were valid under Portuguese law, *lex fori*, and that no exclusionary rule would apply. Seemingly, the violation of the *lex loci* was not invoked. The forgery of the record of the act of seizure had also been invoked, which the court found not to be verified. The Court did consider the possibility of this being an irregularity under Portuguese criminal procedural law, which it also found not to be verified, meaning that it did control whether there had been a violation of the *lex fori*. Even so, the Court stated that this issue would always be governed by *lex loci*.

There is another relevant decision of the Lisbon Court of Appeal, where Portugal was a requested state.[81] Read in the reverse situation, it would mean that the *lex fori* would apply to the issues on admissibility in matters of seizure of correspondence, leaving the *lex loci* a limited formal role. The Lisbon Court of Appeal decided that the Portuguese judge, when ordering the execution of a letter rogatory received in Portugal from Germany requesting the seizure of correspondence, only had to verify compliance with the 'formal legality' of the seizure, that is: (i) whether it was permitted for the type of offence in question (punishable by a prison sentence of more than three years); (ii) whether the recipients were included in the catalogue provided for in the CCP (correspondence sent by or addressed to the suspect); (iii) whether the seizure took place at permitted times (between 7am and 9pm).

According to this judgment, only the court of the requesting state could assess issues concerning 'the content of the seizure, whether or not it offends, inter alia, professional secrecy, or whether or not it is relevant as evidence'. In other words,

[80] Judgment of the Coimbra Court of Appeal of 2 March 2005, case 3756/04, Rapporteur Belmiro Andrade at www.dgsi.pt.

[81] Judgment of the Lisbon Court of Appeal 25 November 1998, case 0061363, Rapporteur Santos Carvalho, www.dgsi.pt.

the *lex loci* would apply only to formal requirements concerning the possibility of carrying out the seizure, but not to the control of the possibility of using the seized documentation, which would be governed by the *lex fori*. In my opinion, this decision is not in line with the Portuguese domestic law, as is made clear in Article 11 of Law 144/99 of 31 August (under the heading 'Protection of confidentiality') and the substantive provisions on the protection of secrecy. Article 11 provides:

> 1 – In implementing a request for international cooperation submitted to Portugal, the provisions of the Code of Criminal Procedure and supplementary legislation concerning grounds of refusal to testify, seizure of property, telephone tapping, professional or State secrets, or any other cases in which confidentiality is protected, shall apply.
>
> 2 – The provisions of the preceding paragraph shall apply to any information that according to the request, ought to be given by persons not involved in the foreign criminal proceedings.

Equally, the protection of attorney–client privilege and the corresponding exclusionary rules also apply in the context of cross-border cases, as they constitute a ground for non-recognition or non-execution of a European Investigation Order (EIO).[82]

In my opinion, this ground of non-execution, in what concerns the legal privilege, must be considered as a mandatory ground for refusal in all instances in which our law prohibits searches for or seizure or interception of communications between lawyers and their clients. This position is also in line with further case law of the Courts of Appeal, such as the Évora Court of Appeals, which ruled on the breach of secrecy according to Portuguese law and procedure, in respect of a practising lawyer whose testimony was sought by an incoming letter rogatory issued by the Dutch authorities in a case of drug trafficking and money laundering.[83] The Lisbon Court of Appeal also ruled on the breach of secrecy according to Portuguese law and procedure, in respect of the Market and Securities Commission (CMVM) and a request by means of an EIO issued by Polish authorities to obtain documents resulting from inspections by the said authority, in a case of aggravated general fraud and computer fraud.[84]

[82] Art 11, para 1, *lit.* a), EIO Directive (n 62); Art 22, para 1, *lit* b) Law 88/2017, of 12 August (n 61).

[83] Judgment of the Évora Court of Appeal 6 June 2017, case 615/16.5 T9LLE-A.E1, Rapporteur Maria Leonor Botelho at www.dgsi.pt.

[84] Judgment of the Lisbon Court of Appeal 7 February 2019, case 7078/18.9T9LSB-A.L1-9, Rapporteur Guilhermina Freitas at www.dgsi.pt. The Commission lodged an appeal to the Supreme Court of Justice, which ruled that such appeal was inadmissible – Judgment of the Supreme Court of Justice of 31 October 2019, case 7078/18.9T9LSB-A.L1-S1, Rapporteur Nuno Gomes da Silva at www.dgsi.pt. In the same line, in a civil case, the Lisbon Court of Appeal ruled that in respect of the testimony of an Italian lawyer practising in Italy, the rules on secrecy that applied were not those of Portuguese law but were established in Italian law, which the Court then applied. It should be noted that this was not a case of cross-border gathering of evidence, in the sense that it appears that the said lawyer came 'freely' to the trial hearing in Portugal. Had there been a letter rogatory to Italy, it would be clear that Italian law on privilege could be invoked to refuse cooperation – Judgment of the Lisbon Court of Appeal of 19 April 2012, case 20/2001.L1-2, Rapporteur Sousa Pinto at www.dgsi.pt.

A third problematic area is that of *intercept evidence*.[85] The Lisbon Court of Appeals made incidental reference, in an action for damages against the Portuguese state, to a decision of the 4th Criminal Court of Lisbon, confirmed by the Supreme Court of Justice, concerning the validity of intercepted telephone communications in Brazil.[86] This case involved intercept evidence ordered in a case being conducted in Brazil, with precedence of a court order and supposedly in compliance with Brazilian law (which the Court found to be *similar* to Portuguese law). In the Portuguese files, however, there was no record of the court order authorising the interception, and the precise prerequisites, the formalities and the conditions for ordering the interceptions in the Brazilian case, were not known.

The Portuguese Court held that both the Brazilian law and the Portuguese constitutional and procedural criminal principles were applicable (ie Articles 32, para 8 and 34, para 4 of the Constitution, and Articles 125, 126, 187–189 CCP). In the absence of evidence concerning the authorisation and conditions of admissibility of the interceptions, the Court concluded that it could not assess their admissibility and that, as this was an exceptional means of obtaining evidence, it could not benefit from a presumption of lawfulness, so that the evidence thus obtained could not be used. The Court also considered that the interceptions had been carried out without any *ex post* court control in Portugal (and it was not known whether such a control had been carried out in Brazil), in violation of Article 188 CCP. In this decision, the Court applies the *lex fori* but does not seem to exclude verification of compliance with it through compliance with the *lex loci* of equivalent content – which it concluded had not been the case due to lack of evidence that would permit such an analysis to be conducted.

A fourth topic refers to the *use of foreign criminal convictions*. In this respect, the Évora Court of Appeals applied the principle of mutual recognition to assess whether a criminal record of a French criminal conviction could be considered as an aggravating factor in sentencing.[87] One could say that this decision applied the *lex loci* by stating that, under the said principle, Portugal had to respect the

[85] I also found two cases on international controlled deliveries, in which an exclusionary rule, due to the use of an *agent provocateur*, in violation of Art 32, para 8 and Art 126, para 1 and 2, *lit* a) CCP, was argued and decided – Judgment of the Lisbon Court of Appeal of 21 September 2022, case 108/21.9JELSB.L1-3, Rapporteur Ana Paula Grandvaux at www.dgsi.pt; Judgment of the Porto Court of Appeal of 26 May 2015, case 191/14.3JELSB, Rapporteur Maria dos Prazeres Silva, www.dgsi.pt. The rulings decide on the lawfulness of the controlled delivery under Portuguese law (in this case the *lex fori*), without referring to whether they were also lawful in the state that requested the controlled delivery to Portugal (Spain and UK, respectively). It seems that, on one hand, that issue was not raised; on the other hand, the courts seem to assume that the requests were lawful. These cases could also be considered different in the sense that the evidence was gathered by the Portuguese authorities (when they seized the drugs), which then also opened and prosecuted the offence, which is slightly different from evidence gathered abroad and sent to Portugal. In any event, these judgments seem to follow the line of applying the *lex fori* to assess whether evidence was unlawfully gathered and has to be excluded.

[86] Judgment of the Lisbon Court of Appeal of 4 June 2009, case 1176/03.0TCSNT.L1-8, Rapporteur Ana Luísa Geraldes at www.dgsi.pt.

[87] Judgment of the Évora Court of Appeal of 22 November 2022, case 226/22.6GBTNV.E1, Rapporteur João Gomes de Sousa at www.dgsi.pt.

French court's decision and its consequences, namely in respect of the deadline to cancel the records of criminal convictions. The Court also noted that the ECRI Framework Decision[88] permitted the exchange of criminal records, as long as under French law the conviction decision recorded in the French criminal records had a criminal nature (as opposed to being merely an administrative offence) and had been transmitted according to the Framework Decision. As this was the case, the Court affirmed the decision to use the previous French conviction as evidence of a previous conviction, since under French law the records of such conviction were still in force.

Finally, the courts have also ruled on *violations of international law*. A first case concerned the violation of the 'specialty principle'. A decision of the Lisbon Court of Appeal dealt with the consequences of the Portuguese state's violation of conventional obligations or principles of international law: the principle of specialty established in Article 2 of the European Convention on Assistance in Criminal Matters[89] and the reservation made by the Swiss Confederation to that provision.[90] The defendant argued that evidence consisting of banking documentation was inadmissible.

The Court held that there was no violation of the specialty principle, and that even if such a violation existed, it would not give rise to an exclusionary rule, since exclusionary rules are linked to the violation of fundamental rights, and this was not the case as regards the 'mere failure to verify a condition for the use of documents for a single crime within a case covering several others'. Quoting Andrade, the Court stated that exclusionary rules only applied to 'violations that cause the same social damage of affront to human dignity, to freedom of decision or will or to the physical or moral integrity of persons', or possibly violation of other values or interests that would have to have a dignity that the Court considered not to be verified in this case (having, moreover, considered that there was no issue of violation of privacy or intimacy).[91]

A second case concerned the interviewing of a witness abroad using Skype instead of a letter rogatory requesting for interviewing conducted by the requested authorities or for a videoconference. The defence argued that a letter rogatory was mandatory pursuant to the MLA Convention between China and Portugal,[92] since otherwise it would be possible to bypass the application of the grounds of refusal

[88] Council Framework Decision 2009/315/JHA of 26 February 2009 on the organisation and content of the exchange of information extracted from the criminal record between Member States [2009] OJ L93/23 (ECRI Framework Decision).

[89] European Convention on Mutual Assistance in Criminal Matters of 20 April 1959, ETS 30 at https://rm.coe.int/16800656ce.

[90] Judgment of the Lisbon Court of Appeal of 13 July 2010, case 712/00.9JFLSB.L1-5, Rapporteur Carlos Espírito Santo at www.dgsi.pt.

[91] Andrade, *Sobre as proibições de prova* (n 3) 209.

[92] Agreement between the Government of the Portuguese Republic and the People's Republic of China on Mutual Legal Assistance in Criminal Matters, of 9 December 2005 at https://gddc.ministeriopublico.pt/instrumento/acordo-entre-republica-portuguesa-e-republica-popular-da-china-sobre-auxilio-judiciario.

contained in that Convention, and in addition because there would be no authority from the requested state attending the videoconferencing, which would mean that there was no surety that the testimony was transparent and that the witness had not been constrained somehow or was reading his answers from a paper, or in extreme cases, would have violated state secrecy.[93]

The Court considered there was no violation of the Convention since this instrument established a means for cooperation but did not exclude other 'alternative means', that is, those permitted by the CCP in Article 318, para 8 and 319, which made provision for hearing witnesses in their domicile in special cases when they could not attend on reasonable grounds, and also permitting the hearing of such witnesses from abroad by video from their residence. Furthermore, in casu, there was no reason to believe that the testimony had not been free from constraints and reliable. I believe this decision is flawed for the reasons argued by the defence, but also because under international law this would constitute the practice of an act of *ius imperii* in the territory of another Member State, resulting in the violation of the principle of non-interference and sovereignty of the state where the witness was located. It may also result in the violation of the rights of the witness (who may have a right to refuse testimony in the state in which he or she is located but is not informed about it or given a chance to invoke it) and of the accused (in case he or she is not able to properly test the free and spontaneous character of the testimony, or to assert other grounds, which, under the requested state law, could have led to a refusal of cooperation, eg, *ne bis in idem*).

It is true that it should be easier to hear witnesses by such means, but if states want to accept that, then they will have to agree upon it in international instruments (as they do for service of documents allowing direct service in some cases). And it would also be necessary to establish proper safeguards to protect the rights of the witness and the accused, and possibly special rules in respect of the evidential value or corroboration of such testimony.

C. Conclusions on Portuguese Law on Exclusion of Evidence Gathered Abroad

Looking at the Portuguese case law, there is not a clearly stated and uniform decision-making criterion in respect of exclusionary rules for evidence obtained abroad. As outlined above, it seems, however, that a principle of admissibility under the law of the forum (*lex fori*) applies. In some cases, courts also refer to the *lex loci*. However, consequences do not always seem to be drawn from reference to the *lex loci* – reference is made to its applicability, but compliance with *lex loci* is not assessed (sometimes for lack of elements or of a challenge by the defendant, sometimes it is simply not analysed). Alternatively, reference is made

[93] Judgment of the Lisbon Court of Appeal of 8 October 2019, case 920/17.3S6LSB.L1-5, Rapporteur Agostinho Torres at www.dgsi.pt.

to the applicability of the *lex loci* but linking it to the enforcement of the *lex fori*. It does seem that in some cases, however, such as professional privileges, the *lex loci* would be the applicable criterion.

In respect of interference with privacy, though, it seems that most case law follows the *lex fori* in the sense that the substantive requirements of Portuguese law must be complied with (substantive prerequisites and equivalent formalities). There seems to be a tendency, on the other hand, to consider that compliance with the *lex fori* is assessed based on respect for certain standards or principles in a more flexible or 'fuzzy' way, using a kind of 'substantial equivalence', and not based on respect for precise rules with a criterion of 'strict compliance' or strict legality. As referred to in section IV.A, Article 11, para 3 of Law 88/2017 of 21 August (implementing Directive 2014/14/EU in Portugal) supports the *lex fori* principle. So does Article 85 of Law 144/99 of 31 August. However, the fact that, when executing EIOs or letters rogatory, Portuguese law will also apply and may lead to a refusal to gather evidence (or an exclusionary rule in relation to evidence obtained in violation of Portuguese law), and that an appeal may be lodged against decisions of the Portuguese authorities, acting in their capacity as executing authority, to challenge 'judicial decisions concerning the formalities and procedures of execution of the investigative measure' requested by the issuing authority (under Article 45, para 4 of Law 88/2017 of 21 August), in my view also supports a recognition of the significance of the *lex loci*.

My position in respect of our domestic law is as follows. Under our domestic constitutional law, we should apply national (extrinsic) exclusionary rules to cross-border evidence, including that obtained through an EIO (or a letter rogatory), in accordance with the following fundamental principles:[94] (i) only evidence that would be admissible in Portugal may be requested from another country (*prohibition of circumventing the law*); (ii) in every outgoing request or order, compliance with formalities essential to the validity and admissibility of the evidence must be requested;[95] (iii) evidence obtained upon request or spontaneously may only be used if it does not contradict exclusionary rules of evidence (or 'prohibitions of evidence') of a 'constitutional nature' as established in the Portuguese legal system,[96] in the country where evidence has been gathered[97] or at 'supranational' level (*no evidence laundering* and *assimilation of protection of constitutional interests*).

[94] I first expressed this opinion (which is product of the development of my unfinished research) orally in presentations disseminated online, and then published as VC Ramos, 'Meios processuais de impugnação da decisão europeia de investigação – subsídios para a interpretação do artigo 14.º da Directiva com uma perspectiva portuguesa' (2018) 7 *Anatomia do Crime* 113, 166–69.

[95] For example, formalities regarding the formal declaration of a person as accused, information about rights of refusal to testify, judicial intervention for interception of communications, participation rights of the subjects of the proceedings, etc. In the same sense, see Caeiro and Costa (n 53) 290, stating that the evidence 'can only be used if it is valid in light of Portuguese law' (namely, if it would have been possible to gather it in accordance with national criminal procedure). Nevertheless, the authors do not state that requiring the formalities is mandatory but only 'sensible'.

[96] In this sense, see also Caeiro and Costa (n 3) 576–77; and Caeiro and Costa (n 53) 284–85, 290, 316.

[97] Caeiro and Costa (n 53) 310, 315, 316 also agree with me that in the event that Portugal requested cooperation from another country to gather evidence, and it is then established that such cooperation

In some cases, the application of the last criterion will not pose any major difficulties, but difficulties may be unavoidable in those cases where our constitutional prohibition is relative. That is, where the Constitution itself allows restrictions on fundamental rights 'in accordance with the law', since in this case the question will have to be asked whether the existing legislative authorisation in the executing state (or simply the *lex loci* state that transmitted the evidence spontaneously or upon a request for transfer of criminal proceedings) is sufficient, provided the evidence is gathered in accordance with the respective legal requirements, or whether the normative criterion defined by our ordinary legislator still prevails (a paradigmatic case is that of the recording of conversations or images).

This is increasingly relevant in a time where the space or territory of the location of the evidence is not always clearly defined or is seen as a composite reality where multiple laws apply. I also believe that the judgment of constitutional conformity with the norms of our legal system should not be one of *strict compliance* but of *substantial correspondence*. However, as far as privacy intrusion is concerned, it will always be necessary to consider the fundamental rules on which citizens may base their expectations of protection, particularly since there is a lack of harmonisation in EU law on the requirements for such intrusions.

The rationale behind the exclusionary rules in Article 126 CCP is specifically to safeguard fundamental rights, particularly those set out in Article 32, para 8 of the Constitution.[98] In the Portuguese legal system, it seems uncontroversial that the exclusionary rules laid down in this provision are part of the right to a fair trial and the guarantees of defence enshrined in Articles 20, para 4 and 32, para 1 of the Constitution. These include not only substantive fundamental rights, but also, in the part referring to personal integrity, procedural fundamental rights.[99] The *supranational* exclusionary rules established by the ECHR[100] – which the CJEU seems to follow[101] – were established on the basis of violations of rights equivalent to fundamental rights protected in the Portuguese Constitution (while there is a striking difference in respect of the treatment of evidence obtained by means of a breach of privacy).

should not have been granted, the evidence should not be used. In the EU context, the authors state that the decision declaring the evidence to be unlawful should also be *recognised* under the principle of mutual recognition. However, they underline that this is a position *de jure condendo*. Interestingly, a judgment of the Supreme Court of Justice of 3 April 2013, case 157/05.4JELSB-N.S1 at www.dgsi.pt, rejected an extraordinary appeal to review a conviction based upon a Spanish decision declaring intercept evidence unlawful in Spain, arguing that the latter could have no effect in Portugal unless subject to *review and confirmation proceedings* to grant it an *exequatur*. The Court also stated that the Spanish decision (an acquittal based on the unlawfully gathered evidence) had been proffered under Spanish law, and in the Portuguese case the courts had already ruled on and rejected the argument that the intercept evidence was unlawful and that, in any event, other evidence sustained the conviction.

[98] In this sense, see the literature cited in n 3.

[99] Mendes, 'O efeito-à-distância' (n 33); Correia, 'A distinção' (n 3).

[100] See VC Ramos, 'Novos problemas em matéria de proibições de prova: a dimensão internacional: regras de exclusão da prova obtida em violação da Convenção Europeia de Direitos Humanos na jurisprudência do Tribunal Europeu de Direitos Humanos' in J de Faria Costa et al, *Estudos em Homenagem ao Prof Doutor Manuel da Costa Andrade*, vol II (Instituto Jurídico, FDUC, 2017) 739, 742–68; Ramos (n 90) 159–61; K Ligeti, B Garamvölgyi and M von Galen, 'Admissibility of Evidence in Criminal Proceedings in the EU' (2020) 3 *eucrim* 201, 205.

[101] Ramos (n 94) 160–61; Ligeti, Garamvölgyi and von Galen (n 96) 205.

Taking into account the understanding that, in light of the Constitution – as seems to me most appropriate – Article 32, para 8 enshrines a right inherent to a fair trial, preventing the use of evidence obtained in violation of fundamental rights, I believe that it makes sense that, in all cases of violation of an ECHR or EU Charter right equivalent to those referred to in Article 32, para 8, the domestic law remedies provided for in the law and in the Constitution (ie the exclusion of evidence) should apply. Furthermore, it would not make sense to distinguish the consequence according to whether the protection of the equivalent fundamental rights violated derives from the Constitution, on one hand, or the ECHR or the Charter, on the other hand, since Article 32, para 8 itself makes no such distinction.[102] The same reasoning applies in the context of the Charter and the EIO Directive, and is particularly called for under the principle of *equivalence* with respect to the Charter's right to an effective remedy.

This reasoning may be taken even further, in the horizontal context within the EU, as I have proposed. Considering that the EU Member States, in other matters, are bound to the principle of assimilation (eg recognising their own criminal provisions as including the protection of legal interests of other EU Member States), they should also, in matters of fundamental rights, assimilate the protections and *remedies of* another EU Member State. For example, it will make sense that when equivalent rules of the executing state are violated, the evidence obtained therein and sent to Portugal cannot be used if this is the *remedy* provided for the violation of the corresponding right in Portugal. In Portugal, this prohibition would be based on a combination of our internal rules (for example, Article 32, para 8 of the Constitution; Article 126 CCP) with the principle of the highest level of protection of fundamental rights and the principle of assimilation, extended to fundamental rights in the horizontal sense, or even of mutual recognition of decisions on fundamental rights. This matter necessitates further research and to be substantiated in a more consolidated way, since these principles have not been applied in this sense. However, these may be foreseeable developments of trans-state constitutionalism and, at the EU level, suffer the influence of the rights of citizenship and free movement, for example. This works in the sense of safeguarding the right to effective judicial protection of the fundamental rights or persons accused, laid down in Article 47(1) of the EU Charter and in Article 20, para 1 of the Portuguese Constitution, regardless of whether the evidence travel across borders within EU Member States.

V. Admissibility of E-Evidence in Criminal Proceedings

The PT-Cybercrime Law (implementing the Budapest Convention[103]) does not explicitly establish direct rules on the admissibility of e-evidence or its exclusion.

[102] Already in this sense, see Ramos (n 100) 769, 771.

[103] See Council of Europe Convention on Cybercrime (adopted 23 November 2001), ETS No 185.

There are no specific rules governing the admissibility of e-evidence in criminal proceedings in other legal instruments either. The general rules of admissibility apply equally to e-evidence as they do to any other items of evidence. This is confirmed by the PT-Cybercrime Law, which refers back to the CCP (eg Articles 16, para 3, 5 and 6). In this sense reference should be made to the rules outlined in section III.

Nonetheless, there are provisions that may be relevant to the debate, namely on the proportionality of electronic searches and seizure. See, for example, Article 16, para 7

> 7 – The seizure of computer data, whichever is most appropriate and proportionate, taking into account the interests of the case, may in particular take the following forms:
> a) seizure of the media where the system is installed or seizure of the media where the computer data are stores, and the necessary devices for their reading;
> b) production of a copy of the data on an autonomous media;
> c) preservation, by technological means, of the integrity of the data, without making a copy or removing them, or
> d) removing in a non-reversing way or blocking the access to the data.

Practitioners and scholars have nonetheless criticised the lack of practical implementation of the requirements of the proportionality principle in the context of electronic searches and seizures.[104]

Another interesting provision is Article 16, para 3 of the PT-Cybercrime law:

> In case of seizure of computer data or computer documents which content is likely to disclose personal or intimate information, that would jeopardize the privacy of its owner or a third party, under penalty of nullity, the data or documents shall be submitted to the judge, who will consider its seizure regarding the concrete

In my opinion, violation of these provisions may give rise to exclusionary rules under Article 32, para 8 of the Constitution or Article 126 CCP. There is at least one decision to this effect.[105] The accused had consented to a search of his mobile phone, which had not been validated by the Public Prosecutor. Since such validation is mandatory within 72 hours, there was a nullity (due to lack of a mandatory procedural act, under Article 120, para 2, *lit* d) CCP). However, the Supreme Court considered that such a nullity would only be considered subject to an exclusionary rule under Article 126 CCP and Article 32, para 8 of the Constitution, where the data contained anything likely to impinge upon privacy or intimacy, which would fall within the scope of the rights protected by those provisions. In casu, the Court

[104] PS Mendes, 'A privacidade digital posta à prova no processo penal' (2021) 2 *Quaestio facti* 225at https://revistes.udg.edu/quaestio-facti/article/view/22487; RC Pereira, '*A pesquisa de dados informáticos – Exigências práticas do princípio da proporcionalidade*' (2021) 31 *Revista Portuguesa de Ciência Criminal* 569, 590–91.

[105] Judgment of the Supreme Court of Justice of 28 August 2021, case 1/20.2F1PDL.S1, Rapporteur Nuno Gonçalves at www.dgsi.pt.

adopted a position that such infringements had not been raised, and even records of communications via chats and messaging recorded by the smartphone did not fall under that provision.

As outlined in section III, Article 14, para 5, 6 and 7 of the the PT-Cybercrime Law also prohibits production orders in respect of e-evidence directed at the suspect, systems holding information under practising lawyers' professional secrecy, medical, banking and media secrecy, and systems subject to state secrecy or official secrecy. However, there is case law permitting a court order to obtain such information from a bank (which would also be permitted in the context of a search).[106]

There is also some case law in civil cases on the admissibility of digital documents, accepting them as valid evidence.[107]

In criminal cases, it was decided that 'the proof of ownership of the Facebook account and the content disclosed therein does not obey any principle of legal proof of digital nature, to be obtained through the search of computer data and its seizure, being subject solely to the principle of free assessment of evidence'.[108] In another area, it was ruled that

> the lack of expert evidence, when such evidence is mandatory, constitutes a curable nullity or irregularity, depending on the case. However, determining whether or not certain email accounts have become inaccessible or unusable does not require any special technical or scientific knowledge – therefore, it does not require expert evidence. The proof of these facts can be made by any means of evidence (including testimonial evidence from users).[109]

From a defence lawyer's perspective, I would like to outline that in practice, I have been confronted with the refusal of judicial authorities to provide me with access to e-evidence stored in my client's smartphone and personal computer

[106] See Procuradoria-Geral da República, Gabinete Cibercrime (n 45) 22.

[107] See Procuradoria-Geral da República, Gabinete Cibercrime (n 45) 22–23, notably Judgment of the Porto Court of Appeal of 7 December 2018, case 2905/18.3T8OAZ-A.P1, Rapporteur Fátima Andrade at www.dgsi.pt (email is an electronic document subject as such to the regime of electronic legal documents and acts, under Law Decree no 290-D/99 of 2 August. If a certified qualified electronic signature is not affixed, its probative value, namely as to its authorship, will be assessed under the general terms of law); Judgment of the Coimbra Court of Appeal of 14 November 2017, case 2840/12.9TBFIG.C2, Rapporteur Maria João Areias at www.dgsi.pt (SMS and emails, as electronic documents, fall within the concept of documentary evidence. While electronic documents with a qualified signature are given the full probative force of a signed private document, underart 376 Civil Code, other documents, such as SMS, which do not bear such a signature are assessed 'under the general terms of law'); Judgment of the Lisbon Court of Appeal of 12 July 2018, case 82328/14.0YIPRT.L2-2, Rapporteur Jorge Vilaça at www.dgsi.pt (the exchange of correspondence by email has become perfectly natural between people in general and between business partners in particular. Therefore, insofar as it can be printed, the electronic message has the same probative force as any other private document under arts 373 and following of the Civil Code. In civil proceedings, if the existence of an email account attributed to the defendant is not in question, the burden to prove that a message was not in fact received is upon the recipient, ie the defendant).

[108] Procuradoria-Geral da República, Gabinete Cibercrime (n 45) 23, referring to the Judgment of the Porto Court of Appeal of 13 September 2017, case 498/15.2GBPNF.P1, Rapporteur João Pedro Nunes Maldonado at www.dgsi.pt.

[109] ibid 27, referring to the Judgment of the Lisbon Court of Appeal of 27 June 2019, case 1429/09.4JDLSB.L2-9, Rapporteur João Abrunhosa at www.dgsi.pt.

throughout the investigation stage.[110] The reasons given were that it was necessary to protect the investigation since it was a serious offence (drugs trafficking); and other persons suspected could be contacted by the accused if he had access to his phone, this notwithstanding his being held in pre-trial detention and knowing of, but obviously not remembering entirely, the contents of his own devices. A position confirmed by the Court of Appeal.[111]

In my opinion, as was later shown, this was baseless, since no investigation against the said persons was undertaken (and in fact the accused stated he wanted to help to identify the persons involved and have them investigated). Also, in the end, after the trial, it was shown that the offence was a lesser one and the accused received a suspended sentence, which reinforces my belief that the refusal to grant access had been ill-founded.

The Court of Appeal in its reasoning outlined that the rejection of the accused's claim had to satisfy the constitutional and legal requirements of stating reasons, by a dialectical comparison of the arguments put forward by the accused and the prosecution, showing an impartial assessment of the pertinence and factual and legal relevance of each argument, and not simply an uncritical choice as to why the arguments of one or the other party were the most appropriate.

This had not been the case, but the Court of Appeal then made its own assessment and concluded that the refusal was lawful. The Court stated that secrecy of the investigation could not be an automatic and definitive impediment to access to the evidence, since the objects were seized from the accused and referred to his communications and other aspects of his private life, and the law (Article 89, para 6, *lit* b) CCP) established that secrecy could be derogated from in order to provide persons with evidence essential to the exercise of their rights, provided that no prejudice or risk of compromise to the investigation would result therefrom. In the case at hand, the appellant had argued in all his applications, and also in the appeal, that access to the seized devices was essential for the exercise of his rights of defence, an argument which the court found 'plausible'.

The Court also considered that delays in the gathering of evidence by the police and judicial authorities should not have the effect of aggravating the legal and procedural situation of the accused, under penalty of violating the 'due process of law', which aimed at uncovering crimes and their perpetrators while respecting the fundamental rights of those affected and any applicable procedural formalities. The arguments of the accused thus required

> consideration balancing the principle of fair trial and defence safeguards (arts 20 and 32 Constitution) against the public interest in the administration of criminal justice with

[110] During the trial stage, it was also impossible to immediately obtain a copy of the smartphone in question, in order for the defence to make a direct analysis. Only after several trial sessions did the court finally obtain data extracted by the police experts and deliver a copy of it to the defence (which was initially provided in a format that it would be very difficult to search, since there was no interface but just bulk data from the data storage devices; only later was it provided in a more legible format).

[111] Judgment of the Lisbon Court of Appeal of 29 September 2021, case 88/21.0JELSB-C.L1, Rapporteur Cristina Almeida e Sousa, unpublished.

> the purposes of the investigation, as regards the obtaining of evidence and the preservation of its integrity, with a view to uncovering the truth about the crimes charged and the identities of their perpetrators.[112]

Due to the nature of the crime under investigation and the fact that it was often committed with international contacts, as in the case at hand, the Court found that it was justified not to allow unrestricted access to the data.

Finally, it is essential to note that following the *Digital Rights* and *Tele2* case law of the CJEU,[113] there were disputes as to whether evidence obtained under the Portuguese legislation implementing the Data Retention Directive should be excluded for a violation of EU law.[114] In April 2022, the Constitutional Court declared the unconstitutionality with general binding force of the Portuguese Data Retention Law (Law 32/2008 of 17 July), adhering to the grounds outlined in the CJEU decisions, considering the reasoning also to be applicable under the domestic constitutional privacy and data protections (Articles 26, para 1 and 35.1 of the Constitution) and the right to effective judicial protection (Article 20, para 1 of the Constitution), since the data retention regime is in the field of EU law.[115]

The Court held that Article 4 of the Portuguese Data Retention Law, in conjunction with Article 6, violated the provisions of Article 35, para 1 and 4 (right to access, rectification and update of personal digital data, right to know the purpose of the data treatment, prohibition on accessing third parties' personal data) and Article 26, para 1 (right to protection of moral integrity), in

[112] ibid, unpublished.

[113] Judgment of the Court of Justice of the European Union (CJEU) [GC] of 8 April 2024, Joined Cases C-293/12 and C-594/12 (*Digital Rights Ireland and Seitlinger and Others*); Judgment of the CJEU [GC] of 21 December 2016, Joined Cases C-203/15 and C-698/15 (*Tele2 Sverige AB and Watson and Others*).

[114] Directive 2006/24/EC of the European Parliament and of the Council of 15 March 2006 on the retention of data generated or processed in connection with the provision of publicly available electronic communications services or of public communications networks and amending Directive 2002/58/EC [2006] OJ L105/54 (Data Retention Directive). See, eg, DS Ramalho and JD Coimbra, 'A declaração de invalidade da Diretiva 2006/24/CE: presente e futuro da regulação sobre conservação de dados de tráfego para fins de investigação, deteção e repressão de crimes graves' (2015) 147 *O Direito* 997, 1039–44 (arguing that the Portuguese implementing law was still in force, and this meant that it could be applied by private persons but not by public authorities – eg the courts – to the extent it was contrary to EU law. However, the lack conformity with EU law would only have effects *ex tunc*, from the date of the *Digital Rights Ireland* judgment onward, 8 April 2014. This would prevent the judges, from that date onwards, from asking for retained data, and would mean that the evidence obtained thereby since such date should be excluded under Art 126 CCP, without prejudice to the cases finally disposed of, which would not need to be re-opened). See also A Silveira and PM Freitas, 'The recent jurisprudence of the CJEU on personal data retention: implications for criminal investigation in Portugal' (2017) *UNIO Eu Law Journal* 45, 53 (arguing that the lack of conformity with the Directive is evident). On the other hand, it is worth outlining the position expressed by the General Attorney's Office, as described in Silveira and Freitas, ibid 53–55; and DR Nunes, 'Impedirá o Acórdão do Tribunal Constitucional n.º 268/2022 a obtenção e a valoração, paru fins de investigação criminal, de metadados conservados pelos fornecedores de serviços de comunicações eletrónicas ao abrigo da lei atualmente em vigor?' (2022) 170 *Revista do Ministério Público* 9, 22 (with further references in respect of the different positions in literature at fn 10, arguing that Portuguese law already had sufficient guarantees since it went beyond the Directive and thus did not contradict EU law).

[115] Judgment of the Constitutional Court no 268/2022 of 19 April 2022, case 828/2019 at www.tribunalconstitucional.pt/tc/acordaos/20220268.html.

conjunction with Article 18, para 2 (proportionality in the restriction of fundamental rights) of the Constitution. Additionally, the Constitutional Court declared the unconstitutionality of the transmission of stored data to the competent authorities for the investigation, detection and suppression of serious crimes, in respect of the lack of notification to the person concerned that the stored data were being accessed by the criminal investigation authorities, as long as such notification was not likely to jeopardise the investigations or the life or physical integrity of third parties, for violation of the same constitutional provisions as well as Article 20, para 1. Consequently, evidence obtained from unlawfully retained data must be excluded under Article 32, para 8 of the Constitution and Article 126 CCP.[116]

An example of a judgment of the Supreme Court of Justice (in an ordinary appeal) confirms this. However, *in casu*, the Court found that while it was correct to state 'that the investigation collected "metadata" during the course of the investigation … the contested judgment will only be null and void, pursuant to art 126, para 3 CCP, to the extent that it makes it clear that the facts are based on such data'.[117] And since the data retained under the said legislation, namely traffic data including the cellular location of a witness, was only referred to incidentally 'in a footnote', and the relevant facts in respect of the identification of the person speaking to an accused resulted from other evidence, 'it would be disproportionate to declare the judgment null and void under the provisions of art 126, para 3 of the CCP and order the appealed court to decide the same fact in a new judgment without recourse to that traffic data', in other words, the appealed judgment was not affected by the evidence that should have been excluded.[118] There are currently abundant disputes ongoing before our Supreme Court as to whether cases finally disposed of, in which such evidence was used, may be subject to an extraordinary appeal based on a decision declaring the unconstitutionality of a law, or the 'discovery' that the evidence obtained was prohibited and thus had to be excluded.

VI. Case Law and Practical Problems Regarding Cross-Border E-Evidence and its Admissibility

The PT-Cybercrime Law regulates the gathering of e-evidence in cross-border cases under Articles 20–26. However, some consider that other provisions also

[116] On the other hand, see Nunes (n 114) 47–53, arguing that some of the data collected by providers for the purposes of invoicing their services can be used, under a different legal basis (for subscriber data, location data and traffic data).

[117] Judgment of the Supreme Court of Justice of 15 September 2022, case no 5553/19.7T8LSB.L1.S1, Rapporteur Orlando Gonçalves at www.dgsi.pt.

[118] ibid.

apply in cross-border cases. There is a legal dispute around the interpretation of Article 15, para 5 of the PT-Cybercrime Law, which provides:

> When, during a of search, there are reasons to believe that the information sought is stored in another computer system or in a different part of the previous system, but these data are legally accessible from the initial system, the search can be extended by authorization of the competent authority in accordance with paragraphs 1 and 2.

This provision implements Article 19(2) of the Budapest Convention. However, the words 'in its territory', which appear in that provision of the Convention, have been removed in the text of the PT-Cybercrime Law. Thus, scholars argue that this allows for transborder remote searches of non-publicly available data even without the consent of the holder of the data, as long as the initial access occurs in Portugal and is lawful.[119] The position and the practice of the Public Prosecutions Office is that where an electronic search is permitted and conducted in Portugal under Article 15, it also allows the extension of the search in the event that the authorities discover that the evidence is in another system that may be lawfully accessed from the first system, even if the latter is outside the Portuguese territory, since the limitation of Article 19 of the Budapest Convention in respect of territory was not included in the wording of the PT-Cybercrime Law.[120]

This possibility is not to be confused with the direct gathering of evidence abroad, for example using *malware*, which is not lawful without a request for mutual legal assistance, as noted in the Portuguese literature.[121] The Public Prosecutions Office also states that it is not possible to use Article 15 for 'cross-border direct access to electronic information', and therefore a 'judicial cooperation request

[119] On this topic, see DS Ramalho, *Métodos ocultos de investigação criminal em ambiente digital* (Coimbra, 2017) 84–87 (explaining that there are two possible readings of the Portuguese law, one in line with the Convention, which does not permit transborder searches in the context of lawful access to a system located in Portugal; the other arguing that the elimination of 'in its territory' was intentional and therefore allows for such searches. The author adheres to the latter argument. This interpretation does not, however, extend to the use of *malware* to extract information directly from systems abroad. which the author later in his work attaches to the provision on undercover operations); DS Ramalho, 'A recolha de prova digital através de pesquisas informáticas transfronteiriças' in AAVV, *O domínio do imaterial: prova digital, cibercrime e a tutela penal de direitos intelectuais* (Centro de Estudos Judiciários, 2018) at https://cej.justica.gov.pt/LinkClick.aspx?fileticket=tQdHZg1ZPVc%3d&portalid=30 (outlining that in practice, law enforcement accesses systems located abroad); RS Pereira, 'O acesso (unilateral e sem recurso a mecanismos de cooperação judiciária internacional) a dados armazenados em sistemas informáticos localizados no estrangeiro' in JL Moutinho et al, *Homenagem ao Professor Doutor Germano Marques da Silva* (Universidade Católica, 2020) 2685, 2689 (arguing that Art 15, para 5 is unconstitutional when it permits transborder searches without resorting to international cooperation mechanisms; and that the evidence thereby obtained must be excluded as a matter of constitutional significance, including the concepts of sovereignty and territoriality/jurisdiction as a relevant part of the domestic system of protection of fundamental rights).

[120] In the same sense, Ramalho, *Métodos ocultos* (n 119) 89 (noting that since the gathering of evidence is lawful at domestic level, there is no place to even discuss whether an exclusionary rule under Art 126, para 3 CCP would be applicable; and arguing that the violation of international law has no effect on the validity of the evidence). Cf Pereira (n 119) 2713–2715 (arguing that the evidence thereby obtained must be excluded as a matter of constitutional significance, including the concepts of sovereignty and territoriality/jurisdiction as a relevant part of the domestic system of protection of fundamental rights).

[121] Ramalho, *Métodos ocultos* (n 119) 89–91.

is needed to obtain evidence abroad from public or private providers'. It equally outlines that prosecutors need to obtain permission from the investigative judge in the event that they want to conduct an electronic search, and they also must present a copy of the evidence obtained to the judge within 15 days and submit it to judicial control.[122]

In this context, albeit referring to interception of mobile phone conversations, an interesting case is cited by Ramalho, in which the Supreme Court of Justice concluded there was no unlawfulness because the interception concerned a Portuguese phone number operated by a provider located in Portugal and was made via this provider. For that purpose, the Court considered it was irrelevant that the other party was abroad and/or had a foreign phone number, stating that as long as the Portuguese communications network was used (which could also be via *roaming*), the interception could be ordered by the Portuguese courts. The Supreme Court affirmed, *obiter*, that

> the violation of sovereignty by acts of criminal procedure carried out outside the national territory would only exist if the intercepts were made, either by devices installed outside Portuguese territory, or with the use of a foreign operator, without the 'roaming' of the national operator, which was not the case.

As the author notes, Portuguese authorities lack jurisdiction to order such an intercept and Portuguese law is not applicable thereto, which would mean that the evidence thus obtained would lack any legal basis and would be prohibited pursuant to Article 126, para 3 CCP.[123]

In respect of production orders served abroad, I found no case law. But it has been sustained that Article 14 of the PT-Cybercrime law is a sufficient basis for cross-border production orders.[124] It is worth noting that the position and the practice of the Public Prosecutions Office is that it is allowed to issue those orders to online service providers, which may provide the required information voluntarily, limited to basic subscriber information, including IP addresses used to establish a specific communication.[125] Foreign authorities may also access data stored in a computer system located in Portugal, where publicly available, or receive, or access through a computer system located in its territory, the data stored in Portugal, via the lawful and voluntary consent of the person legally authorised to disclose

[122] European Union Agency for Law Enforcement Cooperation, '4th Annual SIRIUS EU digital evidence situation report' (2022) 42 at www.eurojust.europa.eu/publication/sirius-eu-digital-evidence-situation-report-2022.

[123] Ramalho, *Métodos ocultos* (n 119) 91 (text at fn 148), citing the Judgment of the Supreme Court of Justice of 5 July 2012, case 911/10.5TBOLH.E1.S1, Rapporteur Santos Carvalho at www.dgsi.pt. The author argues – on the contrary – that in the case of cross-border access under Art 15, para 5 of the PT-Cybercrime Law, the domestic legislator made Portuguese law applicable to the case – knowing it was allowing the authorities to conduct extraterritorial procedural acts with effects in another jurisdiction and therefore not in line with Art 6 CCP establishing the applicability of Portuguese procedural law to the Portuguese territory and to foreign territory *under the limits established in international law*.

[124] European Union Agency for Law Enforcement Cooperation (n 122) 32.

[125] ibid 29.

it (see Article 25 of the PT-Cybercrime Law).[126] Similarly, it has been sustained that production orders for subscriber information from online service providers outside Portugal are permissible, provided such information is in possession of those providers or they have control over the data and offer the services in the territory of Portugal (and, upon entry into force of the Second Protocol to the Budapest Convention, even in the absence of a territorial link; as well as in case of production orders directed at providers of domain names registration).[127] In this report, the Portuguese authorities also noted that as long as a request to an online service provider is lawful, the evidence obtained thereby may be used in court, since 'according to the Portuguese legal framework, it is allowed to obtain evidence in any circumstance, unless it is forbidden by law'.[128]

In respect of practical problems, the Portuguese authorities reported in 2022: (i) delays in the execution of requests due to reduced capacity; (ii) an increase in cases connected to cybercrime; (iii) difficulty in identifying sets of data that could be requested.[129]

VII. What Exclusionary Rules of Evidence Could be Agreed at EU Level?

Taking into account the exclusionary rules of evidence in criminal proceedings in Portugal, what exclusionary rules of evidence could be agreed at EU level?

It follows from the foregoing discussion that Portuguese case law admits as a principle that evidence obtained in violation of fundamental rights is inadmissible, in particular in the context of the violation of rights protected by the sanction of the exclusionary rule established in Article 32, para 8 of the Portuguese Constitution (and Article 126 CCP). Despite controversy in its application to individual cases, a significant part of the scholarship and case law also links the violation of fundamental criminal fair trial rights to those provisions.

The opinions I expressed in section IV.C also hint at my position: I see exclusionary rules in criminal cases as an effective and necessary means to protect *fundamental rights*,[130] *including the rights of defence*, and would support their adoption at EU level. This is only reasonable. However. if those rules are categorical,

[126] Ramalho, *Métodos ocultos* (n 119) 86–87 (outlines the disparate treatment of the Portuguese legislator in this respect: Art 15, para 5 allows for unrestricted cross-border access by Portuguese authorities to content located abroad, irrespective of the consent of the person – eg, if police authorities have access to their credentials, logging into a webmail account – while limiting the access of foreign authorities to those cases in which the data are publicly available, or where there is lawful and voluntary consent of the person legally authorised to disclose the data).

[127] ibid 31–32, 34–35.

[128] ibid 31–32, 39.

[129] ibid 46.

[130] In this sense, see Dias and Brandão (n 13); MT Sousa, 'A prova ilícita em processo civil: em busca das linhas orientadoras' (2020) LXI *Revista da Faculdade de Direito da Universidade de Lisboa* 15, 19.

bright-line rules, that is rules that are not subject to judicial balancing *in concreto*, which would otherwise make them virtually inapplicable because they would never be applied, thereby undermining their rationale and purpose.[131] Equally, their adoption – *since I am referring to rules to protect fundamental rights and not to just any procedural rule* – should not replace domestic constitutionally based exclusionary rules, but rather create an additional layer of protection.

In respect of testimonial privileges (often supplemented with limitations on seizure of intercept evidence), Portuguese law envisages several cases in which evidence may have to be excluded to safeguard a legally protected interest protected by the privilege. As these are familiar rules, there should be no obstacle to foreseeing similar rules at EU level.[132] However, some of these privileges (if not all) have constitutional underpinning, and thus their regulation at EU level would require a thorough assessment in order not to undermine or preclude domestic constitutionally based rights (eg, the absolute nature of the clerical privilege may be tied to the right of freedom of religion or even conscience).

In respect of the exclusion of evidence in violation of the right to confrontation of persons who gave their statements abroad, adoption at EU level would not contradict the Portuguese legal framework, and additional EU rules could be considered pertinent and provide some clarification.[133]

From another perspective, I believe that some degree of harmonisation is needed in respect of the requirements for the gathering of evidence that is normally of a cross-border nature or even impossible to attribute to a particular territory (this may apply to financial transactions data in the digital world, communications data, electronic data that allows for identification, etc). In this way, it will be possible to properly protect the rights of those affected by the gathering of evidence in this field via exclusionary rules, but without excessively hampering the effectiveness of criminal investigations that can only be achieved by access to such data.

Finally, addressing this matter at EU level should entail tackling the procedural obstacles that have been identified to date (mainly, the rule on non-inquiry in respect of evidence gathered abroad; the gaps in protection due to the refusal of executing or requested state authorities to deal with evidence already sent back to the requesting or issuing state; and the lack of recognition by issuing and requesting states of the

[131] In this sense, in respect of a theory of modern exclusionary rules, see SC Thaman, 'Balancing Truth Against Human Rights: A Theory of Modern Exclusionary Rules' in SC Thaman (ed), *Exclusionary Rules in Comparative Law* (Springer, 2013) 403, 441–42 (arguing that once violation of constitutional importance has been ascertained, there should be a presumption that any evidence directly or indirectly gathered as a result of the violation should be excluded, with only very narrowly construed exceptions, and that judicial balancing should have 'free rein' only where the violation is truly not of constitutional significance).

[132] Thus, it would even be acceptable to establish rules that go beyond the European Court of Human Rights (ECtHR) case law, including exclusionary rules to protect privacy rights, familial, religious and professional privileges (ie legal privilege), the freedom of the press and state secrecy.

[133] In fact, I believe our case law is mostly also in line with that of the ECtHR, and the exclusionary rule derived therefrom is also binding as a matter of EU law. But I have not dealt with this case law here. For an account of such case law, see L Bachmaier Winter, 'Transnational Criminal Proceedings, Witness Evidence and Confrontation: Lessons from the ECtHR's Case Law' (2013) 9 *Utrecht Law Review* 127.

decisions of executing or requested states declaring evidence inadmissible). Effective minimum procedural remedies need to be established in this respect.

VIII. Evidence Obtained in Administrative Proceedings and in Internal Investigations

This section provides just a brief overview of some of the main issues in respect of two topics: evidence obtained in administrative proceedings; and evidence obtained in internal investigations in the field of compliance programmes.

In respect of the use of evidence obtained in administrative proceedings, in general terms, based on my practice and previous research, I can confirm that several independent authorities have jurisdiction for preliminary administrative investigations or even inspection procedures, and the evidence obtained thereby may be used in criminal cases.[134] However, witness evidence must be repeated during the trial in formal criminal proceedings, unless one of the exceptions under Article 356 CCP applies.[135]

If evidence (including documents) was obtained under legal compulsion by administrative authorities, though, in particular by independent regulatory authorities, in principle it cannot be used in formal criminal proceedings. Nevertheless, there is scholarly debate around the issue. Case law does admit that evidence obtained in formal administrative offence proceedings,[136] by inspection or under 'supervision powers' by compulsion, can be used in formal administrative offence proceedings instituted by the same regulatory authorities, and even in formal criminal cases.[137] This also occurs in respect of tax crimes and the administrative

[134] For in-depth analysis of this topic, see AS Dias and VC Ramos, *O Direito À Não Auto-Inculpação (Nemo Tenetur se Ipsum Accusare) No Processo Penal e Contra-Ordenacional Português* (Coimbra Editora, 2009) 43–60, 67–81; JF Dias and MC Andrade, 'Poderes de supervisão, direito ao silêncio e provas proibidas (Parecer)' in AAVV, *Supervisão, direito ao silêncio e legalidade da prova* (Almedina, 2009) 11; FC Pinto, 'Supervisão do mercado, legalidade da prova e direito de defesa em processo de contraordenação (Parecer)' in AAVV, *Supervisão, direito ao silêncio e legalidade da prova* (Almedina, 2009) 62; PS Mendes, 'O problema da utilização de elementos recolhidos em ações de supervisão como meios de prova em processo sancionatório' (2012) 3 *Revista de Concorrência e Regulação* 307; PS Mendes, 'A regulação financeira, o direito penal e a utilização em processo penal das provas produzidas por autoridades reguladoras financeira' (2015) 1 *Anatomia do Crime* 129; MC Andrade, 'T.C., Acórdão n.º 340/2013 (Nemo tenetur se ipsum accusare e direito tributário. Ou a insustentável indolência de um acórdão (n.º 340/2013) do Tribunal Constitucional)' (2014) 3898 *Revista de Legislação e Jurisprudência* 121; SO Silva, *O Arguido como Meio de Prova contra si mesmo* (Almedina, 2018).

[135] This is not the case in formal administrative proceedings, for which the law and case law foresees the possibility of using the evidence collected at the administrative stage.

[136] I use this wording because in my view (and of further scholars) under the ECHR and the case law of the ECtHR (ie the 'Engel criteria'), these cases should be considered as criminal in nature.

[137] See Judgment of the Constitutional Court no 360/2016 of 4 January 2017, case 563/2015 at www.tribunalconstitucional.pt/tc/acordaos/20160360.html (constitutionality of the rules in the Market and Securities Code and the Legal Regime on Credit Institutions and Financial Companies permitting the use of evidence obtained under legal compulsion from the persons subject to supervision outside of the scope of a punitive procedure by the regulators in future punitive proceedings; it should be noted

activities of the tax authorities, but in this case there is a tendency to exclude such evidence if it circumvents the protections established for the accused in the criminal proceedings.

An example may be found in the case law of the Constitutional Court.[138] Although the Court found that there was no constitutional obstacle to the use of evidence gathered during tax inspection proceedings under the duty of cooperation of the taxpayer in a criminal case, it also stated that once there is suspicion that a person has committed a criminal offence, the evidence must be obtained within the criminal proceedings and not via the inspection procedures (using powers to compel the taxpayer to provide information), otherwise there would be a violation of the right against self-incrimination. The judgment states:

> [T]he use of documents obtained during tax inspection activities as evidence in criminal proceedings will be prohibited, under the terms of art 126, para 2, lit a) CCP, when it is revealed that the inspection entity has deliberately triggered or prolonged the inspection phase in order to gather evidence for the criminal proceedings to be opened thereafter, abusing the taxpayer's duty to cooperate.[139]

The Constitutional Court later decided that rules permitting use as evidence in criminal proceedings of tax-relevant documents obtained under the duty of cooperation during a tax inspection *while* a criminal investigation for a tax crime was pending against the taxpayer, and without the previous knowledge or decision of the competent judicial authority, was unconstitutional.[140] However, it has recently decided that the rule according to which documents obtained during a tax inspection under legal compulsion and the duty to cooperate *before* the opening of a criminal investigation may be used as evidence was not unconstitutional (in the reasoning of the case, the Court outlines that there had been no *bad faith* and the tax authorities had immediately reported the suspicion of an offence to the criminal authorities, but it also admits that some documents had been gathered when the criminal investigation was already ongoing).[141]

In respect of the use in criminal proceedings of evidence gathered in administrative proceedings, there is a different problem that has been brought to public attention by a report of the General Attorney's Office.[142] The report expressed reservations in respect of a practice that consisted of maintaining administrative

that this was a ruling pronounced in a criminal case); see also Judgment of the Constitutional Court 461/2011 of 11 October 2011, case 366/11 in respect of administrative offence proceedings instituted by the competition authority.

[138] Judgment of the Constitutional Court no 340/2013 of 17 June 2013, case 817/12 at www.tribunalconstitucional.pt/tc/acordaos/20130340.html.

[139] ibid. This is in line with the proposal in Dias and Ramos (n 134) 55–60.

[140] Judgment of the Constitutional Court no 298/2019 of 16 July 2019, case 1043/17 at www.tribunalconstitucional.pt/tc/acordaos/20190298.html.

[141] Judgment of the Constitutional Court no 279/2022 of 16 July 2019, case 1093/2021 at www.tribunalconstitucional.pt/tc/acordaos/20190298.html.

[142] Procuradoria-Geral da República, 'Relatório de Inspecção aos Serviços do Departamento Central de Investigação e Acção Penal – Processo de Inspecção nº 117/2013 – RMP – DCIAP' (28 March 2014) at www.ministeriopublico.pt/sites/default/files/documentos/pdf/relatorio_inspecao_dciap_2014.pdf.

'preliminary' proceedings of a secret nature, with the aim of monitoring and gathering evidence for criminal cases, which often could be 'parallel' to criminal investigations but which would not be known to the accused since they were strictly confidential. Scholars addressing the topic have voiced strong criticism of this practice, which they find clearly unconstitutional, with the consequence that the evidence obtained thereby would have to be excluded.[143]

Is evidence collected by internal investigations carried out in the field of compliance programmes admissible in the criminal proceedings against the company or persons employed by the company? In principle yes, but once again there are doubts around possible violations of the right against self-incrimination. Would that right apply if the evidence been gathered in a criminal investigation? If so, the evidence would likely not be used. In respect of individuals, the answer to this question is fairly clear. However, in respect of legal persons, the legal landscape is not is more blurred (both in case law and commentary). There are difficulties in defining the scope of the right against self-incrimination of legal persons, and in knowing whether such a right may be subject to derogations and, if so, which derogations would be constitutionally admissible.

The legal person's right to be present and to be heard is exercised through its procedural representative under Article 61, para 1, *lit* a) and b) and 7 CCP. In respect of the personal scope of the right, that is the right to remain silent, the representative will also be primarily responsible for exercising the right of the legal person to remain silent (Article 61, para 1, *lit* d) CCP) in the same way as natural persons. However, the personal scope of the right to remain silent (and not to incriminate oneself) of the legal person cannot be limited to the procedural representative. Imagine that the Public Prosecutor or the Court intends to hear legal representatives of the legal entity other than its representative for the case. In what capacity will they be heard? Can they also invoke the right of the legal person not to incriminate itself, and refuse to make statements? Prior to the legislative reform operated by Law 94/2021 of 21 December, there were doubts about the capacity in which a legal representatives other than the procedural representative should be heard: (i) as mere witnesses, with a duty to answer truthfully to the facts of which the legal person is accused (Article 132, para 1, *lit* d) CCP) and, if so, possibly allowing them to invoke the right to refuse to answer questions that could result in the incrimination of the legal person (Article 132, para 2 CCP, by analogy); (ii) as mere witnesses, but to whom a right to refuse to testify analogous to that of relatives (under the terms of Article 134 CCP) would be recognised; (iii) or as a person with a broad right to silence equal to that of the legal person accused? What if the legal representatives at the time of the commission of the offence no longer had such capacity: would the rules be different? Article 133, para 1, *lit* e) CCP, introduced by Law 94/2021 of 21 December, now states that '[a] representative

[143] AS Dias and RS Pereira, *Sobre a Validade de Procedimentos Administrativos Prévios ao Inquérito e de Fases Administrativas Preliminares no Processo Penal* (Almedina, 2018).

of the legal person or similar entity in the proceedings in which the latter is an accused may not testify as a witness'.

The new Article 134, para 1, *lit* c) CCP now establishes a right to refuse to testify for '[a] member of the governing body of the legal person or similar entity who is not its representative in the proceedings in which the legal person is an accused'. This provision covers any of the current members of the bodies of the legal person, because they are all part of its structure and the reasons that justify the right to refuse to testify are valid for all.[144] However, the right is not regulated in a broad manner but only in respect of the declarative dimension, that is the right to silence, and this in an incomplete manner. For example, the personal scope of application of the right of a legal person against self-incrimination has not been fully clarified: the law is mute about whether it should extend to former members of the bodies, to people holding leadership positions who are not representatives, or to simple employees or people acting on behalf of the company.[145]

Beyond the personal scope of application of the right not to incriminate oneself, there are questions relating to its material scope of application, namely: (i) whether it covers the right to refuse to hand over documents (applicable to natural persons) or not; (ii) whether there is a difference between formal administrative offence proceedings and formal criminal proceedings, the right not applying in the former; and, if so, (iii) whether such documents obtained in administrative offence proceedings under compulsion can be used in criminal cases. I believe that the right of legal persons will be identical to that of natural persons, even though I have already defended a limitation of this right with regard to documents the existence of which the law requires.[146]

Scholars argue that the decision to submit, or refuse to submit, documents in respect of the 'connecting facts' or 'internal facts of the legal person' is the sole responsibility of the legal person's representative in the proceedings. Thus, requests for materials must be addressed to that person, who may then exercise the right to refuse.[147] Note that according to scholars, the right of refusal by the legal person will not cover documents relevant *only* to the responsibility of an accused who is a natural person. It has also been argued, however, that this distinction is only possible if one is able to fully separate the facts of which the individual is accused from those of which the legal person is accused. And that, in any case, their evaluation

[144] GM Silva, 'Responsabilidade penal das pessoas colectivas – questões processuais', conference paper (Centro de Estudos Judiciários, 2022) para 5.2. (I). Text kindly provided by the author.

[145] Note that under Portuguese law, the actions of (say) persons holding leadership positions may in certain cases attribute criminal liability to the legal person. For further development in commentary, see MJ Antunes, *Processo Penal e pessoa colectiva arguida* (Almedina, 2020) 65–72; TQ Brito, 'Processo contra pessoas colectivas: algumas propostas de adaptação (urgente) do Código de Processo Penal português' in P Pinto de Albuquerque, R Cardoso and S Moura (eds), *Corrupção em Portugal. Legislative Evaluation and Reform Proposals* (Universidade Católica Editora 2021) 477, 504–05; Silva (n 144) para 5.2. (II).

[146] VC Ramos, 'Corpus Juris 2000: imposição ao arguido de entrega de documentos para prova e nemo tenetur se ipsum accusare'(2006–2007) 108–109 *Revista do Ministério Público* 125, 57–96.

[147] Antunes (n 145) 66–67.

should be subject to a regime 'parallel to that of the statements of the co-defendant' (see Articles 343, para 4 and 345, para 4 CCP).[148]

The most serious problems are to be found at the intersection of the personal and material scope of the right against self-incrimination of the legal person. For example, the reform did not touch Article 14, para 5 of the PT-Cybercrime Law, which states that a production order for access to 'specific and determined computer data, stored in a certain computer system', 'cannot be addressed to a suspect or accused in such proceedings'. How does this prohibition operate as regards a legal person? Might the production order be addressed to an employee (eg, of the IT department), who would not be covered by the right of the legal person against self-incrimination and could thus be compelled to provide the data, subject to criminal punishment for disobedience in the event of non-compliance? Although the data are available to that employee, they are so because only he or she is legitimised by virtue of his or her employment. Therefore, I believe that this production order may not be addressed to an employee. If an employee receives such a production order, he or she should forward it to the representatives of the legal person, who may refuse to comply with it.

Scholars have also argued[149] that people holding leadership positions who do not represent the legal person in the proceedings, and those who do not have such a position but hold evidence in the name and on behalf of the legal person, should be able to refuse to hand it over. This is the only way to guarantee the right of the legal person not to incriminate itself. Otherwise, the accused legal person would be deprived of 'the right to decide on the submission of evidence to the proceedings'. Of course, this does not preclude the coercive obtaining of such documentation through search and seizure.[150] Less clear is the situation in which, in the scope of a search in the facilities of the legal person, the aforementioned employee is asked to cooperate in a search of the computer system, for example by providing a cryptographic key or a password.

Whatever solution eventuates in the development of case law, I believe that one should not put too much emphasis on the obligations to cooperate to be imposed on companies or their employees. These hardly lead to the obtaining of reliable evidence in cases of real fraud or criminal intentions (where collaboration may be misleading, providing unreliable or incomplete elements). In my opinion, in cases of serious corporate crime, there is no way to avoid the need to use (proportionate) computer searches where the authorities are prepared to act without the collaboration of the legal person and its employees and representatives or managers. Perhaps a better incentive to obtain reliable evidence would be the establishment of an attractive reward scheme for the company, making it more advantageous to adopt voluntary collaborative conduct, thus overcoming the obstacles in the gathering of evidence, with proper safeguards to avoid abuse.

[148] Brito (n 145) 477, 505.
[149] Antunes (n 145) 66–67.
[150] In the same sense, Brito (n 145) 477, 505.

Lastly, on another topic in respect of internal investigations, it is not to be excluded that, in practice, courts may consider the probative value of evidence collected in internal investigations weaker than that of evidence obtained by the authorities, but there is no explicit provision stating this. This issue has not been clearly dealt with by case law, but I am aware of cases in which such internal investigations or audits are used but where the prosecution offices additionally seek to obtain confirmation and further evidence during their investigation. In any event, the limitations on the use of elements of internal investigations resulting from the limitations on reading previous witness statements, or from rules on hearsay evidence in force in criminal proceedings,[151] should remain applicable, making it more difficult to rely on internal investigations without additional investigation within the scope of the criminal case. It should also be noted, as relevant for this field, that there is at least one case in the area of labour law stating that corporate email accounts may not be monitored in the absence of clear rules forbidding personal use, which makes such evidence inadmissible when obtained by the company in an internal investigation without the explicit consent of the employees, due to violation of data protection rules.[152]

[151] See text at n 38.

[152] See Judgment of the Porto Court of Appeal of 15 December 2016, case 208/14.1TTVFR-D.P1 at www.dgsi.pt.

9

Admissibility of Evidence, Transnational E-Evidence and Fair-Trial Rights in the UK

JOHN JACKSON

I. Introduction: The Common Law Legacy

Within the United Kingdom (UK) there are three distinct legal jurisdictions, each with its own legal system, distinct history and origins: England & Wales, Scotland and Northern Ireland. There has never been one systematic code governing the admissibility of criminal evidence, or indeed criminal procedure more broadly, in any of these jurisdictions, in contrast to many Continental jurisdictions that have codified their criminal procedure. Instead, the admissibility of such evidence has traditionally been governed by the common law, a judge-made system of law developed by case law. Over the centuries, judges developed a series of rules to forbid juries from relying on certain kinds of suspect or prejudicial evidence (eg confessions obtained by threats or inducements, accomplice evidence, hearsay, bad character, etc). The common law system of evidence is often contrasted misleadingly with the Continental system of 'free proof', whereas in fact, under the harmonising influence of European fair-trial rights and Article 6 of the European Convention on Human Rights (ECHR), contemporary Continental procedural systems place a variety of constraints on the use that can be made of certain types of evidence that are similar in many ways to the common law.[1]

It is true, nevertheless, that the rules governing criminal evidence in the common law world have had a peculiar exclusionary effect that is not seen in many Continental processes, as a result of the bifurcated nature of common law decision making, whereby the judge as the tribunal of law decides issues of law

[1] J Jackson and P Roberts, 'Beyond Common Law Evidence: Reimagining, and Reinvigorating, Evidence Law as Forensic Science' in DK Brown, JI Turner and B Weisser (eds), *The Oxford Handbook of Criminal Process* (Oxford University Press, 2019) 787, 788.

and juries in the most serious cases decide issues of fact.[2] This has meant that judges are able to screen inadmissible evidence from juries in a manner that is not possible in unitary tribunals, with the result that juries may never get even to hear the inadmissible evidence. In this manner, 'admissibility' is a term of art in the common law world, referring to the process whereby the judge at trial sifts each piece of evidence submitted by the parties and determines whether it should be heard by the tribunal of fact. The very existence of a lay jury that can be cocooned from large swathes of evidence in this way has provided a distinctive rationale for exclusionary rules, as lay persons were considered unable to give certain types of suspect evidence their due weight.[3]

Another distinguishing feature between common law and civil law evidentiary systems is that the common law developed a discrete and unified Law of Evidence disaggregated from procedural regulation, which stretched across all types of adjudication processes.[4] In recent decades, however, the common law rules have become more anchored in the procedural settings in which they are applied, as legislatures have increasingly taken on the role of law reform from the courts. A major transformation in criminal justice has seen the emergence of criminal justice legislation, eclipsing case law as the predominant source of criminal law and procedure, and taking a variety of forms, including primary legislation but also embracing a range of secondary, delegated or 'soft law' sources.[5] One of the sources that has gained considerable importance has been the use of Codes of Practice to govern the way evidence is to be obtained and disclosed in pre-trial criminal procedure.[6]

This transformation has not yet resulted in the codification of evidence law, but it has meant that legislatures have been increasingly codifying certain rules of criminal evidence that were once the domain of judges. A turning point came in England & Wales in 1965, when the Judicial Committee of the House of Lords, then the highest court in the land, declared that judges no longer retained the common law power to create ad hoc exceptions to the hearsay rule. This rule had been developed by judges at common law to exclude out-of-court statements of witnesses when they were used to prove the truth of facts. Over the years, judges created a number of exceptions to the rule where such statements were likely to

[2] This point about the peculiarity of common law rules was made originally by JB Thayer, *A Preliminary Treatise on Evidence at the Common Law* (Little Brown, 1898) 1–2. For more on the 'peculiar' effect of common law exclusionary rules, see JD Jackson and SJ Summers, *The Internationalisation of Criminal Evidence* (Cambridge University Press, 2012) 32–33.

[3] For the view that the common law rules were the 'child of the jury', see Thayer (n 2) 47.

[4] Jackson and Roberts (n 1) 788.

[5] P Roberts, *Roberts & Zuckerman's Criminal Evidence*, 3rd edn (Oxford University Press, 2022) 35. Roberts focuses on England & Wales. Northern Ireland has very similar legislation to that in England & Wales. Scotland has had its own criminal justice system, quite distinctive from the English system, for centuries. Many of its criminal procedure rules are contained in the Criminal Procedure (Scotland) Act 1995 and the Scottish Criminal Procedure Rules 1996.

[6] See, eg, the PACE Codes of Practice governing police conduct under the Police and Criminal Evidence Act (PACE) 1984 and the Code of Practice governing disclosure of evidence under the Criminal Procedure and Investigations Act 1996.

be reliable (eg, for public documents and official records), but in *Myers v DPP*[7] the House of Lords held that it had no discretion to admit factory records to prove the identity of stolen cars. Parliament swiftly reversed this decision by creating a dedicated statutory exception to the hearsay rule for business documents, and in 2003 it enacted a 'statutory code', contained within the Criminal Justice Act (CJA) 2003, to govern the whole of the law of criminal hearsay.[8]

The process of law reform and increasing codification has also gone hand in hand with a relaxation of many of the rigours of the old rules of evidence, as a view has prevailed that as juries become 'better educated and more literate', they can be trusted more to give evidence the weight it deserves without the need to shield them from what may be perfectly probative, if potentially prejudicial, evidence.[9] Thus the hearsay reforms in the CJA 2003 admitted much more hearsay evidence than ever before, and the Act also contained provisions to relax the admissibility of bad-character evidence, which had hitherto been subject to judge-made exclusionary rules at common law.[10]

II. Fair-Trial Rights

One counter-tendency to this movement towards 'free proof', however, has been the harmonising effect of the ECHR. The enactment of the Human Rights Act (HRA) across the UK in 1998 has meant that the UK jurisdictions have had to ensure that any new laws are compatible with Convention rights not only as a matter of international law (as the ECHR is an international treaty) but also as a matter of domestic law. The courts have the power to make a declaration of incompatibility where legislation is in breach of Convention rights, although this does not have the effect of nullifying any such legislation.[11] The HRA 1998 also requires that legislation must be read in a way that is compatible with the ECHR so far as it is possible to do so.[12] There are notable evidentiary examples where the courts have applied this interpretive provision to 'read' legislation in an ECHR-compliant manner under the HRA 1998. So in a number of instances, the UK courts have considered that Article 6(2) ECHR, which declares that everyone charged with a criminal offence shall be presumed innocent until proved guilty, requires that statutory provisions that appear to place a legal burden of proof on the defence

[7] *Myers v DPP* [1965] AC 1001.

[8] CJA 2003, pt 11, ch 2. For a summary of the provisions in the 'code', see *R v Horncastle* [2009] UKSC 14, [2010] 2 AC 373 [31]–[38].

[9] *R v H* [1995] 2 AC 596, 613, per Lord Griffiths: 'Today with better educated and more literate juries the value of those old restrictive rules of evidence is being re-evaluated and many are being discarded or modified.' See also M Redmayne, 'Evidence, criminal' in P Cane and J Conaghan, *The New Oxford Companion to Law* (Oxford University Press, 2008).

[10] CJA 2003, pt 11, ch 1.

[11] HRA 1998, s 4.

[12] ibid s 3(1).

should be 'read down' so as to impose a mere evidential burden of raising evidence on contested issues.[13]

Under the HRA 1998, the UK courts are also required to 'take into account' the decisions of the European Court of Human Rights (ECtHR).[14] Although this does not mean that the courts are bound to follow the judgments of the ECtHR, there was a tendency when the HRA 1998 came into force to let the ECtHR take the lead on the approach to be adopted towards fair-trial rights.[15] Within the last 15 years, however, the new UK Supreme Court (UKSC) seems to have been prepared to take a more divergent stance from the ECtHR.[16] A turning point in regard to criminal evidence came in 2009, when the Supreme Court refused to endorse a ruling of the ECtHR in *Al-Khawaja and Tahery v UK* that Article 6 ECHR forbade convictions based solely or decisively upon the unexamined statements of absent witnesses.[17] The rule against hearsay has helped to support the right to confrontation, under which accused persons have a right to cross-examine witnesses who testify against them. However, the statutory exceptions built into the hearsay rule under the CJA 2003 were crafted in such a way that they still gave discretion to judges to exclude hearsay statements where it would be unfair on the accused to admit them, and the UKSC considered that this and other safeguards in the Act were sufficient to protect the accused's fair-trial rights. It followed that an inflexible rule that the ECtHR had developed to prevent convictions based solely or decisively on unexamined statements was not necessary.[18]

The UKSC's growing determination to scrutinise for itself what is required by Convention rights may be welcomed as part of an ongoing 'dialogue' between domestic courts and the ECtHR, which may in the end lead to greater mutual respect and understanding. In a later Grand Chamber decision, the ECtHR conceded that the sole or decisive rule should not be applied in an inflexible manner, and considered that the question in each case was whether there were 'sufficient counterbalancing factors', including strong procedural safeguards, to permit a fair and proper assessment of the reliability of the evidence to take place.[19] When the Court went on to examine the safeguards in the CJA 2003, it accepted that they were in principle 'strong safeguards designed to ensure fairness'.[20] Although critics have considered that this apparent climbdown by the ECtHR amounted to a considerable dilution

[13] See, eg, *R v Lambert* [2001] UKHL 28, [2002] 2 AC 545; cf *R v Johnstone* [2003] UKHL 28, [2003] 1 WLR 1736 and *Sheldrake v DPP; Attorney General's Reference (No 4 of 2002)* [2004] UKHL 43, [2005] 1 AC 264.

[14] HRA 1998, s 2(1).

[15] J Jackson, 'Protecting the Right to a Fair Tral in an Era of Criminal Justice Transformation' in B Dickson and C McCormick (eds), *The Judicial Mind: A Festschrift in Honour of Lord Kerr of Tonaghmore* (Hart Publishing, 2021) 261.

[16] ibid. For analysis of the approach the UKSC has taken more generally towards rulings of the ECtHR, see B Dickson, *Human Rights in the UK Supreme Court* (Oxford University Press, 2013).

[17] *Al-Khawaja and Tahery v UK* (2009) 49 EHRR 1.

[18] See *R v Horncastle* [2009] UKSC 14, [2010] 2 AC 373.

[19] *Al-Khawaja and Tahery v UK* (2012) 54 EHRR 23 [147].

[20] ibid [151].

of the right to confrontation,[21] the broader point is that constructive dialogue can lead in the end to greater convergence on the interpretation of fair-trial rights.[22]

Greater understanding at a global level of what fair-trial rights require is, however, threatened by the current UK Government's post-Brexit policy of wishing to distance itself more radically from the rulings of the ECtHR. Although the Government has indicated that it does not intend to withdraw from the ECHR, a recent proposal to replace the HRA 1998 with a new Bill of Rights Act was intended to '[clarify and re-balance] the relationship between courts in the United Kingdom, the European Court of Human Rights and Parliament', and to give primacy to decision-making by Parliament, rather than any court, in instances where competing rights and interests are at stake.[23] The new Bill would no longer have required the UK courts to interpret laws compatibly with the ECHR 'so far as it is possible to do so', and removed the requirement on courts under the HRA 1998 to 'take into account' the judgments of the ECtHR in cases where human rights are at stake. Instead, the UKSC was stated to be the 'ultimate judicial authority on questions arising under domestic law in connection with the Convention rights'.[24] The Bill has since been shelved, allegedly because of drafting difficulties,[25] but it remains to be seen how long the present HRA 1998 will remain intact.

Against the background of the gradual relaxation of the old exclusionary rules of evidence subject to the need to comply with European fair-trial standards, we can now come to the specific issues of the admissibility of cross-border evidence and electronic evidence ('e-evidence').

III. The Admissibility of Cross-Border Evidence

The general principles governing the admissibility of cross-border evidence are no different from those governing the admissibility of any other kind of evidence. However, the orality principle, under which courts in all three UK jurisdictions have a preference for live in-court testimony, has made it more difficult to admit the evidence of witnesses who are overseas. Unlike witnesses within the UK, who can be required to attend by the courts, there is no legal mechanism by which it is possible to force a witness to travel to the UK to give evidence if the witness is not prepared to do so. Various statutory provisions have been enacted over the years

[21] See, eg, L Hoyano, 'What is Balanced in the Scales of Justice? In Search of the Essence of the Right to a Fair Trial' [2014] Crim LR 4; J Jackson and S Summers, 'Seeking Core Fair Trial Standards across National Boundaries; Judicial Impartiality, the Prosecutorial Role and the Right to Counsel' in J Jackson and S Summers, (eds), *Obstacles to Fairness in Criminal Proceedings: Individual Rights and Institutional Forms* (Hart Publishing, 2018) 99.

[22] See JD Jackson, 'Common Law Evidence and the Common Law of Human Rights: Towards a Harmonic Convergence?' (2019) 27 *William and Mary Bill of Rights Journal* 689.

[23] Bill of Rights Bill 2022, cl 1(2).

[24] ibid cl 3(1).

[25] See J Elgot, 'Liz Truss halts Dominic Raab's bill of rights plan' *The Guardian* (7 September 2022).

to make it easier for witnesses to give their evidence from outside the UK, without however being forced to do so. The Crime (International Cooperation) Act 2003 provides a mechanism under which courts and 'designated prosecutors' in the UK can make mutual legal assistance (MLA) requests to courts and other legal authorities overseas in order to have witnesses examined in other jurisdictions. But the Act does not provide that statements obtained in this way are then admissible in the UK.[26] Unlike in Scotland,[27] there is no provision for criminal courts in England & Wales and Northern Ireland to grant applications for evidence to be taken on commission where witnesses are unavailable to give oral evidence at the trial, and for such evidence to be admissible in the trial.[28]

Another way in which evidence may be taken abroad is for witnesses to testify in court outside the UK by means of a live video link. Section 32(1) of the CJA 1988 enabled evidence to be given from abroad through a live television link by a person other than the defendant and subject to the leave of the court, in trials on indictment, appeals and proceedings in the youth courts. This provision applied equally to prosecution and defence witnesses. When arranging a video link with a witness abroad, however, the laws of other jurisdictions have to be consulted. Most jurisdictions require local law enforcement to be informed of any contact with witnesses by foreign authorities, and some jurisdictions require, or prefer, video-link hearings to be arranged using MLA. Where MLA is required, a request must be issued by a court or designated prosecutor in line with section 7 of the Crime (International Cooperation) Act 2003. In 2020, as a result of the global Covid pandemic, emergency legislation was introduced permitting any person, *including the defendant*, to testify or otherwise take part in all manner of criminal proceedings through live link, whether within or outside the UK.[29] This provision has since been made permanent, and has been extended even further by permitting legal representatives as well as jurors to participate in the proceedings by live link.[30] Section 32 of the CJA 1988 has been amended to reflect this considerable expansion of the scope for taking live-link evidence from witnesses overseas, although before a direction is made to facilitate it, the judge has to take a number of circumstances into account and be satisfied that it is in the interests of justice for the evidence to be given in this manner.[31]

An alternative way of admitting the statements of witnesses which are made outside the United Kingdom is by means of an exception to the hearsay rule. The hearsay rule reinforces the orality principle's reference for live testimony in

[26] See JR Spencer, *Hearsay Evidence in Criminal Proceedings*, 2nd edn (Hart Publishing, 2014) para 15.15.

[27] See Criminal Procedure (Scotland) Act 1995, s 272.

[28] Spencer (n 26) para 5.15.

[29] Coronavirus Act 2020, s 53, sch 23(2), temporarily replacing and substituting s 51 of the CJA 2003, which previously permitted any witness other than the defendant located within the UK to give evidence by live video-link where the court was satisfied that it was in the interests of the efficient or effective administration of justice.

[30] See Police, Crime, Sentencing and Courts Act 2022, s 200 and sch 20.

[31] ibid s 200(4), (5), (6).

court by excluding as we have seen out of court statements admitted in order to prove the facts. But as mentioned above, a number of statutory exceptions now permit hearsay statements to be admitted in certain circumstances. Since 1988 one such exception that has applied in England & Wales and Northern Ireland enables the statements of persons outside the UK to be admitted at trial where it is not reasonably practicable to secure their attendance at trial.[32] A similar exception has applied in Scotland since 1995.[33] Given that it is not possible to force witnesses to travel to the UK to attend trial, the courts have to consider what efforts have been made to persuade witnesses to come, taking into account the seriousness of the case and the importance of their evidence to the case as a whole.[34] Another consideration is whether it would have been reasonably practicable to enable their evidence to be given in other ways that would have secured some of the traditional safeguards associated with oral testimony, such as giving evidence on oath and having the evidence cross-examined, both of which are possible where evidence is given by a video link.[35] Another statutory exception to the hearsay rule that might enable statements made overseas to be admitted is through what is known as the business documents exception which extends to police statements.[36] Where the statement has been obtained from overseas by using formal procedures for mutual assistance, there is no need for the extra conditions that apply to the admission of police statements in England & Wales and Northern Ireland to be satisfied.[37]

Apart from these provisions facilitating the giving of evidence from outside the UK in criminal courts across the UK, there are also special evidentiary provisions under the Criminal Jurisdiction Act 1975 permitting extraterritorial terrorist offences committed in the Republic of Ireland to be tried in Northern Ireland. The Act enables a Northern Ireland court, for the purposes of a trial of such an offence, to issue a letter of request for the taking of evidence by a judge of the High Court in the Republic of Ireland from a witness specified in the letter of request. Any statement taken in this manner may be admitted as evidence in the trial or in any preliminary proceeding. The accused has a right to attend the examination of any such witness in the Republic of Ireland. There are reciprocal arrangements contained in the Criminal Law (Jurisdiction) Act 1976 in Ireland. These provisions have been little used. The Director of the Public Prosecution Service in Northern Ireland told the parliamentary Northern Ireland Affairs Committee in 2009 that there had been just 18 cases, but he stressed 'That does not in any sense diminish the usefulness of the legislation as the land border [between Northern Ireland and the Republic of Ireland] clearly

[32] CJA 1988, s 23(2)(b); Criminal Justice (Evidence etc) (NI) Orde 1988 (SI No 1847 (NI 17)), Art 3(2)(b). See now CJA 2003, s 116(2)(c); Criminal Justice (Evidence) (NI) 2004 (SI No 1501 (NI 10)), Art 20(2)(c).

[33] Criminal Procedure (Scotland) Act 1995, s 259(2)(b).

[34] See Spencer (n 26) para 6.17.

[35] ibid para 6.19.

[36] See CJA 2003, s 117; Criminal Justice (Evidence) (NI) Order 2004 Art 21; Criminal Procedure (Scotland) Act 1995, s 279, sch 8.

[37] See CJA 2003 s 117 (4)(b); Criminal Justice (Evidence) (NI) Order 2004, Art 21(4)(b).

makes it relatively easy for individuals to flee from one jurisdiction to another ….'[38] The Committee recommended that a full review of offences be undertaken, including human trafficking, sexual offences, e-crime, money laundering and fraud, with a view to extending the range of offences contained in the Acts, so that offenders who commit such crimes in Northern Ireland may be tried in the Republic and vice versa. But this recommendation has not been acted on.

IV. The Admissibility of E-Evidence

The general rules governing the admissibility of evidence in criminal proceedings apply equally to e-evidence as they do to other items of evidence. One exception is that there is a ban on the admissibility of domestic intercept evidence, originally imposed under section 9 of the Interception of Communications Act 1984. There is no such bar on foreign intercept evidence, nor is there a bar on the admission of bugged (as opposed to intercepted) communications or the products of surveillance or eavesdropping, even where these surveillance measures were not lawfully authorised and were in breach of the right to respect for private life under Article 8 ECHR.[39] The rationale for the ban on intercept evidence is to ensure the secrecy of surveillance operations, as it has been claimed that using intercepted communications as evidence would reveal the authorities' capabilities, and to ensure that interception for intelligence purposes is not impeded by the imposition of complex procedures to meet evidential requirements.[40] There was some debate following the events of 9/11 that the ban would inhibit the prosecution of terrorist offenders. A review in 2003, which considered that a balance has to be struck between the public interest in prosecuting particular cases and the public interest in maintaining the effectiveness of intelligence-gathering techniques and capabilities, considered that the balance was not struck in the right place if intercepted communications can never be used evidentially.[41] The review found that few other jurisdictions have such a blanket ban.[42] However, successive UK governments have resisted any change to the law, and the re-enactment of the ban in section 56 of the Investigatory Powers Act 2016 effectively ended the debate on whether there should be some relaxation of it.[43]

E-evidence, like any other evidence, will be inadmissible if it falls foul of the hearsay rule. Although, as mentioned in section II, a number of exceptions to

[38] Northern Ireland Affairs Committee, *Second Report, Cross-Border Co-operation between the Governments of the United Kingdom and the Republic of Ireland* (2009) at https://publications.parliament.uk/pa/cm200809/cmselect/cmniaf/78/7802.htm.

[39] See, eg, *R v Khan* [1997] AC 558.

[40] Privy Counsellor Review Committee, *Anti-terrorism, Crime and Security Act 2001 Review: Report* (2003) HC 10, paras 208–215 (Newton Report).

[41] ibid para 212.

[42] The UK position has been described as 'idiosyncratic': see D Giannoulopoulos, *Improperly Obtained Evidence in Anglo-American and Continental Law* (Hart Publishing, 2019) 97.

[43] I Dennis, *The Law of Evidence*, 7th edn (Sweet & Maxwell, 2020) 324.

the hearsay rule permit hearsay evidence to be admitted more commonly than hitherto, the first question that arises is whether material generated by electronic devices is hearsay in the first place. In determining this question, the courts have to consider the function that the device was performing and the sources of information on which it performed that function.[44] If a computer is recording and printing out material keyed into it by a human operator, the content of the printout will be information that has passed through a human mind and the printout will be hearsay when it is sought to be relied upon for the truth of its statements. But if it was operating as no more than a mechanical calculator or programmer, any printout is merely an item of 'real evidence' and will be admitted.[45] Even if a computer printout constitutes hearsay because it contains information provided by the human mind, it may be admissible under the business documents exception in section 117 of the CJA 2003. Documents are given a wide definition under the Act to include mechanical recordings, but section 129 of the CJA 2003 provides that representations of fact made by a machine that depend for their accuracy on information supplied by a person are not admissible as evidence of the fact unless it is proved the information was accurate.

When the possibility of computer-produced evidence first emerged in the 1960s, there was concern about the reliability of such evidence, and special conditions were enacted before it could be admitted. Section 69 of the PACE 1984 provided that

> a statement in a document produced in a computer shall not be admissible as evidence of any fact therein unless it is shown—
>
> (a) that there are no reasonable grounds for believing that the statement is inaccurate because of improper use of the computer; and
>
> (b) that at all material times the computer was operating properly, or if not, that any respect in which it was not operating properly or was out of operation was not such as to affect the production of the document or the accuracy of its contents ….

As the use of computers became more widespread, however, the fear of unreliability diminished, and concern about the difficulty in proving these conditions led to the section's repeal in 1999.[46] As a result, it is no longer necessary to prove that a computer was operating properly and was not used improperly before any statement in a document produced by the computer can be admitted in evidence. Computer evidence must now follow the common law presumption of proper functioning of machines, which means that a presumption will exist that the computer producing the evidential record was working properly at the material time and that the record is therefore admissible as real evidence.[47] That presumption may

[44] ibid 507.

[45] See *Castle v Cross* [1985] 1 WLR 1372; *R v Spilby* (1990) 91 Cr App R 186.

[46] Youth Justice and Criminal Evidence Act 1999, s 60. See Law Commission, *Evidence in Criminal Proceedings: Hearsay and Related Topics* (1997) pt XIII.

[47] Law Commission (n 46) paras 13.13–13.14. See S Mason and D Seng, *Electronic Evidence and Electronic Signatures*, 5th edn (University of London, 2021) ch 5.

be rebutted, however, if evidence to the contrary is adduced. In that event, it will be for the party seeking to produce the computer record in evidence to satisfy the court that the computer was working properly at the material time.

Prosecutors have reported that the repeal of section 69 of PACE 1984 has been particularly helpful in cases where chains of linked computers are involved, for example internet fraud.[48] However, any presumption that computer software is reliable is questionable in the light of what has been described as the UK biggest miscarriage of justice, where 700 former Post Office sub-postmasters and mistresses were wrongfully convicted, between 2000 and 2015, for false accounting and theft, after bugs in Fujitsu's Horizon retail transactions and accounting software falsely showed shortfalls of cash at their branches.[49] Given the defects in computer software, it has been suggested that a court should start with the presumption that any software system contains or is influenced by errors that make it fallible, and that in assessing the weight to be placed on specific computer evidence, the trier of fact should ask 'How likely is it that this particular evidence has been affected in a material way by computer error?'[50]

Given that digital data are inherently malleable and mutable, the process of acquiring, copying and handling e-evidence should be carried out to the highest standards.[51] The Association of Chief Police Officers (ACPO) has issued Good Practice Guidance on Digital Evidence, which sets out four principles as follows:

> Principle 1: No action taken by law enforcement agencies, persons employed within those agencies or their agents should change data which may subsequently be relied upon in court.
>
> Principle 2: In circumstances where a person finds it necessary to access original data, that person must be competent to do so and be able to give evidence explaining the relevance and the implications of their actions.
>
> Principle 3: An audit trail or other record of all processes applied to digital evidence should be created and preserved. An independent third party should be able to examine those processes and achieve the same result.
>
> Principle 4: The person in charge of the investigation has overall responsibility for ensuring that the law and these principles are adhered to.[52]

These are not legal requirements and their use is voluntary. However, it is arguable that non-adherence to them may lead to the exclusion of evidence on the ground that it does not comply with section 78 of PACE 1984, which enables courts to exclude evidence obtained unfairly (see section VI).

[48] See CPS, *Computer Records Evidence – Legal Guidance* (2017) at www.cps.gov.uk/legal-guidance/computer-records-evidence.

[49] Only a minority of those convicted have so far had their convictions quashed. See *Hamilton and others v Post Office Ltd* [2021] EWCA Crim 21.

[50] P Ladkin et al, 'The Law Commission presumption concerning the dependability of computer evidence' (2020) 17 *Digital Evidence and Electronic Signature Law Review* 1.

[51] Mason and Seng (n 47) para 9.27.

[52] *ACPO Good Practice Guide for Digital Evidence* (2011) section 2.

V. Transnational E-Evidence

A distinction needs to be made between issues relating to obtaining e-evidence overseas and the admissibility of such evidence in criminal proceedings. While the rules governing the admissibility of transnational e-evidence are no different from those governing the admissibility of domestic e-evidence, it is much more difficult for law enforcement bodies to obtain certain types of important e-evidence from overseas in time for use at trial. According to Article 32 of the Budapest Convention on Cybercrime:

> A Party may, without the authorisation of another Party:
>
> …
>
> (b) access or receive, through a computer system in its territory, stored computer data located in another Party, if the Party obtains the lawful and voluntary consent of the person who has the lawful authority to disclose the data to the Party through that computer system.[53]

But this is based on voluntary cooperation, and a recent Sirius report has outlined some of the challenges there have been when requests are made for data disclosure held by foreign online service providers (OSPs).[54]

As regards mandatory cooperation, there are limits to which existing domestic court orders can be used to obtain electronic data abroad either because such an order cannot be made where the data are not located in the UK, or, where an order can be made, it cannot be served extraterritorially. There are various statutory provisions that allow law enforcement agents to acquire information that is within the UK compulsorily in electronic form. Section 19(4) of PACE 1984, for example, empowers police officers to require the production of 'any information stored in any electronic form and accessible from the premises'. However, there is a presumption that UK legislation is generally not intended to have extraterritorial effect, which is rooted in both the requirements of international law and the concept of comity founded on mutual respect between states. In a decision in 2018, the Divisional Court held that section 2(3) of the CJA 1987 (which permits the Serious Fraud Office (SFO) in England and Wales to issue notices requiring the production of documents) extends extraterritorially to foreign companies in respect of documents held outside the UK when there is a sufficient connection between the company and the UK.[55] But this ruling was overturned more recently by the Supreme Court, which held that there was no basis for the Divisional Court's finding that the SFO could use the power in section 2(3) of the 1987 Act to require foreign companies to produce documents held outside the UK if there is a sufficient connection between the company and the

[53] See Council of Europe Convention on Cybercrime (adopted 23 November 2001) ETS No 185.

[54] See *Sirius EU Digital Evidence Situation Report* (2020) at www.eurojust.europa.eu/sirius-eu-digital-evidence-situation-report.

[55] *R (on the application of KBR Inc) v Director of the Serious Fraud Office* [2018] EWHC 2368 Admin.

UK.[56] Implying a sufficient connection test into section 2(3) was inconsistent with the intention of Parliament and would involve 'illegitimately re-writing the statute'.[57] The Court reasoned that since 1987, successive UK Acts of Parliament have developed structures in domestic law that permit the UK to participate in international systems of MLA to facilitate criminal proceedings and investigations. These systems are subject to protections and safeguards, including provisions that regulate how documentary evidence may be used and make provision for its return and which are fundamental to the mutual respect between states and comity on which the system is founded. The UKSC considered that it was unlikely that Parliament would have intended them to operate alongside a broad unilateral power to permit the SFO to compel foreign companies to produce documents held outside the UK, under threat of criminal sanction and without the protection of any safeguards.

Thus MLA has been the main mechanism used by law enforcement agencies when they are seeking to obtain evidence overseas. But there has been frustration with this process. According to the UK Government, it takes an average of 12 months for an MLA request sent from the UK to the United States (US) to result in the production of the requested data (assuming they materialise at all).[58] The Crime (Overseas Production Orders) Act 2019, which came into force on 9 October 2019, now enables officers of specified investigative agencies to apply to a Crown Court judge for the production of stored electronic information located or controlled outside the UK, for use in the investigation and prosecution of indictable offences. This power can only be exercised where a designated international cooperation arrangement exists between the UK Government and the government of the country where the electronic information is located or from which it is controlled. In October 2019, such an arrangement was entered into by the UK and the US. This is significant given the huge amount of messaging on platforms run by US tech companies like Facebook and Google. Overseas production orders have the potential to reveal the existence of crucial evidence, but it remains to be seen how the legislation will work out.[59]

VI. Unfairly Obtained Evidence in the Human Rights Era

As already indicated, the courts at common law developed a number of exclusionary rules based on the need to exclude certain unreliable kinds of evidence. However, without a constitution on which to base strong (American-style)

[56] *R (on the application of KBR Inc) v Director of the Serious Fraud Office* [2021] UKSC 2. See also *Serious Organised Crime Agency v Perry* [2012] UKSC 35, holding that s 357 of the Proceeds of Crime Act 2002 did not permit a disclosure order to be imposed on persons outside the UK.

[57] *KBR v SFO* (n 56) [65].

[58] G Patterson, 'Overseas Production Orders: A New Tool to Obtain Foreign Electronic Evidence' (2020) *6KBW* at https://blog.6kbw.com/posts/overseas-production-orders-a-new-tool-to-obtain-foreign-electronic-evidence.

[59] ibid.

exclusionary rules, the UK courts never developed rules mandating the exclusion of evidence that has been improperly or illegally obtained. The approach taken by the common law towards improperly obtained evidence was immortalised in the famous dictum of one judge that '[i]t matters not how you get it: if you steal it even, it would be admissible'.[60] This approach may be contrasted with that in the Republic of Ireland where, in the latter half of the twentieth century, the courts developed one of the strictest exclusionary rules to be seen in the common law world when evidence was obtained in breach of constitutional rights.[61]

The lack of regard to how evidence is obtained has been tempered in recent years by the need to comply with certain statutory requirements that mandate the courts to pay more attention to fairness when determining the admissibility of criminal evidence. Section 78 of PACE 1984 directs the courts to reject evidence on which the prosecution propose to rely 'if it appears to the court, that having regard to all the circumstances in which the evidence was obtained, the admission of the evidence would have such an adverse effect on the fairness of the proceedings that the court ought not to admit it'. This provision encouraged the courts to take a more robust attitude towards evidence unfairly obtained, and was buttressed by the general requirement imposed by the HRA 1998 on courts as public authorities to act compatibly with Convention rights, which include the right to a fair trial under Article 6 ECHR.[62] As mentioned in section II, a further requirement of the HRA 1998 is that the UK courts take into account the decisions of the ECtHR.

Although the UK has left the European Union (EU) and will not be a party to any EU agreement between the Member States on exclusionary rules of evidence, the requirement under the HRA 1998 that the courts must act compatibly with Convention rights and take account of ECtHR jurisprudence suggests that, at least so long as the UK remains within the Convention system, it would broadly subscribe to any exclusionary rules that are recognised by that system, although, as noted, it remains open to its domestic courts to depart from decisions of the ECtHR. Although the ECtHR has stated in numerous cases that the rules on the admissibility of evidence are 'primarily a matter for regulation under national law',[63] the Court has come to accept that the use in criminal proceedings of evidence obtained by way of torture will violate the right to a fair trial, as will the use of incriminating statements obtained in defiance of the will of the accused.[64] Beyond this, it has a developed presumptive rule that prevents convictions based solely or decisively on witnesses' unexamined statements, although as noted in section II, in reaction to the UKSC's hostile reception to such a rule, it has held that it should not be applied inflexibly.[65] It has also developed a presumptive rule that convictions should not be based

[60] *R v Leatham* (1961) 8 Cox 498, 501, per Crompton J.

[61] J Jackson, 'Human Rights, Constitutional Law and Exclusionary Safeguards in Ireland' in P Roberts and J Hunter (eds), *Criminal Evidence and Human Rights* (Hart Publishing, 2012) 119.

[62] HRA 1998, s 6.

[63] *Schenk v Switzerland* (1991) 13 EHRR 242 [46]; *Delta v France* (1990) 16 EHRR 574 [35].

[64] See eg, *Saunders v UK* (1996) 23 EHRR 313; *Harutyunyan v Armenia* App no 36549/03 (ECtHR, 28 June 2007).

[65] *Al-Khawaja and Tahery v UK* (2012) 54 EHRR 23.

on statements obtained from suspects in breach of the right of access to a lawyer, although this would seem to be subject to an overall assessment as to whether the use of such statements would make the trial overall unfair.[66] By contrast, the ECtHR has been much less prescriptive about whether the use of evidence obtained in breach of Article 8 ECHR would lead to a violation of Article 6 of the Convention.[67]

VII. The Admissibility of Evidence Obtained in an Administrative Procedure

Traditionally, as we have seen, the rules of admissibility at common law were applied in an undifferentiated manner to all judicial proceedings, but this has changed as the rules were relaxed in civil and administrative proceedings and tightened in criminal proceedings in order to protect defendants' procedural rights. The hearsay rule, for example, has now been abolished in all proceedings other than criminal proceedings, although, as we have seen in section III, there has been a considerable relaxation of the rule even in these proceedings, to the detriment of the orality principle and the right to confrontation. Witnesses and defendants can still invoke the privilege against self-incrimination in criminal proceedings, but the ECtHR has made it clear that compulsory powers to answer questions outside criminal investigations do not infringe Article 6 ECHR.[68] A large number of regulatory bodies in the UK have compulsory powers to compel persons and corporations to give information that may incriminate them. In *R v Hertfordshire CC, ex parte Green Environmental Industries*, the House of Lords held that the privilege against self-incrimination could not be invoked in extra-judicial inquiries.[69] However, according to *Saunders v UK*,[70] the use of answers and statements obtained in such inquiries may not be used in any subsequent criminal proceedings, except on a charge of giving false information. This extends to include exculpatory remarks or mere information on questions of fact that may later be deployed in support of the prosecution case.

VIII. The Admissibility of the Results of Internal Corporate Investigations

The ECtHR has recognised that the privilege against self-incrimination and the right to silence are fundamental principles at the core of the right to a fair trial,

[66] See *Salduz v Turkey* (2008) 49 EHRR 421; *Ibrahim and others v UK* (2015) 61 EHHR 9, *Beuze v Belgium* (2019) 69 EHRR 1. For discussion of how the ECtHR has 'back-tracked' on the *Salduz* rule, see Giannoulopoulos (n 42) ch 5.

[67] For more detail, see Jackson and Summers (n 2) 169–75.

[68] See eg *Fayed v UK* App no 17101/90 (ECtHR, 21 September 1994); *Saunders v UK* (n 64).

[69] *R v Herts CC, ex parte Green Environmental Industries Ltd* [2000] 2 AC 412.

[70] *Saunders v UK* (n 64) [71].

which protect accused persons from being compelled to answer questions at trials or during the course of criminal investigations.[71] But it has made a distinction between statements made by an accused under compulsion, which may attract the protection of the privilege, and the compulsory production of pre-existing documents, material or reports, which involves no infringement of the privilege.[72] This would seem to include the results of internal investigations that have come into the hands of investigation authorities.

A further question, however, is whether companies may be able to resist handing over the product of their internal investigations by invoking other privileges. Communications between a party/their lawyers and third parties for the purpose of obtaining information or advice in connection with existing or contemplated litigation attract litigation privilege so long as:

(a) litigation is in progress or reasonably in contemplation;
(b) the communications are made with the sole or dominant purpose of conducting the litigation;
(c) the litigation is adversarial, not investigative or inquisitorial.[73]

The question whether litigation privilege extends to internal investigations has not always been easy to determine and has been the subject of recent case law. In *R v Jukes*, the Court of Appeal refused privilege for a statement by an employee to his employer's solicitors following a fatal accident, some six weeks after the accident, at a time when the Health and Safety Executive were investigating the accident but no decision on prosecution had been made.[74] The Court considered that criminal proceedings have a higher threshold for the contemplation of proceedings than civil proceedings. This statement was not approved by a differently constituted Court of Appeal in *Director of the Serious Fraud Office v ENEC*, where an internal investigation had been launched by ENEC following whistleblower allegations of fraud, bribery and corruption.[75] Lawyers were engaged by the company in early 2011 to carry out a fact-finding investigation, followed by forensic accountants a few months later. The SFO initiated discussions with the company in August 2011 following a press report, and in April 2013 the SFO began a criminal investigation. As part of its investigation, the SFO sought disclosure of certain documents generated during the internal investigation, which had continued in the interim. The Court of Appeal held that on the facts, litigation (ie an SFO prosecution) was in reasonable contemplation when the company initiated its internal investigation, and certainly when it received a letter from the SFO in August 2011. This was so notwithstanding that the letter expressly stated that the SFO was not carrying out a criminal investigation at that

[71] *Funke v France* (1993) 16 EHRR 297.
[72] *Saunders v UK* (n 64).
[73] See *Three Rivers DC v Governor and Company of the Bank of England (No 6)* [2004] UKHL 48, [2005] 1 AC 610 [102].
[74] *R v Jukes* [2018] EWCA Crim 176.
[75] *Director of the Serious Fraud Office v ENEC* [2018] EWCA Civ 2006.

stage but instead made reference to 'recent intelligence & media reports concerning allegations of corruption and wrongdoing by [ENEC]'. The Court of Appeal further held that 'where there is a clear threat of a criminal investigation, even at one remove from the specific risks posed by the SFO should it start an investigation, the reason for the investigation of … allegations must be brought into the zone where the dominant purpose may be to prevent or deal with litigation'.[76] The Court considered that it is in the public interest that companies should be prepared to investigate allegations from whistleblowers or investigative journalists, prior to going to a prosecutor such as the SFO, without losing the benefit of legal professional privilege for the work product and consequences of their investigation. Were they to do so, the temptation might well be not to investigate at all, for fear of being forced to reveal what might have been uncovered.[77]

If an internal investigation is carried out by lawyers instructed by a company, another possibility would be to claim legal professional advice privilege. In *Three Rivers DC v Governor and Company of the Bank of England (No 5)*,[78] the Court of Appeal narrowed the definition of 'client' so that only communications between lawyers and those individuals at the corporate client authorised to seek and receive legal advice on behalf of the company will be protected by legal advice privilege. Given that the documents in the *ENEC* case were covered by litigation privilege, the Court did not have to go on and consider whether they would have been covered by legal advice privilege. If it had to decide this question, it considered that it would have been bound by the *Three Rivers* case, but it saw much force in the argument that a narrow interpretation of 'client' was wrong. In its view large corporations need, as much as small corporations and individuals, to seek and obtain legal advice without fear of intrusion. For large corporations, the information upon which legal advice is sought is unlikely to be in the hands of the main board or those it appoints to seek and receive legal advice. If a multi-national corporation cannot ask its lawyers to obtain the information it needs to advise that corporation from the corporation's employees with relevant first-hand knowledge under the protection of legal advice privilege, that corporation will be in a less advantageous position than a smaller entity seeking such advice.

Commentators have observed that the Court of Appeal's willingness to widen the ambit of privilege for internal investigations may not have the effect of encouraging internal investigations if the SFO requests a company that is cooperating with it to waive privilege over them and then considers that any refusal to do so is inconsistent with cooperation, thus precluding an invitation to enter into Deferred Prosecution Agreement (DPA) decisions.[79] This raises important questions about

[76] ibid [109].

[77] ibid [116]. See also A Williams and J Gare, 'ENC v SFO Court of Appeal Judgment: English Legal Professional Privilege Lives On' (2018) *HFW Briefings* at www.hfw.com/ENRC-v-SFO-Court-of-Appeal-Judgment-September-2018.

[78] *Three Rivers DC v Governor and Company of the Bank of England (No 5)* [2003] EWCA Civ 474.

[79] See S Harbur-Kelly and S Melrose, 'The Director of the Serious Fraud Office v Eurasian Natural Resources Corporation' (2019) *Mondaq* at www.mondaq.com/uk/white-collar-crime-anti-

how best to achieve corporate compliance and governance that go well beyond the scope of this chapter, but from an evidential perspective it highlights the distinction between privileged material, which can always be waived by parties under investigation, and material that is inadmissible as a matter of law.

IX. The Future: E-Admissibility, Human Rights and Law Enforcement

In this chapter we have noted a general shift in the UK away from exclusionary rules that forbid the admissibility of certain kinds of evidence at trial towards regulating evidence more by means of pre-trial codes, subject to a judicial discretion at trial to exclude evidence obtained in breach of these codes on the ground that it would be unfair on the defence to admit it. Codes of practice regulating the way evidence is obtained by the police under PACE 1984 are a prime example of this. Much less attention, however, has been given to the dangers of e-evidence,whether it be the use of unreliable computer software or the way in which e-evidence may be falsified or manipulated. We have seen that it is questionable whether the presumption that computers are working properly is justified. Police chiefs have issued guidance on the handling of digital evidence, but it has been argued that the four principles in the guidance are in need of updating, with greater detail given to the quality and robustness of particular investigatory methods.[80]

While there are concerns as to whether there has been enough rigour imposed on the way e-evidence is obtained and used, which can be detrimental to the interests of the accused (highlighted in the recent Post Office scandal), there are concerns the other way when it comes to the uncertainties and difficulties law enforcement bodies face when seeking to obtain e-evidence from overseas to the detriment of the effective prosecution of cross-border criminality. The use of MLA can be a protracted method of procuring evidence. After Brexit, the UK lost access to valuable EU law enforcement tools such as the European Arrest Warrant, although efforts have since been made to ensure effectiveness in the field of judicial cooperation in criminal matters, particularly the continuation of speedy cooperation in extradition and MLA. While the UK will not be subject to any EU directive on the mutual admissibility of evidence, the legislative proposal based on minimal rules of exclusion recognised by the ECtHR and more robust standard setting on the admissibility of e-evidence offers much that the UK could accept in terms of protecting the rights of the defence, while the effective prosecution of crime would be enhanced by a mutual admissibility regime to which the UK could in time become party.

corruption-fraud/806598/the-director-of-the-serious-fraud-office-v-eurasian-natural-resources-corporation-limited.

[80] G Horsman, 'ACPO Principles for Digital Evidence: Time for an Update?' (2020) 1 *Forensic Science International Reports* 100076.

INDEX

www.ingramcontent.com/pod-product-compliance
Ingram Content Group UK Ltd.
Pitfield, Milton Keynes, MK11 3LW, UK
UKHW020814290926
15470UKWH00003B/1154

9 781509 971992